8/04

W9-BRS-569

THE HALLIBURTON AGENDA

The Politics of Oil and Money

DAN BRIODY

WILEY

JOHN WILEY & SONS, INC.

Published by John Wiley & Sons, Inc., Hoboken, New Jersey.
Published simultaneously in Canada.

For general information on our other products and services, or technical support,
please contact our Customer Care Department within the United States at
800-762-2974, outside the United States at 317-572-3993 or fax 317-572-4002.

Wiley also publishes its books in a variety of electronic formats. Some content that
appears in print may not be available in electronic books. For more information
about Wiley products, vis

Library of Congress Cataloging **-** *ublication Data*

Briody, Dan.
  The Halliburton agenda : the politics of oil and money / Dan Briody.
     p.   cm.
  Includes bibliographical references.
  ISBN 0-471-63860-9 (cloth)
  1. Halliburton Company—History. 2. Brown & Root, Inc.—History. I.
Title.
  HD9569.H26B75   2004
  338.7′622338′0973—dc22

                                                              2004002217

Printed in the United States of America

10 9 8 7 6 5 4 3 2 1

ACKNOWLEDGMENTS

Many thanks to my research assistant Sarah Fallon for her enthusiasm, diligence, and attention to detail. Also, thanks to my editor Jeanne Glasser and agent Daniel Greenberg of Levine Greenberg.

Thanks to the many people who agreed to be interviewed for this book, and the journalists and writers who have followed the Halliburton story over the years, including Dan Baum, Pratap Chatterjee, Barry Yeoman, and Peter Singer. Thanks to the Rice University Woodson Research Center; the Lyndon B. Johnson Library in Austin, Texas; the Burnham Library of Bridgewater, Connecticut; The Gunn Memorial Library of Washington, Connecticut; the Ruth A. Haas Library of the University of Western Connecticut in Danbury, Connecticut; and the New York City Library.

And finally, thanks to my family, my wife Michelle, and my son Sam.

CONTENTS

PART III
From Vietnam to Iraq

PROLOGUE

When he was asked, during the 2000 vice-presidential debate with Joe Lieberman, about his financial success during his time as Halliburton's CEO, Dick Cheney responded, "I can tell you, Joe, the government had absolutely nothing to do with it." But even Dick Cheney himself didn't really believe that.

Four years earlier, in his second year as CEO, Cheney wrote the foreword in a Halliburton corporate biography entitled *The Legend of Halliburton.* In it he said, "But no matter how well we position ourselves in the market, I am struck by the extent to which the success or failure of a project is as much of a political decision as it is an engineering decision. Many times the engineering and technical aspects of a project can be relatively easy, but the project may be thwarted by unresolved political issues."

The truth is that Dick Cheney's appointment as CEO of Halliburton had everything to do with the government. Having been a lifelong public servant with no business experience, Cheney was hired by Halliburton in 1995 because of his understanding of the nation's political tendencies and his extensive contacts both on Capitol Hill and at the Pentagon. And he delivered on that expectation. In the five years of his stewardship,

Halliburton increased its government-backed loans from the Export-Import Bank from $100 million the five years prior to his arrival to $1.5 billion over his tenure. The company's government contract business nearly doubled, from $1.2 billion to $2.3 billion over that same period. Halliburton went from seventy-third to eighteenth on the Pentagon's list of top contractors. It is the embodiment of the *Iron Triangle,* the nexus of the government, military, and big business that President Eisenhower warned America about in his farewell speech. America has seen crony capitalism in action before. Indeed this behavior as exhibited by the Carlyle Group was the subject of my previous book.

But Halliburton has taken military industrialization to a whole new level, and as you'll read in this book, the company has had decades to hone its skills and cultivate beneficial relationships within our government. *The Halliburton Agenda* untangles a decades old web of political back scratching from one of the world's most powerful and connected companies. The chapters that follow chronicle the rise of Halliburton from its meager beginnings in 1920s' Texas to a monolithic corporation that has become a crucial vendor to the U.S. military that reached its pinnacle with the appointment of former Halliburton CEO Dick Cheney as vice president of the United States.

Since Cheney left the company to become George W. Bush's vice presidential running mate late in the summer of 2000, Halliburton has been hit with a wave of government agency investigations and political criticism that has vaulted the company from the relative obscurity of an oil-field services business to a lightening rod of political controversy and a symbol of profiteering to the antiwar crowd. The Securities and Exchange Commission (SEC) is currently investigating accounting changes that were made at Halliburton during Cheney's time as CEO that significantly increased the company's reported earnings—changes that were not reported to shareholders. It was also investigated by the U.S. Attorney's office in Sacramento for possible criminal activity in overcharging the government for work done at Fort Ord in 1997 in California—the criminal investigation was dropped, but in 2002, Kellogg Brown & Root (KBR) paid $2 million to settle a civil case. The company was also under investigation by the Nigerian government for a bribe it paid to a tax official in that country. The company admitted to paying the bribe.

Today, Halliburton, because of its ties to Cheney, is under a microscope the likes of which no military contractor has ever seen. The company has been excoriated by lawmakers for the business it did in Iraq, Iran, and Libya while Cheney was CEO just six years ago, between Cheney's first and second wars with Iraq—first as secretary of defense in 1991, then as vice president in 2003. Every move Halliburton makes in Iraq today is being watched by dozens of journalists, waiting for them to overcharge the taxpayer, as the Pentagon suspects they have done in importing fuel from Kuwait. Halliburton has transcended its existence as an unromantic provider of oil-well cementing and Army logistics support to become a political chess piece in a match that won't be decided until November 2004.

Though Cheney took the game to a new level, it's always been played this way, at least by KBR, the subsidiary of Halliburton that is attracting all the political attention with its role in the $2 billion (and counting) contract to rebuild Iraq's oil infrastructure. KBR was first formed (then called Brown & Root) in 1919, and the company was a political animal from the very beginning. Building roads in rural central Texas, Herman and

George Brown learned early how to influence public officials in pursuit of lucrative county contracts. Their relentless and brazen brand of politicking evolved steadily over the years and culminated in their relationship with Lyndon Johnson, an unprecedented business and political association that propelled both the Browns and Johnson to the top of their respective professions.

Throughout its whole existence—from the early road contracts to their current role in Iraq—KBR has lived with charges of political influence peddling. Even Donald Rumsfeld, as an Illinois congressman in the 1970s, accused the company of currying favor with politicians through campaign donations in exchange for government contracts. Meanwhile, Halliburton, KBR's parent company since 1962, has remained relatively free of controversy until recently, at least in its core business of oil-well cementing. In Part I of this book, you'll be introduced to Erle Halliburton, who founded the company in 1919. Ironically, given the reputation of his company today, Erle was an honorable, hard-working man who intensely disliked politicians and built his company on the backs of roughnecks and roustabouts like himself. He was a man who would never have allowed his company, and his surname, to be associated in the public's mind with war-profiteering and political influence.

Yet, the story of Halliburton, and more accurately KBR, is more than just a tale of the confluence of business and politics in America. It is also the story of how government contracting and outsourcing has evolved over the past 100 years, and how the military came to advocate the privatization trend. What we are seeing today in Iraq—the secret letting of no-bid contracts, the strange and arcane bureaucracy behind military outsourcing, the army's dangerous dependency on KBR—all can be explained by following the trajectory of KBR, from its early days of Navy shipbuilding in World War II to its role in building air strips and prisoner cells in Vietnam. The cycles of KBR's war business are repetitive, but distinct. During World War II, no one criticized the company for the role it played in supporting the war effort. Vietnam brought with it heavy criticism from the antiwar, antiprofiteering element, but little talk of the company's ties to prominent politicians. The Iraq War has cast a light on the potential for politicians to influence the government contracting process.

In all of the controversy surrounding Halliburton, some subtleties, and quite possibly the real danger of the current situation in Iraq have been lost. Whether Dick Cheney had a hand in doling out contracts to his former company is unimportant, not to mention unprovable. Everyone in the industry and the military, with few exceptions, agrees that Halliburton was the right company for the job in Iraq because of its experience and the speed with which it was able to operate. The real issue for taxpayers is that of cost overages, an issue of little concern to the people in the Pentagon who are more interested in getting the job done quickly. As you'll read, this is a pattern repeated by Halliburton throughout its history. And the question that no one has been asking is: How did Halliburton become the only company with a realistic chance of doing this work—in essence chasing other worthy competitors out of the market?

The whole purpose of privatization in the military, as with any industry, is to encourage open competition between profit-driven companies, thereby ensuring the government gets the most effective service at the best price. But in the case of Halliburton and the monster army logistical support contract known as LOGCAP, the idea of free competition has been virtually abandoned. It is true that the LOGCAP contract is put out for bid by the U.S. Army, but it has never been a fair competition. KBR designed the contract in the first place, giving the firm an unfair advantage in competing for it. And the contract was designed so that only two, possibly three, companies in the world would have been able to fulfill it.

Since then, the army has found that it is nearly impossible to give its support work to anyone but KBR. When, in 1997, KBR lost the overall LOGCAP contract to Dyncorp, the majority of the support work, mostly in Bosnia, was carved out of LOGCAP and kept in the hands of KBR until the company won back the contract in 2001. Peter Singer, author of *Corporate Warriors: The Rise of the Privatized Military Industry,* told me that the two incentives that keep the free market an efficient economic model—competition and penalties—have been lost when it comes to KBR because the army has become so dependent on them. "In the free market, when a company works with someone, there is a competition incentive," says Singer. "Once a company gets a contract, the competition incentive falls by the wayside, and the job is to avoid the penalties. But there is no record of penalties in this case. They never have to pay, because the army can't penalize them. Then, if you have a built-in profit margin, and you know you're never going to lose this contract, there is no price to pay for not doing the job. We have forgotten the two corrective forces of the market."

Kellogg Brown & Root holds the LOGCAP contract for the next 10 years, and holds similar contracts with both the U.S. Navy and U.S. Air Force. It is entirely likely that no other company will ever again be able to compete seriously with KBR for military logistical support, a market that will only grow in the coming years. KBR is essentially the newest branch of the U.S. military.

Partisan interests will continue to pick apart the Halliburton story over the course of the next year at least. What history can teach us is that eventually the story will die down, elections will be won and lost, Halliburton may pay a fine, and life will go on as it has for the better part of a century. Time will pass, new conflicts will arise, and Halliburton will again find itself the target of political watchdogs. But as you will learn from the history divulged in this book, the company will rest easy, as it does now, in the knowledge that this cycle has been repeated several times over the course of its existence, and nothing has been able to bring it down.

Throughout its history, Halliburton, in its defense, has consistently played the patriotic card. But the fact that a company is profiting from its military outsourcing business does not excuse the manner in which that business was gained or how it was carried out. All it means is that they are doing their job, a job that pays them a guaranteed profit.

As for the role of politics in Halliburton's business, that too is not likely to change. When Dick Cheney was addressing a crowd as the Halliburton CEO at an oil conference in 1997, he aptly characterized the revolving door of Washington, DC, "The biggest problem I faced as Secretary of Defense was the United States Congress," he said. "Now that I'm chairman and CEO of Halliburton, the biggest problem I face is the United States Congress."

Ironically, as vice president of the United States, the biggest problem Dick Cheney has faced so far is Halliburton.

PART I

The Early Years

1

Erle P. Halliburton and the Million-Dollar Boast

Before there was a $13 billion company, before the World Wars and the Texas oil boom, before there were pet presidents and vice presidents, campaign contributions and government contracts, union busting and sanction dodging, there was simply a man, fiercely struggling to escape poverty, doggedly pursuing his piece of America's manifest destiny. At the time of his birth, September 22, 1892, in a small farming town on the outskirts of Memphis, Tennessee, the name Erle Palmer Halliburton stirred no national emotion. It held no political intrigue. It had no impact on government or business. It was only the name of one of five sons of Edwin Gray Halliburton, an anonymous jack-of-all-trades, who would not live to see Erle's thirteenth birthday. Halliburton, as a name, meant virtually nothing to anyone outside of Henning, Tennessee. But Erle Halliburton was determined to change all of that.

As a young boy, Erle Halliburton showed a natural inclination toward mechanics, often dismantling and reassembling devices for pure recreation. While boys his age in Henning were playing with toy trucks in sand boxes, Erle was tinkering with gears and repairing simple machines. His curiosity drove him to understand how things worked. He was an excellent student, completing both elementary and high school courses over an eight-year span by age fourteen. Yet, even then, Erle Halliburton was uninterested in the idle trappings of youth. In what would become one of his trademark characteristics, he was intensely focused on higher aims.

After his father passed away in 1904, the Halliburton family was left with little money and even less opportunity. Two years later, hopelessly impoverished at age fourteen, Erle decided it was time he left home and pursued his fortunes elsewhere. Diminutive in stature at just 5 foot 5 inches, the future of the Halliburton clan was resting on Erle's narrow shoulders, the new man of the house. But he brimmed with confidence, promising his family he would not return to Henning until he had pocketed a million dollars, a claim that no one could have taken seriously at the time. Underestimating Erle Halliburton would be a mistake that many of his contemporaries would repeat over the years, for as author and Texas historian J. Evetts Haley put it, Halliburton was "fired by the stern disciplines of hunger and want."

Alone, directionless, and penniless, Halliburton embarked on a worldwide journey that would take him from Brooklyn to Manila, working dozens of jobs as varied as driving a locomotive to selling automatic stokers. At age eighteen, he joined the U.S. Navy and received the first formal training of his young life, serving two tours and working engineering and hydraulics before leaving the service in 1915. The work suited Halliburton's mechanical mind, and he ultimately ended up in Los Angeles, running a pressure irrigation project for the Dominguez Irrigation Company, pulling down $100 a month. It was there that Erle met and married his wife Vida Taber, and settled in—for the moment. It was a far cry from the $1 million he had vowed to earn, but for a dirt-poor kid from Henning, Tennessee, it was good work and a good life.

· · ·

At about this time, life in America was changing dramatically. While Halliburton had found himself a quiet, decent living in the easy climes of California, the real action was taking place all around him, as oil fever gripped the nation. In the late 1860s, after Edwin L. Drake first struck oil in the hills overlooking Oil Creek in Titusville, Pennsylvania, localized oil booms had sprung up like wildfires, first in Ohio in the 1880s, then in California, and finally in Texas, when a strange-looking hill called Spindletop in Beaumont spewed 75,000 barrels of Texas crude into the sky on January 10, 1901.

It is not surprising that Halliburton did not immediately recognize the impact of oil on the average American, and indeed, the worldwide economic landscape. Oil was originally produced for illumination, to replace the expensive and increasingly scarce whale oil that powered most lamps in the home. With Thomas Edison's new invention, the heat-resistant incandescent light bulb, it seemed for a time that the oil boom was destined to be nothing but a short-lived frenzy, a mineral-based Internet boom, as the price of oil fluctuated wildly and the number of light bulbs in use soared from just 250,000 in 1885 to 18 million in 1902. Kerosene, the by-product of refined oil that was to be the future of illumination, was quickly relegated to a rural niche necessity, severely limiting its market potential and throwing the future of the oil industry into doubt.

But the predicted demise of oil was so short-lived that it was practically unnoticeable. At the same time as the specter of electric light loomed over the kerosene industry, a market with almost the same amount of potential as electric illumination was springing to life: the internal combustion engine. The "horseless carriage" had slowly begun to insinuate itself onto the muddy, bumpy American roads by 1905. At first, the noisy, smelly contraptions were not taken seriously, often met with derisive shouts of "Get a horse!" from disgusted onlookers.

Up to this point, gasoline had been a largely useless, and sometimes cumbersome, by-product of the oil-refining process on the way to making quality kerosene. Refiners were lucky to unload it for two cents a gallon as fuel for stoves. With the explosion of the automobile onto the scene, however, gasoline, the ugly stepchild of oil refining, was revitalized. Automobile registrations in the United States ballooned from 8,000 in 1900 to 902,000 in 1912. The oil industry was back, and the automobile was its impetus. It was a rapid turn of events that would forever change the life of young Erle Halliburton.

After nine years of wanderlust and job-hopping, Erle Halliburton found the oil industry. In 1918, he took a job as a driver in the Perkins Oil Well Cementing Company in California. Though oil well drilling was still a nascent industry, it had already seen several waves of change since the first successful well was drilled at Oil Creek. The first wells, like that of Colonel Drake, had steam-powered cable-tool rigs, crude machines that repeatedly pounded through rock and dirt with a massive chisel on the end of what looked like a giant see-saw. These early rigs literally punched holes in the ground. It was effective for the rocky terrain in rural Pennsylvania, but in the softer sands and clay of the Southwest, the cable-tool method of drilling was futile because the unstable earth around the hole caved in and filled the hole as quickly as it was made. This resulted in a great deal of extra work since drillers or roughnecks needed to constantly remove the cuttings from the drill hole, severely slowing down the process.

By the 1920s, cable-tool drill rigs were approaching obsolescence as rotary drilling emerged as its successor. Rotary drilling uses a drill bit with teeth attached to a long, hollow pipe that turns and grinds, lifting the earth up as its weight pushes the drill bit further and further down. As the bit bores ever deeper, roughnecks add lengths of pipe to the drill, extending its reach. The biggest advantage to rotary drilling was that highly pressurized fluid, called drilling mud, could be pushed down the hollow piping and out of the drill bit, forcing the cuttings back up to the surface, while cooling and lubricating the bit.

The early days of oil drilling were riddled with problems, stemming from the fact that few in the industry had a good understanding of how oil reservoirs worked, where they were to be found, and how to best mine the oil. Wildcatters peppered the landscape of every oil discovery, randomly drilling every inch of the earth in a desperate attempt to strike it rich. Entire oil fields were pumped dry in weeks, leaving much of the valuable crude still locked in the pores of the earth. Often, careless drilling allowed water and underground gases to seep into wells and contaminate the oil, rendering it useless. It was a time of wild speculation, trial and error, and many dashed dreams.

It was in this frenzied environment that Erle Halliburton now found himself, working for Almond A. Perkins and his oil well cementing company. At the time, oil well cementing was unheard of, and the oil industry regarded the practice with skepticism. The process consists of forcing a cement "slurry" down the hollow pipe of a rotary drill, forcing the cement back up through the walls of the hole, and sealing out the water and other unwanted contaminants from the well. It also served to stabilize the drill itself.

After laboring as a truck driver for Perkins, Erle was soon promoted to cementer and learned the craft of oil well cementing firsthand. It's hard to imagine a less romantic job, but the work excited Halliburton and his enthusiasm for the oil business fired his imagination. He began to relentlessly offer suggestions to his new boss on ways to improve the company, but Perkins was not a man open to suggestion, and Halliburton, just one year later, found himself between jobs once again. As it turned out, this break was exactly what Halliburton needed, as he himself would go on to say, "The two best things that ever happened to me were being hired, then fired, by the Perkins Oil Well Cementing Company."

• • •

Down on his luck, but bitten by the oil bug, Halliburton and his wife Vida picked up and moved to Wichita Falls, Texas, a place that had already been thoroughly gripped by oil fever. Two nearby oil fields were in full swing, and Halliburton, armed with his new knowledge of oil well cementing, aimed to capitalize in full. He began working the Burkburnett oil fields, selling drillers on what he called the "Halliburton process."

Halliburton was a tireless salesman, constantly figuring and re-figuring ways to build his young business up. Nevertheless, business went "a-begging." Drillers were a salty, greedy, dis-trustful bunch, and to them it looked as if this nervous little man from Tennessee was trying to sell them nothing more than snake oil. Besides, the wildcatters who had struck oil were already rich and didn't need any help, and the ones that hadn't struck oil were as poor as Halliburton himself. Boomtowns at-tracted every kind of would-be entrepreneur and scam artist, and to the drillers and rig owners, it was impossible to tell into which category Halliburton fit. There were even clairvoyants who claimed they could sniff out oil, for the right price. His was one voice of a thousand trying to sell everything from oil barrels to drill bits.

Even in the face of this adversity, Halliburton would not back down. His stubbornness and ambition intact, he again moved his wife and two kids to another boomtown, Wilson, Ok-lahoma. The town was already overrun with wildcatters and roughnecks, so the Halliburton family set up shop in a one-room house on the side of the road, built in two days by Erle himself, where they lived and worked. The conditions were atrocious and the rent for the land astronomical. No electric-ity, water, or gas. Just a telephone and a makeshift office, which Vida ran. She dutifully answered business calls and kept the books, all while raising their kids. Oil towns in those days were no place to raise a family. Whiskey-fueled fights broke out nightly, some ending in death, and many of the workers ended up in jail over weekends. The Halliburtons seemed to have hit rock bottom. Still, Erle was undeterred. "At any other time and place, his self-confidence, radiating in fluent, cocky self-assurance from his tiny frame, might have been insufferable.

But in this feverish rush for fortune, time was of the essence, and nothing counted but success," says the historian Haley.

Erle bought a wagon and pump, convinced some friends to invest $1,000, and called his new project the New Method Oil Well Cementing Company. Business was not forthcoming. It was a hectic time, as prospectors "drilled, drained, and abandoned site after site." Halliburton was chasing down business all over the region, driving endless days and nights through mud-drenched roads, to little or no avail. Money had gotten so tight, that Vida would later recall their bank account was "low, seriously low. . . . The lamp shone on my ring and I sat there admiring it when the thought came to me, 'Here is the money we need.'" Erle reluctantly agreed to pawn Vida's wedding ring as a last attempt at saving the business.

With the money from the ring, Halliburton bought materials to enhance the oil well cementing process, despite the almost total lack of interest in the process from the drillers. His belief in the process, fostered during his year stint with Perkins, was unshakeable. He designed a measuring line that could gauge the depth of the cement in the well, adding more precision to cementing. He patented the measuring line, which would eventually become a standard device in the oil well cementing business. But still, the family struggled to make ends meet, selling off its furniture to pay its workers on one occasion. Halliburton needed something to happen, and he needed it soon. They had very little left to sell. As far as he had come since leaving Henning, Tennessee, he was rapidly approaching utter poverty. The Halliburtons were, once again, broke. The company had a balance of only $50.27, a mere $999,949.73 short of the $1 million Erle was still aiming for.

Halliburton's unyielding faith in his business and process paid off in January 1920. As was common in those days, an oil well was spewing oil into the air, wasting thousands of dollars worth of crude. The well, in Hewitt Field, outside of Wilson, Oklahoma, belonged to William G. Skelly, president of the Skelly Oil Company, and he was losing money by the barrelful. Erle Halliburton called Skelly and offered to subdue the well using the Halliburton process of oil well cementing. Skelly, not in a position to argue, gave the cocky little man the go-ahead, and shortly thereafter, the well was under control and Skelly was regulating the flow of oil with precision. It had worked. Oil well cementing really worked. And word began to spread throughout the drilling communities in Oklahoma and into Texas that a fiery Tennessean had a new method to control their wells. The Halliburtons had their first big break, and poverty would never again show its sallow face in their house.

• • •

It was an exciting time for Erle, Vida, and their children. Orders began to come in from the dozens of oil fields dotting the landscape. Halliburton kept busy driving from town to town, field to field, throughout the Southwest. Vida handled the financial side of the business while Erle racked up miles on the family truck. It was not uncommon for Erle to drive for days to reach a potential customer, sometimes putting 700 miles behind him before bedding down for the night. Outfitted in his corduroy cap and leather jacket, Erle was as much a roughneck as he was an entrepreneur, lending him the credibility he needed when cutting deals with his peers. He did business over a scotch-whiskey, and he was more at home in the mud and grime of the drilling floor than he was in the office crunching numbers and doling out payroll to his crews.

The work itself was brutal but relatively simple. Each job consisted of first getting a cement truck to the well site, no easy task with the deplorable state of Texas roads in the 1920s. Often, entire days were lost wrenching a truck out of waist-high mud. Once at the site, the roughnecks mixed bags of cement with water and rushed to funnel the slurry into the well hole before it hardened. Halliburton, always working on ways to refine the process, would eventually patent the Jet Mixer or Halliburton Cement Mixer, which allowed workers to pour large amounts of concrete mix into a tub that automatically added the water. What seems like an obvious invention today, was nothing short of a revolution in oil well cementing at the time. Halliburton and his New Method Oil Well Cementing Company quickly gained a reputation for innovation and diligence throughout the industry.

While Halliburton devised a number of ingenious enhancements to the cementing process, one fundamental problem with his business remained: Erle Halliburton had not invented oil well cementing. In fact, his old boss Almond Perkins had patented the process long before Halliburton brought the idea to the Southwest. When Perkins got wind of Halliburton's New Method Oil Well Cementing Company, he filed suit for patent infringement. Halliburton did not deny that he had infringed on Perkins' patent. Rather, he was quoted as often telling his own patent attorney, "Don't ever tell me I cannot do something because it will infringe somebody's patent. I started in business infringing." The dispute was settled when Erle gave Perkins

rights to his Jet Mixer process in California, while Perkins con-
ceded the oil well cementing process to New Method in the
Southwest. This would not be the last time that Halliburton tangled with patent attorneys.

• • •

Though Halliburton had gained a reputation for a hard-
nosed, blue-collar work ethic, he was equally effective at
negotiating deals. In the year 1920 alone, his crews cemented
500 wells. Halliburton was astute at following the money,
moving the company and his family once again to new oil
fields in Duncan, Oklahoma, in 1921. There he continued to
grow the company from just three cementing trucks in 1920
to twenty in 1923. Even so, business was still shaky and incon-
sistent, and payment often relied on the success of a given
well. Erle himself was earning only $260 a month, less than
some of his employees were making. Halliburton knew that
he would have to provide some stability and steady cash flow
to his business. He had proven the value of oil well cementing, now he needed a more solid commitment from the industry. In 1924, Halliburton engineered a deal that would
secure the future of his company and prove that his business
acumen was grossly underrated.

The solution came when Halliburton convinced his seven
largest customers, the biggest oil producers in the area, to invest in his business. He issued 3,500 shares of stock at $100 a
share, and renamed the company the Halliburton Oil Well Cementing Company, or Howco. Magnolia, Texas Company, Gulf,
Humble, Pure, and Atlantic were in for 200 shares apiece,

while Sun bought 100 shares. The Halliburton family owned 1,700 shares, and the Republic National Bank of Dallas held the rest in trust.

By inviting his customers in as investors, Erle Halliburton increased his salary from $260 a month to $15,000 a year. He also took $130,000 in exchange for the use of his patents and used that money to further build the business. Howco now employed 57 people and had achieved the stability and cash flow the company so desperately needed. Suddenly, Erle's million-dollar boast was starting to look more attainable.

• • •

With his investors secured, and his position as president of Howco settled, Halliburton set about the business of building a truly professional corporation. For a company that employed mostly roustabouts and roughnecks, this was no easy task. But Halliburton's hands-on approach and gritty reputation earned the respect of his employees. While his personal fortune grew, Halliburton never lost touch with his down-and-out roots, and his work ethic and diligence remained intact. Howco was a successful company, and its books, now kept by professional accountants, were evidence of that.

A year after the company was incorporated in 1924, it paid a dividend of $30 per share. By 1927, the dividend had increased to $100 per share. With 1,700 shares of their own, the Halliburton's were becoming a wealthy family. They continued to expand the business and bring in other family members. Erle's brothers Paul and George founded the Halliburton Oil Well Cementing Company, Ltd., of Canada. They even began to win international business in 1926 when Howco exported cementing trucks to a British petroleum company.

In an effort to diversify, Halliburton bought a fleet of passenger planes and opened the Southwest Air Fast Express airline, known as SAFEway, which ferried people around the Texas panhandle. The airline would introduce Erle to the role of politics in American business. At the onset of the Great Depression, the airline fell on hard times, and Erle made a final attempt to save it by competing for a contract with the U.S. Postal Service to fly mail in the area. It was an entirely new kind of business for Halliburton, and not surprisingly, his bid was not accepted. In a fit of rage, Halliburton took his fight to Capitol Hill, flying to Washington to plead for the deal. At this point in his professional life, Halliburton was not familiar with the subtleties of government contracting, and his weeks of protest in Washington proved fruitless. Further, the experience engendered a lifelong distrust of politicians, whom he referred to as "those people in Washington." As we now know, this was not an attitude that his company would maintain.

• • •

Another lesson Halliburton learned the hard way was the importance of patent protection. In stark contrast to his early disregard for other people's patents, Halliburton fiercely protected his own patent rights, often filing suit in multiple states throughout the country. His legal battles met with mixed results, but Halliburton was fearless in pursuit of patent justice.

There were myriad cases of small, local companies infringing on Howco patents, like a band of blacksmiths in Guthrie,

Oklahoma, who were using Howco's Jet Mixer process without permission. Cases like that were cleared up quickly, and usually found in Howco's favor. But in 1926, Howco tangled with the most powerful corporation in the world at the time—none other than John D. Rockefeller's Standard Oil. The claim was that Standard Oil was using the oil well cementing process patented by Perkins but licensed by Howco in Louisiana. Halliburton was undaunted by Standard's sheer mass and endless parade of expert attorneys and settled the case by requiring Standard to pay $75 for every well drilled below 200 feet deep.

As the drilling field became more and more advanced, innovation and patent protection grew in importance to Halliburton's business. Oil field services was a rapidly maturing area, and the pressure on Howco to stay ahead of the curve mounted daily. In an effort to do so, Erle bought the rights to something called the Simmons Drill Stem Tester, a device used to collect samples of rock and fluid at a drill site for analysis. Halliburton met the inventor, John Simmons, and over a drink paid him $15,000 on the spot for the device. Unfortunately, for Halliburton, Simmons was not the only person working on that type of device, and he soon found himself involved in yet another patent dispute.

Because there were multiple applications for similar devices being filed at the U.S. Patent Office, the regulators set up an Interference Proceeding, which Howco won. One of the men who had contested Howco's ownership of the patent in Texas skirted the ruling, however, by setting his brother up in California, using the same process. Halliburton was enraged, writing angry letters to oil companies throughout California who were using the process. He sued both the company that was selling the tester and the oil companies that were using it. The plan backfired, and Halliburton inadvertently galvanized the oil companies, many of whom were his customers and investors, against Howco. The California court found in favor of the defendants. In court, Halliburton lived up to his fiery reputation, banging the bench with his fists and prompting the judge to rebuke him repeatedly.

Halliburton would not let go, though. He took the battle all the way to the State Supreme Court, which ultimately found Howco's patent to be invalid. Upon the rendering of the decision, Halliburton commented that "If the courts will not sustain my patents, I am not going to respect anybody else's." He fought hard, worked hard, and lived hard, and though life for Erle Halliburton had certainly improved since his days in Tennessee, you wouldn't know it from looking at the stern, leathery face of a man always determined to do more.

By the end of the 1920s and the onset of the Great Depression, Howco was by all measures a successful company. The work remained arduous, back-breaking labor that required constant vigilance and endless hours of driving. But Erle Halliburton had made good on his promise of making $1 million, and he continued to pour every ounce of his considerable energy into the business. Despite his remarkable success, he would never rest easy.

2

The Road to Riches

The story of Herman and George Brown, the founders of Brown & Root, is the story of how American politics and entrepreneurship evolved together, through the entire twentieth century. At first, Brown & Root, like Howco, was built on the backs of determined men, slogging their way through the mud of rural Texas in pursuit of financial independence. But whereas Howco continued to thrive through the years on innovation and classic salesmanship, Brown & Root veered into the complicated world of government contracting and political influence. The Browns were drawn early to the easy money to be gained through cultivating political benefactors, a style of business that would carry the company through successive decades of war and profit cycles. Though the nature of America's military engagements, and the political zeitgeist that served as the context for each, would change constantly, Brown & Root's ability to play the game would only improve with time. In the early 1900s, the company would cut its teeth on the immature and business-driven political environment of Texas. It was the new Wild West.

It is hard to imagine a state in more flux and disarray than Texas at the turn of the twentieth century. Overrun by wildcatters, torn apart by political scandal, and laced with numerous pockets of abject poverty, the state was going through a severe and wrenching identity crisis. From 1870 to 1900, the population of the region had increased from 818,579 to 3,048,710. Speculators and the disenfranchised from the East in search of cheap land made up the bulk of the newcomers, and the state was ill equipped to handle the influx. There was very little infrastructure of any kind. Entire regions were without electricity or running water. The state government was virtually penniless. Compounding the problem was the fact that Texas had some of the worst roads in the country.

The importance of good roads to a state experiencing the type of growth that Texas was seeing cannot be overstated. While an extensive highway system is something that Americans take for granted today, at the turn of the last century, bad roads could cripple industry, restrict passenger travel, and delay mail delivery for weeks. This wasn't about a few potholes on the interstate. This was about primitive trails of cleared brush, dusty in the dry months and quagmires in the rainy season.

Up to this point, most roads in Texas were old Indian trails that had been widened and matted down from repeated use. Some of the paths had improved considerably when the cattle trade sent seas of longhorns thundering across the landscape, pounding down the dirt and trampling down grass and brush. But still, by the early 1900s, some roads were no better than openings of "endless and everlasting mud."

The situation was intolerable for a state with the dawning potential of Texas, hindering the state's economic growth as it became bogged down in an endless cycle of poverty. Due to the poor roads, growth industries spurned most areas of the state, resulting in more poverty and an inability to fund new roads. There were few bridges, and travelers were often up to their waists in rushing water while crossing rivers that meandered so much they blocked a direct path three or more times a trip. The existing roads did not intersect, making it impossible to navigate the terrain without leaving the road. General Roy Stone, head of the U.S. Office of Road Inquiry, publicly berated the state for the lack of progress it had made in building better roads in 1895, singling out Texas as having the worst roads in America.

Yet, it was on these roads that Erle Halliburton slogged back and forth across the state in search of new business for Howco, and it was on these roads that Herman and George Brown, two kids from Belton, Texas, would grow rich beyond their dreams.

• • •

Central Texas in the early 1900s was a tough area to live in for more reasons than the bad roads. Tired of the harsh winters of Ohio, in 1879 Rhinehart "Riney" Brown moved to Belton, a budding commercial center in Bell County, and what he found there was not entirely to his liking. The majority of the residents were independent out of necessity, unable to move freely about the state due to the horrid conditions of the roads. They were farmers and cattle herders mostly, and there was little community in the area. Theft, vagrancy, and even murder were not uncommon in Belton, and Riney Brown was appalled by what he saw upon arriving: "More deceitful people in Texas than anywhere I've been—every man for himself, and everybody trying to steal from or cheat his neighbor."

This was the Belton of Herman and George R. Brown, two sons of Riney born in 1892 and 1898, respectively. Riney ran a dry goods store in town, and his initial instincts about Texans proved tragically accurate when one of his business partners in The Brown Hardware Company stole money and merchandise and left town for the sunny climes of South America. These hard-learned lessons were passed on to Riney's sons who worked hard from a very young age, selling newspapers and doing odd jobs around town. Riney also taught his sons the importance of saving money. Instead of buying fireworks for the family, Riney explained his homespun thinking to his boys: "They were just as pretty to look at when the other fellow was shooting them and cost us nothing."

When Herman was twelve, the family moved to Temple, Texas, a town more centrally located on the local rail line. At Temple High School, Herman earned a reputation for his intensity and work ethic. He drove a grocery truck, worked at the family store, and did chores around the house. He went on to the University of Texas at Austin, but quickly discovered that academics were not his strong suit, and instead took a job at the Bell County Engineering Department. Various accounts of Herman Brown describe him as serious, contentious, and fantastically hardworking. With his young career in construction at the County Engineering Department now beginning, Herman put those traits to work, and the results were nothing short of phenomenal.

Pulling down $2 a day checking building materials for the county was decent work for a kid from Belton, but the money was inconsistent because rain would regularly wash out days of work at a time. In a theme that would repeat itself throughout his life, the simple county job was not enough for the ambitious Herman Brown, and he took his talents elsewhere. Herman took a foreman's job with Carl Swinford, a local road contractor who was struggling to keep his business afloat. The position paid $75 a month, but Brown didn't get to see much of that money. In fact, he rarely got paid. Swinford eventually ran the business into the ground, offering up his mules and road scraper in exchange for Herman's back pay. Herman was finally in business for himself, albeit with a team of tired, old mules and some outdated equipment. "I had not been paid any salary for approximately two years, so I was given part of his worn-out mule outfit from which to collect my back pay, as if, and when I had paid off the mortgage . . . I struggled on, not only paying it off, but managing to buy additional teams on credit."

• • •

George R. Brown, six years his brother's junior, had an entirely different disposition than his older brother. Whereas Herman Brown was intense, brooding, and at times distant, George Brown was affable and engaged. He was a born salesman: charming, handsome, and well liked. He sold rabbits to his neighbors, he sold the *Saturday Evening Post* around town, and, most importantly, he sold himself. In high school, he was involved in activities as far ranging as the glee club, debate team, and business clubs. He was utterly aware of his allure and not the least bit modest.

After high school, George enrolled at Houston's Rice Institute, which later became Rice University and the object of much of the Browns' philanthropy. Life in Houston was far different than Belton or Temple. By 1916, when George arrived, the city was already being transformed by the oil boom into one of the fastest growing municipalities in the country. He thrived on the energy of the big city. But he cut short his education at Rice to join the U.S. Marines during the First World War, though he never saw any combat action. After the war, he enrolled at the Colorado School of Mines, intending to become an engineer. Having grown up in Central Texas, where floods and bad roads routinely disrupted life, George Brown recognized early on the growing need for public works projects, most of which required the skills of trained engineers. He enjoyed tremendous success in Colorado, graduating in 1922, with an inscription in his yearbook that read, "gains his power through his ability to make friends." It was a simple but powerful phrase that would foretell the roots of the Brown brothers' remarkable success.

With his new degree in hand, George headed to Butte, Montana, to work in the mines of the Anaconda Copper Company. It was dangerous and difficult work, exploring cavernous underground mines for veins of copper. One night, while exploring 2,200 feet underground, the walls of the mine caved in around George and left him bleeding from the head and with a fractured skull and cracked ribs. He spent the night alone, pressing his head against a rock to stem the bleeding, unable to move, waiting for help on a twelve-inch wide beam overlooking a bottomless chasm. "I pressed the vein in my head against a rock, with that side of my head down, and when I became unconscious, that shut off the bleeding." He was rescued 12 hours later, returning home to Texas to convalesce. That was enough for Herman who offered George a job with his nascent road-building business for $100 a month. And that was the end of George Brown's mining career.

• • •

By this time, Herman Brown had built up a decent business in road building. Much like Erle Halliburton and his wife, Herman and his wife, Margaret Root, a schoolteacher from Georgetown, Texas, started out living hand-to-mouth, honeymooning in a tent near one of Herman's work sites. Herman spent endless hours performing heavy labor, moving dirt from one place to another, grading and paving roads with his beat-up mules. He drove more than 75,000 miles in one year bidding on work and hustling for contracts. Along with his mules, Herman commanded small crews of reckless day laborers, working them hard all week and bailing them out of jail every Monday. The growing demand for roads in Texas, bolstered by the onslaught of cheap automobiles in 1917, provided enough work for a small-time contractor like Herman Brown to feed his family.

The only problem was that Herman Brown never wanted to be a small-time contractor. Like Halliburton, he was always on the prowl for bigger jobs, never content to scrape out a living. He had already imagined his future well beyond the dusty roads of Texas, and it was big. He needed to grow the business, and fast, but he confronted a major obstacle: His creditors were growing anxious and threatening to pull their funding in the middle of Herman's largest job to date. That money was to be the source of his expansion. Facing an abrupt end to the fairy tale he'd yet to complete, he tapped a new, more familiar, source of capital: Margaret's brother, Dan Root.

The owner of an enormous ranch near Granger, Texas, Dan Root used his good credit to lend Herman $20,000 to grow the fledgling business. After paying off his creditors, Brown thanked Root by naming the company Brown & Root. Dan Root had little interest in the road-building industry and was virtually uninvolved in the day-to-day activities of his brother-in-law's company. He died in 1929, but the name survives to this day.

In sharp contrast to Dan Root, Herman Brown was intimately involved in the workings of his company. The same inexorable force that drove Erle Halliburton's oil well cementing business was driving the road-building business—the automobile. By 1925, there were 975,000 automobiles registered in the state of Texas, and the enormity of the road-building job was daunting. Most of the work consisted of clearing, grading, and sanding roads, unlike paving that would later become the standard. Herman Brown lived with his crews in sprawling tent cities along the side of the roads they were building. He mixed well with the motley crews, even giving his men money to shoot craps. One night, he was arrested and fined along with the rest of his crew for gambling, but was back at work the next day. Like Halliburton, Brown gained the respect of his crews through his grit and hard work. He was considered one of them as he later acknowledged, "I grew up in the days when the relationship between myself and my employees was a personal one. If he had a grievance, he could come to me with it. There was no disinterested third party between us." Herman Brown was, and would continue to be, the heart and soul of Brown & Root. Though his brother George would play an increasingly important role in the development of new business ventures, it was Herman's ambition and determination that fueled the company.

• • •

Road contracting was a business that required more than just hard labor. A tremendous amount of business acumen, political finesse, and relationship building was necessary as well—this was particularly true in 1920s' Texas. At the time, government funding of road projects was nothing short of a political crapshoot. Power struggles between the state and county governments were routine, and the issue of Texas roads was repeatedly used to obtain political power, and to abuse it. By 1925, the politics of Texas roads had evolved into full-blown scandal—the Wild West of government contracting. Like it would do eighty years later when it hired Dick Cheney, Brown & Root needed to identify the political power base in its highly competitive business and curry favor with the key players. Relationships were everything.

As the rush to build new roads for the influx of people and automobiles reached a fevered pitch, allegations of waste, mismanagement, and favoritism began to surface against the newly formed Texas Highway Department, the statewide oversight commission for all new roads in Texas. In one case, a highway commissioner, who also happened to be in insurance and real estate, granted numerous contracts to Jim Smith of Smith Brothers Contractors. As it turns out, the commissioner also sold Smith a life insurance policy and collected $11,500 in real estate commissions. In another case, the American Road Company, which had close friends on the Texas Highway Commission, was issued several contracts without participating in the mandatory competitive bidding process. The company was eventually found guilty of corruption and excessive profits, fined $600,368, and banned from doing business in Texas.

The Texas road scandals went on for years, involving payoffs and kickbacks to everyone from governors to ex-governors and their wives. It was a thoroughly corrupt, highly political, and extremely profitable business. And Herman and George Brown now found themselves smack in the middle of it. In terms of business ethics, it probably could not have been a worse time and place to be learning the ropes in a new business. But for those with a willingness and ability to play the game, there was a lot of money to be made. The Brown brothers learned this lesson quickly. The groundwork was being laid for a pattern of influence peddling that would characterize Texas business and politics to this day.

In the early going, Brown & Root contented itself to take the scraps that the larger road companies left behind. With the sums of money that were required to gain contracts from highway commissioners, it was all Brown & Root could do. They had no great fortune and very little political clout. Paying off politicians was a little over their head. But gradually, they gained experience in how to influence the decisions of policymakers. At first, it was just taking out a commissioner for a nice dinner. Then they learned how to submit a low-bid then ratchet up costs over time. Finally, they became adept at the more sophisticated lobbying of public officials. Herman Brown was not some naïve kid who just happened to become involved in industrial and political intrigue, he was keenly aware of what it took to be successful and grow the business. He reveled in this environment of power, influence, and money and from the very beginning had no qualms about maneuvering within this world. One anecdote that confirms Herman's comfort level at an early age involves how his company obtained its very first job. After he had acquired the broken-down mules, Herman walked into the county commissioner's office and walked out with a contract. Not exactly a standard competitive bidding process, but that was how business in Texas got done, and Herman Brown knew it.

No one knows exactly what took place in that fateful meeting between Herman Brown and the county commissioner, but whatever it was, it went far beyond the open and competitive bidding process that was supposed to be taking place. To Herman Brown, it was strictly business, and in the corrupt world of Texas road politics, probably not that great a sin. But Herman Brown had taken his first steps out onto the slippery slope of inappropriate influence. To him, it probably felt good and right. He knew he could do the job, it was just a matter of getting his foot in the door. Very little has changed since those days, and Brown & Root (now called Kellogg Brown & Root), and its parent company Halliburton, still understand the lessons Herman Brown learned eighty years ago: politics is business, and business is politics.

The Brown brothers realized the nature of the business they had chosen and embraced it completely. While they may have started out with little idea of how to wield political influence, the Texas road business of the 1920s taught them everything they would ever need to know. It was never an issue of right and wrong with the Browns. As Brown brothers' biographers Joseph Pratt and Christopher Castaneda point out, "They had to become more adept at playing the game of political influence. This was a natural part of doing business in the world of public works contracts. They accepted this reality." Though our understanding of business ethics is far more advanced today, the methods of gaining contracts changed little for Brown & Root over the years. Indeed, with the work being done in Iraq today, the company is grappling with the very same issues they did in

Texas in the 1920s, but the level of scrutiny and acceptability of their business practices has changed.

The burgeoning needs for roads eventually drew Brown & Root toward Houston, where George had first gone to college, and where road paving was now the hot new trend. To date, Brown & Root had done mostly grading jobs in which dirt was leveled and compacted, then covered with small rocks to make a smoother ride on what was essentially still a dirt road. As one long time Brown & Root road crew employee, Bill Trott, says, "It was real simple work, you get the water off and the rocks on." Paving was a more complicated and more lucrative procedure that involved either asphalt or concrete. The company was also slowly getting more intricate work, building a few small bridges as part of its longer road-paving jobs. Every day the company became a little more sophisticated, a little more entrenched, and a little more profitable.

As payment for many of the jobs, the Browns took promissory notes that matured over a five-year period. By the late 1920s, the Browns were doing quite well building roads, and in addition to the cash they had made, were sitting on a mountain of promissory notes. The notes were secured by municipal real estate, and as the stock market crash of 1929 approached, the Browns were urged by their financial consultants to liquidate the immature notes. Demonstrating his legendary stubbornness and frugality, Herman continued to accept the notes and refused to cash them in before they had reached maturity. In July 1929, Dan Root passed away and Brown & Root officially incorporated. Upon incorporation, their financial advisor again pleaded with them to cash in the notes. "You're broke and you don't know it. All you've got is paper. Credit's running wild; it's out of hand. I tell you again, sell your paper and sell it quick." Finally, George Brown took the advice and went to Chicago to cash in the notes. The company took a 10 percent hit on the notes, but saved its future—the stock market crashed only a few months later. If not for cashing those notes, Brown & Root would have been just another company that withered and died during the longest and darkest economic winter America has ever known. Instead, the money from the notes sustained the company through the Great Depression, barely, and delivered to them the project that would elevate Brown & Root to the next level.

• • •

With the onset of the Great Depression, the road-building business came to a virtual halt. By this time, Brown & Root had close to 600 employees on staff, fleets of trucks and equipment, and a number of road-paving contracts that were suddenly worth nothing. Up to this point, the company had prided itself on keeping its employees working, all year long, rain or shine. But the Depression was something different entirely, and drastic measures had to be taken if the company itself was to survive, let alone keep its employees busy. The Depression would be the sternest test of Herman Brown's tenacity, and would bring his young company to the brink of dissolution.

For the first few years of the Depression, Brown & Root relied on the money they had made in cashing their promissory notes. Herman and George Brown learned some important lessons during that time; lessons that would serve them well for decades to come and serve as a basis for those that would come to decry the company in 2003.

The first was that the hardest part of their business was obtaining contracts, and they would need to employ any means at their disposal to do this. The second lesson, and perhaps most important to their long-term success, was that in order to adapt and survive, Brown & Root had to be willing to do any kind of work that was available in any kind of economic climate, no matter how demeaning or diverse. They had to scramble for every job; a reality that Herman Brown, who for once saw little use for his pride and stubbornness, readily accepted. By 1932, the situation had become dire. Brown & Root, as a last resort, took on work hauling garbage from the city of Houston. To make the business more profitable, Herman had his men separate the organic waste they collected, feed it to pigs, and then sell the pigs on the side. Times were indeed desperate, and even the garbage-hauling business was hotly contested. Brown & Root soon found itself involved in its first controversy involving municipal contracts—the first of many. As the company would learn, with any public works contract—whether supporting the military, rebuilding the oil infrastructure in Iraq, or even hauling garbage—a higher code of ethics is required. Public money comes with public scrutiny, an unavoidable and warranted fact of the government contracting business. Damage control, like that in which the company is currently engaged in Iraq, is a cost of doing business.

The subsidiary that did the garbage work for Brown & Root was the Houston Public Service Corporation, and it won a three-year contract worth $1,254,000 to collect and dispose of Houston's trash. But at the eleventh hour, another contractor submitted a bid for $750,000. Brown & Root was given the opportunity to rebid, and lowered its bid to $792,000, and won the contract. The Houston press was outraged, and claimed that corruption and favoritism were at play. Yet, the contract stood. "The way things were handled in awarding the garbage contract, nobody else had a chance except Brown & Root," wrote Nat Terence, editor of the *Houstonian*. Herman Brown was putting all that he learned during the 1920s Texas road-building business to work during the Depression, but he was no longer the eager outsider trying to break into the corrupt establishment. He was on the other side now.

Garbage hauling was not the only odd job that Brown & Root would stoop to during these lean years. The company did everything from repurposing World War I surplus equipment to forming the Texas Railway Equipment Company. They also had a brief foray into the transportation business, hauling construction materials by mule over, ironically, unpaved roads to remote construction sites. Though varied and unglamorous, the businesses that Brown & Root adopted during the Depression had two things in common: they all involved unskilled labor and they all, collectively, kept Brown & Root out of bankruptcy.

Herman Brown, the undisputed leader of Brown & Root, had already known hardship in his life growing up in rural Texas. The Depression simply further educated him on the business needs for diversification, frugality, and above all, adaptability. Now forty years old, he more than ever yearned for the big score. He wanted so badly to make his mark on the world with significant projects that having to haul garbage and scrap metal was a bitter pill. He never gave up, though, and continued to look for the one contract that would make the difference. However, despite all of his hard work, scrambling for meager contracts and accepting any and all work that was thrown his way, Herman Brown was slowly going broke. The Depression was steadily sucking the cash out of the company coffers, eating up the money they had so reluctantly secured when George liquidated Brown & Root's paving notes. Herman Brown needed a big score, and he needed it quickly. And he would do almost anything to get it.

PART II

Public Money,
Private Profits

3

The Man Behind the Dam
That Built Brown & Root

Every state in the union, at one time, has had their own version of Alvin J. Wirtz. Seldom are the names and faces that appear over and over in the newspapers, the public figures and politicians that take the brunt of the praise and criticism for government decisions, the driving forces behind those decisions. It is often the case that men operating outside of the spotlight of public office are the ones that really make things happen. We could argue that a certain level of anonymity is, in fact, prerequisite for getting things done. Elected officials are to some extent hamstrung by their constituency, limited by media scrutiny, and at times paralyzed by their thirst for re-election; loathing to make the tough decisions for fear of alienating voters. Alvin J. Wirtz recognized this unfortunate reality of American Democracy early on, leaving his post as a Texas state senator in 1930, and beginning his long career as a behind-the-scenes politician and businessman.

For the average acquaintance, it was very difficult to understand the full extent of Wirtz's power in 1930s' Texas. That was because he went to great lengths to conceal it. Gregarious and sociable, Alvin Wirtz drew people to him, invariably gaining their trust. There was a lot to like about Wirtz. A big man who favored good cigars and mint juleps, he was always relaxed, charming, warm, and generous. He was a wonderful storyteller. He had a quiet, unassuming manner and never needed to raise his voice to command the full attention of a room. He was able to listen silently to a heated and emotional debate on virtually any topic and offer a soft-spoken, measured summary of the topic with stunning clarity. "He was very deliberate in everything he did, even to walking or talking, but it gave people confidence in him because he was slow in reaching any decision," recalled George Brown of his close friend. People actively solicited his opinions and often abided by his judgment. It was this silent, entrancing power that enabled Alvin Wirtz to be a mover of men. In almost any group or organization there is that one individual who operates completely behind the scenes, wielding great power and ultimately pulling every string. Alvin Wirtz was that person in Texas in the 1930s.

Former Senator Wirtz moved effortlessly through the Texas power scene, playing the role of a simple country boy. Lyndon Johnson called him "my dearest friend, my most trusted counselor," adding, "from him . . . I gained a glimpse of what greatness there is in the human race." Lady Bird Johnson dubbed him, "The Captain of My Ship, Any Day." Acquaintances referred to him simply as "The Senator," even decades after his stint in the Texas Senate was over. But Wirtz's inviting, warm, and humble exterior thickly veiled both his seething ambition and a "mind as quick as chain lightning." He thought three steps ahead of everyone else in the room and was always working an angle. He was an indirect operator, aligning political forces against each other, deftly maneuvering men like chess pieces, and working the system to his own benefit. Many of the men who did Alvin Wirtz's bidding were never aware they were being manipulated, including Lyndon Johnson. "A. J. Wirtz, I believe, as you say, had as much influence on Lyndon Johnson's concept of what he should do as a public servant and what his obligations were as any man he came in contact with in his early political life," said George Brown. In many ways, Alvin Wirtz was what Herman Brown would eventually become: a man who subtly but powerfully pulled the strings of government, without the knowledge or consent of the people that government represented.

Ultimately, it was power that Wirtz wanted, and in his position as partner in the law firm of Powell, Wirtz, Rauhut & Gideon, he was in a better role to attain that power than at any time during his eight years in public office. He worked alone in his dimly lit library and hatched plans, sometimes exceedingly complex plans, to further his goals. He burned and shredded documents and memos, instructing the recipients to do the same. During the Depression, most men found it difficult to find work at all, let alone work that would vault them into power and financial fortune. Alvin Wirtz operated outside the constraints of crumbling economies, however, and during the most trying time in America's history, built his fortune beyond reasonable expectations. And he did it, in part, through Brown & Root.

• • •

By 1936, Herman Brown's company was fighting for its life, after nearly two decades of scraping and scrapping for road contracts. Prior to the Depression when times were good, Brown & Root had made it clear that the company was ready and able to take on the more complex tasks in road building, like paving and even constructing small bridges. Getting this work, however, required more than willingness to do the job, as Herman Brown discovered when he saw the larger construction jobs continually being given to larger firms with better connections and more experience. With Texas' public funds circling the drain during the Depression, it was clear that the pittance of roadwork being done was not nearly enough for the company to survive. Brown & Root was slowly sinking, drawing from its limited funds to make payroll, hopelessly casting about for a job that would save the ship. But the company had a powerful ally on its side: its counsel Alvin Wirtz.

Wirtz had already determined that the only available path to personal riches lay in the massive public works' projects being doled out by the federal government under President Roosevelt's New Deal program. These public works projects gave way to a new era of federally funded construction in an effort to put people to work and spur the national economy. It created a number of instant business success stories, like Bechtel, which built the historic Hoover Dam (then known as the Boulder Dam) between 1930 and 1936. Many of the companies that capitalized on government spending during this time became the largest and most powerful heavy construction firms in the world. The New Deal spawned some of the largest government contracting companies on earth, and Brown & Root would be no exception.

Wirtz had already worked on behalf of a large Chicago-based construction company to secure government funding and procure land for the building of several dams along the Guadalupe

River, and he was now angling for another, much larger dam, along the Lower Colorado. The dam was to provide hydroelectric power to the Texas Hill Country, which was at the time largely in the dark. As the chief architect of the deal, which involved some tricky legal maneuvering to obtain the land where the dam was to be built, Wirtz anticipated having a powerful say in how the jobs were distributed, as well as how and where the electricity was distributed. Half way through the project, the company he represented, Insull of Chicago, went belly up, and further financing for the project was not forthcoming.

To remedy the situation, Wirtz pulled off an extraordinary magic act. First, he convinced the Texas Legislature that the purpose of the Hamilton Dam was not electricity production, but rather flood control. The Texas Hill Country was regularly ravaged by flooding of the Colorado. From the start of the century through 1936, the flooding had caused $80 million in damages, flooded the capital of Austin, killed hundreds of people, and left the valley in peril every rainy season. A series of attempts to build flood-control dams along the river had been met with every conceivable form of obstacle, from a dearth of financing to entire construction projects in progress being washed away by the unrelenting flood waters. Persuading the legislature of the need for flood control was the easy part.

Wirtz's gifts were in full display during the second phase of his plan when he manipulated the legislature into forming a new public authority, the Lower Colorado River Authority (LCRA). Designed to take advantage of the $3.3 billion Emergency Relief Appropriation Act, LCRA was ready to receive money that was allocated by the federal Public Works Administration, an organization set up as part of the New Deal. The LCRA was created despite suspicions on the part of the Texas legislature that the new dams were not intended for flood control at all and therefore qualified for public funding, as Wirtz had maintained, but for the generation of hydroelectric power. Wirtz, with his calm reassurance and trademark charm, allayed the fears of the legislature, and the LCRA was formed in 1935. Wirtz was nothing if not convincing; for him to persuade a handful of local politicians, many of whom he had worked with in the past, was hardly a challenge.

Wirtz was appointed chief counsel of the new public authority and immediately set off for Washington, DC, to secure Public Works Administration (PWA) funding for his dam. It was during these trips to the capitol that Wirtz met and befriended Texas Congressman Richard Kleberg's ambitious young secretary, Lyndon Johnson, a relationship that would have a lasting impact on both Wirtz and, eventually, Brown & Root.

Convincing the PWA to authorize funding of the Hamilton Dam was the third step of Wirtz's plan. At first, the PWA was tight-fisted with its massive relief fund and failed to see the urgent necessity of the dam. Wirtz skirted this roadblock by engineering a redistricting of Texas—a technique that Wirtz employed regularly and that Texas politicians use even today—such that the dam now fell under the district of Texas Congressman James P. Buchanan, who also happened to be the chairman of the House Appropriations Committee. In a not-so-subtle nod to the influential congressman, a classic Wirtz maneuver, he renamed the dam; it was now to be called the James P. Buchanan Dam. Buchanan, who was tight with Roosevelt, had little problem securing funding for the dam. The story goes that in the summer of 1936, he met with the president, told him he had recently had a birthday, and the president asked him what he wanted. Buchanan replied, "My dam." The president responded, "Well, then, I guess we'd better give it to you, Buck."

There was one problem: The Buchanan Dam, abandoned and half-completed by this time, was not designed for flood control, and everyone knew it. Wirtz had hoodwinked the entire Texas Legislature and half of Congress into approving a flood-control dam that was clearly meant for hydroelectric power. It simply would not be an effective measure against floodwaters. For Wirtz, this was less a problem than an opportunity. The solution would be to build another dam, downstream from the Buchanan, but bigger—much bigger. This dam, the Marshall Ford Dam, would ultimately cost $10 million to build, and the company in charge was none other than Alvin Wirtz's suffering client, Brown & Root.

• • •

The closest Brown & Root had ever come to constructing a dam was the few bridges they had built before the Depression. But that hardly qualified them for a job of this magnitude and complexity. Realistically, Brown & Root had no business even submitting a bid for the Marshall Ford Dam. However, Herman Brown believed strongly that given enough men and money, his company could do any task. He reviled so-called "skilled laborers" and rejected union workers at every turn. His philosophy was to get the contract at all costs and worry about how to fulfill it later, a business practice that characterizes the company to this day. Securing contracts has become one of the company's greatest skills.

Brown & Root competed against two other bidders, both infinitely more experienced, for the Marshall Ford Dam contract.

So Herman Brown decided he'd better partner with at least one company that knew what it was doing, both to help educate Brown & Root on dam building and share in the risk. "Joint ventures in the early days not only spread the risk for us, it also permitted us to acquire a lot of know-how we didn't have much of," explained George Brown. "When we'd take on a big one, we wanted some company up in that dark alley with us." McKenzie Construction Company went in on the bid with Brown & Root, and the joint venture underbid the nearest competitor, Utah Construction, by a margin of $127,000. In December of 1936, the LCRA and its chief counsel Alvin Wirtz, awarded the construction contract for the Marshall Ford Dam to Brown & Root-McKenzie, also represented by Wirtz.

Brown & Root's lack of experience did not faze the company's ultra-confident leaders in the least. George Brown would later rationalize, "We originally were road builders. To be road builders, you have to know about concrete and asphalt. You have to learn something about bridges. Once you learn these things, it's only a step, if you're not afraid, to pour concrete for a dam. And if you get into the dam business, you'll pick up a lot of information about power plants. . . . Each component of a new job involves things you've done before." It didn't matter that Brown & Root had no idea how to build a dam; they were hungry for work, for the big score. This was the job they had been waiting for, the job that would vault them to a whole new level. And besides, they had Alvin Wirtz there to smooth out all the wrinkles for them. The Browns knew something then that most government contractors understand now: 90 percent of the work in government contracting is getting the job. Once you have the contract in hand, prices can be systematically ratcheted up, and the government's costs for switching contractors midstream exceeds the cost increases being handed down by the current contractor. It's that dependency on the contractor that allowed Brown & Root to grow its contracts once they were obtained, everywhere from Austin to Iraq.

• • •

The wrinkles would be considerable. Though the money ultimately came from the same place as the Buchanan Dam, the Emergency Relief Appropriation Act, the Marshall Ford Dam was not to be funded by the PWA. Instead, the $10 million dam was being funded by a grant from the Department of Interior's Bureau of Reclamation. As such, each project had to be approved by congressional committee. In this case, the relevant committee was the Rivers and Harbors Committee. But the Marshall Ford Dam had not been approved by that or any other committee yet. Because of Roosevelt's informal awarding of the Buchanan Dam to James Buchanan, the appropriations for the Marshall Ford Dam (that had been tied to the Buchanan Dam), money that had already begun to flow to Brown & Root, had not been formally approved. In fact, there had been no hearings whatsoever on the project. Roosevelt had granted the go ahead on a project that required Congress' approval while Congress was not even in session. It appeared that the dam was a nonstarter.

The Comptroller General's office caught the mistake and refused payment on the first of two planned installments of the appropriation, $5 million. Enraged, Buchanan set about convincing the Comptroller General that the authorization of the dam was imminent and would be obtained first thing during the 1937 session of Congress. Against his better judgment, the comptroller relented and approved the $5 million installment. The comptroller was unambiguous though: The second half of the payment would not be made if congressional approval was not obtained.

Brown & Root, meanwhile, had already begun working on the dam. Because they had no prior experience in dam building, the Brown brothers were forced to outlay significant capital just to acquire the proper equipment. Railroads had to be built to the remote location, tent cities erected, and major construction equipment procured. The biggest expenditure was a massive cableway over the gorge of the dam site. The cable carried large buckets of concrete over the dam site and poured the cement down into block forms. The total cost of the planning and preparation of the site was $1,500,000—money that Brown & Root would never see again. Money they had to borrow in the first place. Now the whole project was in jeopardy because of Buchanan's backroom deal.

The situation had the Brown's very much on edge. "The appropriations were for one year at a time—piecemeal," said George Brown. "And they were illegal. Wirtz was telling us all along that the money was wrong, and that if someone in Congress raised a question they would stop it." The way Brown & Root had budgeted the job left them with only a $1 million profit on the first half of the work. That meant that if the second payment never came, they would be out $500,000, deficit enough to break them forever. This project was the biggest gamble the company had ever, or would ever, take. The fate of Brown & Root was resting solely on the shoulders of one politician and his ability to clear the way for congressional approval.

• • •

After Herman and George Brown decided that they had no other option but to risk it, things quickly turned from bad to worse. It turned out that the land on which the Marshall Ford Dam was to be built was not owned by the federal government after all. It was owned by the state of Texas. The Bureau of Reclamation's charter strictly forbade the agency from building anything on land owned by anyone other than the federal government. Not only had the bureau allocated money for a dam that was not authorized, but it had allocated money for a dam that it was, in fact, forbidden to build.

In most states, this would not have been an issue. Upon admittance to the union, most of the western states had given up land rights of their riverbeds to the federal government. Not Texas. The state had guarded its public lands and kept them under state control. Its proud heritage as an independent Republic had dictated that stipulation. Of the 17 western states the Bureau presided over, only Texas had this arrangement.

Of course, Texas could just sign away its rights to the land, and the problem would go way. But when the LCRA was created, part of its charter strictly forbade the state from ever selling its public land, for example, the land that was the proposed site of the Marshall Ford Dam, to anyone, especially the federal government. The idea was to prevent the union from ever "federalizing" its public utilities, like the Tennessee Valley Authority. It worked. And now Brown & Root was stuck in the mother of all legal impasses. As Robert A. Caro puts it, "Under federal law, then, the Bureau of Reclamation was required to own the land on which its dams were built; under state law, it could *not* own the land on which this dam was being built."

George Brown later related Brown & Root's predicament in his own words. "We had put a million and a half dollars in that dam, and then we found out it wasn't legal. We found out the appropriation wasn't legal, but we had already built the cableway. That cost several hundred thousand dollars, which we owed the banks. And we had had to set up a quarry for the stone and build a conveyor belt from the quarry to the dam site. And we had had to buy all sorts of equipment—big, heavy equipment. Heavy cranes. We had put in a million and a half dollars. And the appropriation wasn't legal!"

Alvin Wirtz knew the law and he planned and devised a way around the whole mess. Buchanan would have to persuade Congress to pass a law so specific that it would approve the building of this particular dam on Texas land. If that were to happen, the original issue of land ownership and the laws that governed both Texas and federal land procurement would be so thoroughly obscured, the dam would have no problem getting approved. In other words, Buchanan's law would muddy the waters enough that the comptroller general would appropriate the funds. The plan had a chance, a real chance. In fact, with Buchanan's power in Congress, and the esoteric nature of the laws involved, few congressmen were likely to put up a fight. Understanding Wirtz's plan, Buchanan told the Browns not to worry, he would handle it in March 1937 when Congress reconvened.

Though the company was teetering on the brink of ruin, Brown & Root had faith in Buchanan. He was a powerful force in Washington, and besides, most congressmen couldn't be bothered with such a complicated and seemingly insignificant issue, even if it did violate the law. But Buchanan never got that chance. In February 1937, one month before he was to rectify the situation, Buchanan died of a heart attack. The Marshall Ford Dam was the first project in which Brown & Root was doing business directly with the federal government, and thus far, it was a complete disaster.

• • •

Upon hearing the news of Buchanan's death, a young, impossibly tall, aspiring politician by the name of Lyndon Baines Johnson cut short a meeting with the Kansas director of the National Youth Administration (NYA—another New Deal program), hopped into his Pontiac sedan, and sped from Houston to Austin with dreams of replacing the beloved James Buchanan as the next representative to the U.S. Congress for the Tenth District of Texas. His chances of winning the seat were as slim as his stature. He was a tender 28 years old, and had served only as Richard Kleberg's secretary, and more recently as the director of Texas' NYA. In addition, he was an unknown quantity in the Tenth District, which included Austin. He had been plying his trade as a congressman's secretary in the Fourteenth District, and he faced an unnerving battle against well-known and well-liked allies of James Buchanan in the Tenth. But this man was as ambitious as he was opportunistic, and he knew that a chance like this didn't come around often. Besides, he had a powerful force on his side—good friend and mentor Alvin Wirtz.

Johnson's first stop upon arriving in Austin that day in February was Wirtz's office. Wirtz adored Johnson. He had met him while acting as an advisor to Texas' chapter of the NYA and in his role as counsel to the LCRA, and had treated him like family ever since. With no sons of his own, Wirtz maintained an abnormally close relationship with Johnson, replete with bear hugs and other such uncharacteristic effusiveness. He once gave Johnson a gift, a picture of himself with the words, "To Lyndon Johnson, whom I admire and love with the same affection as if he were in fact my own son."

By the time Johnson had reached Wirtz's office to ask his support, Wirtz had already decided he would throw his considerable weight behind the lanky, young aspirant and had hatched a plan to win Johnson the election. But there was more to Wirtz's support than simple filial loyalty. Wirtz knew that Johnson, and only Johnson, could get him his dam. The other potential candidates, the most prominent being either Buchanan's wife or his popular campaign manager, C.N. Avery, would not be able to get the job done. They were both highly regarded in the community, but lacked the killer instinct that was needed to push through the crucial piece of legislation that would secure the dam. Wirtz had seen what Johnson was capable of during his time in Washington. He had seen the way people took to Johnson. And he knew that Buchanan's wife and Avery didn't have the drive or the personal interest in making the dam, which by now was rapidly approaching termination. Johnson would fight and fight hard because he was loyal to Wirtz. So Wirtz would fight hard to win the election for Johnson.

Wirtz immediately made calls to two of his biggest clients, the Magnolia and Humble oil companies, and shored up campaign contributions from both (the calls were made before Buchanan's funeral). He even dictated what was to be Johnson's strategy in winning the election: Johnson was to promote himself as a fearless supporter of President Roosevelt and a champion of the New Deal. Despite reservations about Roosevelt's programs on the part of Wirtz, the Browns, and Johnson himself, it was Johnson's undying loyalty to the president that would get him elected. He supported the president without reservation on all current and future programs, and if the other candidates supported Roosevelt as well, Johnson would step up his own support.

Buchanan's wife was the clear sentimental favorite in the race. But not willing to slug it out with career politicians, she chose not to run upon hearing of Johnson's candidacy. That meant that his chief opposition would be C.N. Avery. Wirtz pulled all the strings during the campaign. He lined up the money needed to sustain the campaign and obtained the support of Charles Marsh, an influential publisher of the two major newspapers in Austin, the *Austin American* and the *Austin Statesman*. The publisher of the *Johnson City Record-Courier,* Reverdy Gliddon, threw his support behind Johnson without Wirtz's prompting and wrote a glowing editorial that crowed, "He enters his political career with 'clean hands.' No one ever heard of Lyndon Johnson doing anything that was not honorable and straightforward."

To win the seat, Johnson waged one of the most expensive campaigns that Texas had ever seen; some estimate it cost between $75,000 and $100,000. The campaign rested entirely on the Roosevelt platform. By the end of the election, it was hard to tell who was running for Congress, Johnson or Roosevelt himself. Surprisingly, Herman Brown did not support Lyndon Johnson for Congress. Though he contributed a token sum to the campaign to cover his bases, Herman Brown was for Avery because he liked his politics better. Like most Texas business-men, Brown didn't care for Roosevelt's New Deal, despite the fact that he was in line to make millions from it.

After a whirlwind campaign, Lyndon Johnson won the seat in Congress in a contest that wasn't even close. The young man from the Texas Hill Country, bent on power and willing to do whatever he needed to obtain it, had won his first public elec-tion running on a platform he didn't entirely agree with. The Brown's didn't waste much time in getting to know their new representative. Time was not a luxury they had. The Bureau of Reclamation had sent a routine form to the Bureau of Budget regarding the Marshall Ford Dam. The form had been re-jected due to lack of Congressional authorization. It was now unclear as to whether Brown & Root would even get the initial $5 million. And even if they did get it, they would still be out $500,000. The Bureau of Reclamation sent auditors to the dam site to track expenses on an ongoing basis, signaling to the Brown brothers that the money could be stopped at any time. Auditors were watching the company's every move, approving every expenditure, and waiting for the ax to fall.

Johnson was elected in early April 1937 and didn't make his first trip to the Capitol until May 13. In the meantime, a mutual friend of the Browns and the Johnsons, Jim Nash, hosted a din-ner party so that the new congressman could meet the founders of Brown & Root. Johnson knew who the brothers were—Alvin Wirtz had ensured that Johnson knew what his first order of business would be in Washington: to save that dam. George and Lyndon hit it off. Herman was significantly more difficult to be-friend, but knew that Johnson would be the key to Brown & Root's future. He needed Johnson at this moment, more than Johnson needed Brown. But all of that would soon change.

Time was running excruciatingly short for the Browns. The chairman of the Rivers and Harbors Committee in Washington, the organization that would ultimately have to sponsor the legislation that Wirtz and the Browns so desperately needed, the legislation that Buchanan had been ready to push through, was Joseph Jefferson Mansfield, a fellow Texan. Mansfield's committee was to issue a report on the Marshall Ford Dam on May 24. That gave Johnson exactly 11 days to enact Wirtz's master plan and secure funding for the dam. Johnson knew why Wirtz had backed him, and he knew how important the dam was. He went to work immediately. He convinced Mansfield of the need for the dam, and the Rivers and Harbors Committee drew up a bill, which read in part, "The project known as 'Marshall Ford Dam,' Colorado River project, in Texas, is hereby authorized . . . and all contracts and agreements which have been executed in connection therewith are hereby validated and ratified . . ."

The muddying of the legal waters had begun. But there was much more to be done. The bill still needed to be approved by the House and Senate. The comptroller general had started delaying payments to Brown & Root until the full approval was handed down. And whispers around Congress began to spread about the illegality of the dam and the land where it was being built. The possibility of an investigation was broached, an outcome that would surely kill the project altogether. Johnson, just a few weeks on the job, needed to throw a Hail Mary pass.

The recipient of that pass was Thomas G. Corcoran, a White House aide to President Roosevelt and the ultimate Washington insider. Like Wirtz, only far more direct, "Tommy the Cork" or "White House Tommy" was known to be a man who could get things done. Corcoran had been told by Roosevelt, after the president had first met Johnson, to "help him with anything he can." Johnson approached Corcoran and asked him to plead his case with the dam to the president. Corcoran did, and Roosevelt's response is the thing of legends. "Give the kid the dam," he said.

With Roosevelt's stamp of approval, Mansfield was able to push the bill through the House and Senate with very little resistance. The first $5 million for the dam was finally secured, and for the time being, it seemed, so was the Marshall Ford Dam. But one last eleventh-hour wrinkle appeared. An administrator at the Work Relief office noticed that the work on the dam was being done by a private contractor and not a government agency. In addition, the dam was being built by skilled laborers, and as such, violated certain tenets of the work relief program. Corcoran intervened again, persuading the low-level administrator to drop his objections—which he did. Johnson and Wirtz traveled to the White House to finally put the issue to rest, and there received paperwork approving the full $10 million for the dam. Jimmy Roosevelt, the president's son, handed over the papers, telling them simply, "We are doing this for Congressman Johnson."

• • •

Herman Brown had his home run—his big score. Through very little effort of his own, Brown had gained control of one of the largest public works projects ever to grace the state of Texas. He was the beneficiary of a collection of interests independent of his own: Alvin Wirtz's need to control the flow of jobs and electricity in and around the capitol of Austin; Lyndon Johnson's need to make good on Wirtz's political and financial support; Mansfield's need to assert himself in Congress and bring work to his home state. Brown & Root stood to make a $1 million profit on the first half of the $10 million appropriation (minus the $1,500,000 initial investment) and nearly $2 million on the second half. It was far more money than the company had ever seen. And the contract had been skillfully guided through the channels of Washington, fallen to within a breath of its life, and revived again by a freshman congressman with a gift for flattery. By all accounts, Herman Brown should have been thrilled, relieved, and eager to complete a quality job on the dam as a calling card for future dam work. He should have been showering Johnson and Wirtz with gratitude. But perhaps the most amazing part of this saga was that it was not nearly over. Not even close.

Herman Brown knew that Wirtz and Johnson had bent the law to secure the dam. He knew that the dam had been sold as a flood control project and, as such, qualified for public funding. He also knew that, like the Hamilton Dam before it, the dam was really intended for power generation, not flood control, and that, in fact, the dam as it was currently designed and funded, would not be an effective defense against floods. Johnson and Wirtz had managed to obscure this fact throughout their manipulations of the system and had completed the process without anyone noticing this obvious contradiction. Herman Brown decided to press his luck and put the screws to the very men who had worked so hard to get him his precious dam. He decided to push for a bigger dam.

In November 1937, with construction of the dam well under way, a Rotary Club meeting was called at the Driskill Hotel in Austin. Ross White, Brown & Root's construction superintendent, opened the meeting by presenting his case for a higher dam. His argument was, simply, that the dam would not hold back the raging floodwaters of the Colorado. As a result, Austin and the outlying areas would continue to be imperiled. He wanted an additional $17 million to increase the height of the dam, more than the entire cost of the original dam. White's speech was followed by a similar talk by Howard P. Bunger of the Bureau of Reclamation. He was followed by yet another speaker, who again urged the room to consider the need for a higher dam. The meeting had been arranged by Brown himself, who did not speak, but he orchestrated the entire afternoon. A crafty sort himself, he had not warned Wirtz or Johnson of his intent.

Herman Brown, at this time, didn't particularly care for Lyndon Johnson. He had only met him a handful of times, and his wife was appalled by Johnson's sycophantic fawning over her husband, which all but excluded the very erudite Margaret Brown from conversation. Johnson's most powerful political weapon, the ability to make anybody like him, could not penetrate the steely pragmatist that was Herman Brown. Johnson's flattery rang empty and, as such, was far from effective. And Brown disliked politicians in general anyway. To add to this mismatch, Brown was dead set against the New Deal and President Roosevelt, who he thought was taking his money and handing it out to lazier men. He called the New Deal programs "Gimme's." The fact that Johnson had campaigned solely on the New Deal ticket had upset Brown. To Herman Brown, Johnson secured the Marshall Ford Dam for Alvin Wirtz, not Brown.

It took time for Johnson to work his charm on Herman Brown. Johnson knew that with the addition of the dam to Brown & Root's resume, the company was fast becoming a powerful financial force in Texas. It was clear that he needed

Herman Brown behind him, and he set out to get a better read on the fiery businessman. As Johnson would soon discover, Herman Brown didn't want people to agree with him without a fight. He wanted to convince people he was right. He wanted to argue politics and business long into the night, bang his fist on the table, and curse his opponent. He wanted people to be principled and stubborn. The normally malleable Johnson eventually learned to give him what he wanted. Between spring 1937, when Johnson won the final $10 million for the Marshall Ford Dam, and fall 1937, when Brown staged the high dam coup at the Rotary luncheon, Johnson thought he had made significant progress with Brown. Johnson and Brown had many things in common; a history of poverty, unbridled ambition, and Johnson even spent time working on a road building crew in his youth, much like Brown. He spent many nights at the Brown's residence at 4 Niles Road, in Austin in 1937, and had even managed to patch things up with Margaret Brown through the advice of mutual friend and Austin attorney Ed Clark. But with the stunning turn of events now taking hold, the budding relationship, which Johnson had worked so hard on, seemed to be exposed for what it really was to Herman Brown: just business.

• • •

Herman Brown had Wirtz and Johnson over a barrel, and the situation was all the more embarrassing because it was true. The original dam, now standing at an already immense 190 feet, would need an additional 78 feet to be able to hold back the flood waters. The new issue begged the question: If the dam needed an additional 78 feet for flood control, what was the purpose of the first 190 feet? It became suddenly clear that Wirtz and Johnson had sold the dam on false pretenses, and Herman Brown was poised to expose the entire scenario. At first outraged by this betrayal, Johnson, ever the politician, quickly gathered himself and chose wisely not to fight Herman Brown on the issue of the high dam. Johnson knew even then that Brown would become a crucial part of his political career. Swallowing his anger, Johnson did Herman Brown's bidding. He immediately began the process of securing funding for the higher dam.

The problems surrounding funding the higher dam were even greater than those that had been overcome to build the low dam. Johnson needed $17 million, and with no credit left, it wasn't going to come from the LCRA—which wouldn't have spending power again until the dam began generating power. That day was now looking like it might never come. The Bureau of Reclamation meanwhile was only authorized to fund projects for flood control. At this point, it would be impossible to argue that the higher dam was for flood control, without by default making hydroelectric power the purpose of the low dam. This was just the kind of legal morass that Alvin Wirtz thrived on, and he went to work rewriting history.

Using his trademark legal legerdemain, Wirtz redesignated the purpose of the low dam to be power production. It was safe to do this now that the original $10 million had already been obtained. That allowed the Bureau of Reclamation to pay for the additional 78 feet of the dam that would now be designated as flood control. But the Bureau was only authorized, on the high end of the scale, to spend $14,850,000 on flood control, and any additional funds would need to be reimbursable through the sale of hydroelectric power. That money,

along with the $9,515,000 that the LCRA had already commit-
ted to the dam, left a gap of $2,635,000, and nobody left to pay
the bill. That's when all heads turned to Abe Fortas, a Washington attorney and friend of Johnson's.

Fortas was a young and talented lawyer; he sized up the situation and gave the Browns his honest assessment. He was their
last hope for the higher dam, and as George Brown recalls,
"The fellow [Johnson] relied on most of all and became
friends with was the fellow he later appointed to the Supreme
Court, Abe Fortas." Fortas reasoned that he could convince
the PWA to fund the unclaimed portion of the dam, even
though the agency was not authorized to fund flood control
dams or power generating dams. He told Harold Ickes, the
PWA administrator, that if the unclaimed portion of the dam,
approximately 33 feet, were to be designated as neither for
power production nor flood control (because it was in fact for
both), the PWA could foot the bill. That portion of the dam
would cost about $2.5 million, as it happened. Unbelievably,
Ickes agreed.

The impossibly complicated solution for funding the higher
dam still needed to be rammed through the congressional approval process. Johnson had people working on his behalf to
smooth things over in the Department of the Interior, cutting
through endless red tape. But getting Congress' approval on a
transaction so obviously concocted would be no small task.
That burden fell to Charles H. Leavy, the chairman of the
House Appropriations Committee, who, like so many others in
Washington, was doing the bidding of the ambitious young congressman from Texas' Tenth District without fully understanding why or to what end. Leavy added an amendment to the law
governing projects funded by the Bureau of Reclamation that

specifically exempted the Marshall Ford Dam from the usual bylaws. Several congressmen jumped upon hearing this blatant rewriting of the law. Questions flew as to why they were being asked to provide an additional $2.5 million for a dam that was originally intended for flood control, then changed to a power generating dam, then was being called neither. It made no sense, and despite the complicated and esoteric nature of the project, the committee knew it.

Leavy began to feebly explain why the additional funding was necessary, but he was unconvincing. Upon seeing this weak attempt to persuade Congress, Sam Rayburn, the Majority Leader and a loyal Texan, silently stood behind Leavy as his words tapered off. When Leavy's convoluted explanation ended, Rayburn, one of the most powerful men in the House, said, "The gentleman is correct, yes." That was all it took. The House voted to approve the amendment, and the PWA was back in the dam business in Texas. Johnson, along with the help of some of his new friends in Washington and some old friends from Texas, had done it again.

• • •

Legally, there had to be a new bidding on who would build the higher dam. Ostensibly, the work would go to the most qualified, lowest bidder. Brown & Root, already having invested in all of the equipment necessary to do the job, easily outbid the competition. The new cost for the entire project was $27 million, and Herman Brown began slowly ratcheting up the cost even from that lofty plateau to increase his profits on the project. It was a technique the company would employ repeatedly in its government contracting business. Using Johnson as his go-between, Brown was able to get countless requests for additional costs approved. Johnson manipulated Department of the Interior underlings while he feverishly worked on Herman Brown's behalf. He sliced through red tape effortlessly, and Brown & Root reaped the benefits. Each *change order* had to be approved by several people in the Department of the Interior, and Johnson had them all working for him.

It was during this time that Johnson grew very close to George Brown, who served as liaison between him and Herman. George, closer in age and temperament to Johnson, frequently traveled to Washington. And Johnson reported back to Brown sometimes multiple times a day to update his progress. Later in life, George Brown would recall conversations he had with Johnson in which Johnson would characterize himself, Alvin Wirtz, and George Brown as "a joint venture . . . Wirtz is going to take care of the legal part, and I'm going to take care of the politics, and you're going to take care of the business end of it. . . . The three of us together will come up with a solution that will improve the status of all three of us," Johnson would say.

In reading Johnson's correspondence with the Brown brothers at the time, it's impossible not to think that he was spending a great deal of his time working for them. He was very much like a new employee at a firm, eager to impress. "It is needless for me to tell you that we are humping ourselves on the jobs we have to do here and that this little note . . . is being knocked off between conferences," he told Herman in one note. In another telegram from November 1940, Johnson expressed frustration with the orders he was receiving from George Brown: "Why do you send me telegrams and then run out before I can follow your instructions?" Johnson's subservience to Brown indicates just how important he knew the company would be to his future. It seems as if the majority of Johnson's first year in Washington was spent working on behalf of Brown & Root. Tommy Corcoran would later say, "Lyndon Johnson's whole world was built on that dam."

The same could be said for Brown & Root's world. The company had entered the bidding process for the original dam with zero dam building experience, hurtling toward bankruptcy. They made a $2 million profit on the low dam alone, and millions more from the higher dam, particularly as Herman Brown managed to squeeze change order after change order through the Department of Interior. The dam is a still-standing monument to the sheer will of several Texas men. Eventually renamed the Mansfield Dam, after the man who played a key role in its development, the dam served as the foundation for Brown & Root's financial future and Lyndon Johnson's political future.

Though their relationship had been strained, Lyndon Johnson and Herman Brown developed a mutual respect through the process of building the dam that would last through Johnson's presidency. Johnson learned how to spar with Brown on political issues, getting so heated that the two of them nearly came to blows at times. That's what Herman needed to see in order to grudgingly dole out his respect. He needed to know that Johnson was up to the challenge, that he stood firm and defended his views with pragmatism. "Lyndon and Herman would have some knock-down-dragouts, but they would always get back together because they all appreciated each other as a worthy opponent," recalled Lady Bird Johnson. Besides, it didn't hurt that Herman saw how hard Johnson had worked to make him money.

Up to this point, the relationship had been fairly one-sided. Johnson had bent over backwards for Brown, and Brown hadn't even supported him in his first campaign for Congress. But Brown knew what was to be expected of him now. He accepted the terms of the new relationship, for Johnson had more than proven his worth. Herman Brown had graduated from his days of wining and dining local politicians to eek out a living paving roads. He had bulled his way into the world of federal contracting, where the stakes were higher and the payoffs greater. He now had his pet politician on Capitol Hill, and he was going to ride him hard. George Brown would later say, "Listen, you get a doctor, you want a doctor who does his job. You get a lawyer, you want a lawyer who does his job. You get a governor, you want a governor who does his job." Johnson, it seemed, had a new job.

George Brown, understanding what Johnson had done for him and his brother, wrote a note to the freshman congressman. It read, in part, "Dear Lyndon, In the past I have not been very timid about asking you to do favors for me and hope that you will not get any timidity if you have anything at all that you think I can or should do. Remember that I am for you, right or wrong, and it makes no difference whether I think you are right or wrong. If you want it, I am for it 100 percent."

One of the most powerful and influential alliances between a business and a politician was cemented at that moment.

4

Guns and Butter

Whenever a nation enters into armed conflict, the business climate is of course fundamentally, if temporarily, altered. Stock markets plummet, consumers spend less, and corporations are faced with a series of critical decisions as the uncertainty of war sets in. How long will the conflict last? How will it affect our strategy? What should we do in the meantime? How a company answers these questions determines whether it thrives, survives, or dies in wartime.

During time of war, companies find themselves in a position to profit from that war by changing, sometimes dramatically, their core business to serve the needs of the nation and its military. When enough businesses choose this course, production in other areas of the nation's economy inevitably suffers. It is known as the *Guns and Butter Curve,* the economic principle that demonstrates opportunity cost; you can get more of something only if you give up something else. As a nation produces more guns (or any variety of goods and services for the military), it is incapable of producing as much butter (or food, or any other domestic products). The ongoing work of the American military in Iraq and Afghanistan and the promise by President Bush of a long, protracted war on terrorism has forced many companies to reconsider their business models. Halliburton, a company that has been experiencing severe problems of late with its core business, oil field services, is but one of those companies that has seen its balance of revenues tilt toward war-related work, be it through Kellogg Brown & Root's (KBR) support of the army or the rebuilding of Iraq's oil infrastructure. But this is not the first time Brown & Root, or its parent company, Halliburton, has been in this position.

Understanding a company like Brown & Root and Halliburton is nearly impossible without historical context. All of the confusing talk of no-bid, cost-plus contracts in Iraq and the relationship of Dick Cheney to Halliburton make little sense when viewed as an isolated event. It might even seem excusable to the casual observer. Taken with the company's history, particularly its long relationship with Lyndon Johnson and other prominent politicians, an undeniable pattern emerges, one that is far less likely to be overlooked. The abuse of political influence is endemic to Brown & Root, a pathology that repeats itself decade after decade. And the story rarely changes.

In protracted war, like World War II, the effects of the Guns and Butter Curve can be drastic. Companies must adapt to the changes foisted on them, and they must do it quickly, or they will miss out on an opportunity that could cost them their business. Halliburton, the eventual parent company of Brown & Root, came into the World War II era riding high. They had bucked the trend of the Great Depression, generating impossibly high profits during a time when most companies were drowning in red ink. They continued to invest in technology and expansion, even while their competitors filed for bankruptcy. And Halliburton remained focused on the business they knew best: oil well services.

For Halliburton, there was no real need to restructure their business during the war, though they did contribute peripherally to the war effort. They had a thriving business in a field that would only grow in importance during the 1940s, as the country's demand for energy grew exponentially in an attempt to fuel the war machines. By concentrating on extracting more oil from each well in the United States and its allies, Halliburton was set up for an impressive run during the war.

In contrast, as the war approached, Brown & Root had just had its first taste of success in government contracting in building the Mansfield Dam (previously known as the Marshall Field Dam). The company made several million dollars in profit from the job, which George Brown understated as "a nice bit of work" that had vaulted the company onto the federal government's favored contractor list. With their new congressman working hard for them in Washington, the next direction for Brown & Root was all too clear: defense contracting. While the simple and direct Erle Halliburton chose to eschew the sophistry of lobbying and government contracting, Herman Brown had embraced the inner workings of the federal government. Both men loathed the New Deal. Both resented having to pay taxes. And while both men distrusted politicians intensely, each would take very different paths to achieving success during the war. Brown & Root would choose guns. Halliburton would choose butter.

• • •

By 1938, Adolph Hitler had already begun mobilizing the German military in anticipation of successive invasions of Czechoslovakia and Poland in 1939. War in Europe was imminent, but the impact of Nazi aggression in Eastern Europe had yet to spread to the United States. Erle Halliburton had little interest in the events of Eastern Europe, however, as his oil-well cementing company had just pulled down its largest profit ever in 1937: a $2 million windfall that allowed him to expand the business, even buying out his former boss and the Perkins Cementing company. Howco owned a fleet of 100 cementing trucks, painted primary red, that roared from field to field across an ever-expanding geography, and they now had nearly 500 employees. Using new techniques like acidizing and well-logging, Howco was significantly cutting down the time it took to drill wells, while improving the profits from each successful well. Business was booming, but Erle Halliburton was still the same intense, hard-working man who drove endlessly across the southwest drumming up work.

The Depression had come and gone, leaving Howco untouched. The trajectory of Howco's profitability alone suggested the 1930s were a boom time in American business. In 1938, the company began a new type of work that eventually became one of the most important in its portfolio: offshore drilling. It was, at first, an awkward and untested process. Though the cementing crews had experience working in shallow water—marshes and swamps in the Louisiana delta—they had never done work that required barges. In the Gulf of Mexico, Howco loaded its trucks onto enormous barges that floated out to the Creole field, a few miles off the coast of

Louisiana. It was a stopgap solution that met with mixed results. Trucks were obviously not the best means of getting to offshore well sites. Eventually, Howco employed a small armada of ships to do the offshore jobs. But for now, trucks on boats would have to do.

The company also ramped up its international operations. Using a corporate structure that later would allow Halliburton to do business in several countries under United States or United Nations sanctions, Howco set up the Compania Halliburton de Cementacion y Fomento in Venezuela. Establishing this new company made it possible for Howco to take advantage of local incentives for Venezuelan-based companies. This ultimately led to the creation of similar operations in Colombia, Ecuador, and Peru. On the company's international expansion, Erle Halliburton remarked, "It is not my idea to just make money out of a country, but to develop it and raise the economic standards of its people." This is a claim that would be called into question long after Halliburton's death in 1957.

By the end of 1940, Britain, France, Australia, and Canada had already declared war on Germany. Paris was occupied by the Nazis, and the massive German air raids on London had begun. It was clear that the United States would not be able to remain neutral for long. By the summer of 1941, Roosevelt had frozen German and Italian assets in America, cut off relations with Japan, and announced an oil embargo against all aggressor states. It was clear that Howco's business was going to be affected by the coming World War, but how?

Halliburton knew what he was good at and decided not to stray too far from his company's core strengths. The best thing Howco could do for the country after it declared war on the

Axis powers in late 1941 was to help produce oil. The company continued to churn out technological advances during the war, helping the nascent industry grow and evolve.

Demand for oil in the United States skyrocketed through the war years, and Howco's business thrived. When many employees left to join the war effort, Howco increased its work week from 54 to 60 hours to make up the difference. Acknowledging the additional workload on those remaining, Halliburton increased the executive pay at Howco during this time, and established an employee profit-sharing program and retirement benefits package. Just as the Depression had not set Howco back financially, neither did World War II.

Howco was not entirely adverse to war profiteering, despite it's founders political leanings. The company found its way into military contracting, if only for a few years. It established a War Products Engineering division, and made gun mount bearings for the navy, fixtures and dies for Boeing's B-29 bombers, and even got some cementing work, building landing strips for the army air corps. Overall, the work for the war effort was minimal and secondary to Howco's oil well services juggernaut. And Erle Halliburton was not about to change his formula for success, certainly not for the U.S. government. He spent his own money in starting up the war products business and accepted no loans from the government. He became more interested in politics as time went on, fighting against unionization, excessive taxation, and what he saw as the spread of socialism in America. In a 1949 issue of the company newsletter, *The Cementer*, Halliburton aired his views. "As the politicians have become more powerful, the operation of free enterprise and the things that we in our generation have tried to accomplish have become more difficult. If the trend continues . . . the ingenuity and efforts of the next generation will be so sapped through taxation by the politicians that human progress will be reduced to the speed of a snail."

Comments like these hold obvious irony when you consider that huge portions of Halliburton's revenues today come from government contracting paid for by the taxpayers. If Erle Halliburton had his way, his company would never have gone that route. He had managed to isolate and protect his company from both domestic and international crises, but in 1947, after the end of World War II, Halliburton began to withdraw from the day-to-day operations. At the age of 55, he turned over the presidency of his beloved company to his brother, John Halliburton. Erle remained intensely interested in technical innovations and ways to improve the oil well business. Through all of his years, since he first caught the oil bug out in California, until the day he passed away in 1957, Erle Halliburton stayed focused. He was an oilman, an inventor, and an entrepreneur. He died having earned many times over the million dollars he once boasted about making. It was only after his death that the company would, for the first time, stray from the rigid path of the previous four decades, culminating with the purchase of Brown & Root in 1962. It was a future that Halliburton himself could never have imagined and most assuredly would not have condoned.

• • •

While Erle Halliburton remained definitively opposed to entangling Halliburton in the world of political back scratching, Herman Brown took Brown & Root in a markedly different direction. The Mansfield Dam had been a brutal and complicated transaction for the company, albeit a highly profitable one. Herman Brown had seen what the power of one well-placed politician could do for his bank account. Despite his opposition to the New Deal and the creeping socialism it represented, by the start of World War II Herman Brown had transformed his company from a hard labor, simple road-building business to that of a New Deal capitalist corporation. Through its work securing the Mansfield Dam contract, Brown learned a lesson his company would never forget: The right politician at the right time can make you very, very rich.

Brown's politics had not changed, but he had developed an overwhelming desire and uncanny ability to follow the money. During the Depression, the money came from federal hand-outs, and Herman Brown proved himself flexible enough to accept that reality. During World War II, the money was coming from defense contracts, and once again, Brown & Root made a seamless transition from New Deal capitalist to defense contractor in the blink of an eye. As Brown & Root's needs changed, so did Lyndon Johnson's politics. In the face of the approaching war, the supposedly liberal Johnson took on the rhetoric of an anti-union, Communist-hating reactionary, even going so far as to equate the two. "New Dealer or no, again and again he cast his anti-union votes, and by 1947 the alliance (of Brown & Root and Johnson) became common knowledge as his political identity changed from left to right before everyone's eyes," writes Ronnie Dugger, the Johnson biographer that gained unprecedented access to Johnson before, during, and after his years as president. Johnson had thus demonstrated his commitment to Brown & Root, and the time had come for Herman Brown to return the favor.

• • •

The Mansfield Dam had saved Brown & Root from certain bankruptcy and provided enough capital to last for years. But it was important to Brown & Root for other reasons as well. The contract had led to two other dam projects along the Colorado, the Marble Falls Dam and the Wirtz Dam (named after Alvin Wirtz), and vaulted the company into the ranks of the largest construction concerns in the nation. Ironically, building the dams turned out to be a much-needed public service. Flooding of the Colorado virtually ended after the completion of the Mansfield Dam, and the electricity that the LCRA was able to produce from the combination of the dams earned the agency the nickname, "Texas' Little TVA," after the infamous New Deal–era Tennessee Valley Authority (TVA).

Not surprisingly, Brown & Root played large role in bringing electricity to the rural Hill Country of Texas. The Pedernales Electric Cooperative, in charge of electrifying the countryside of central Texas, awarded the company a contract to erect 1,830 miles of electric line. The work consisted of blasting holes in solid rock, accomplished by a combination of dynamite and manual labor and hauling rock fragments out of the hole by hand. The work was subsidized by five-dollar contributions from the residents of the Hill Country, a hefty fee for some of the most impoverished people in the country. Many of the residents bartered their labor in exchange for the electricity the lines would eventually carry to their homes. By the late 1940s, the hillsides were awash in electric light, and all of the legal wrangling that led to the dams supplying the energy was forgotten.

The profits earned from the Mansfield, Marble Falls, and Wirtz Dams only further whetted Herman Brown's appetite for more federal work. With war looming, Brown knew the direction the company must now take. With Johnson on his side, he liked his chances of competing in Texas and abroad for defense work. The first target of Brown's desire was an air base that was being planned for Puerto Rico. In April 1939, Roosevelt was ramping up the country's military spending in earnest and signed a bill for $66,800,000 for the first wave of new air bases. Brown & Root had no experience in building bases, or really in anything of a military nature. But the company had faith in its man in office. And it didn't hurt that Johnson was now on the Naval Affairs Committee.

At this time, the spring of 1939, the Browns and Johnson exchanged several correspondences, all of which are on file at the Lyndon B. Johnson Library in Austin. The letters almost take on the tone of courtship, with increasing professions of devotion and loyalty. One note, from George Brown to Johnson, closed, "I hope you know, Lyndon, how I feel reverence to what you have done for me and I am going to try to show my appreciation through the years to come with actions rather than words if I can find out when and where I can return at least a portion of the favors."

Lyndon replied, "I wish I could dictate as sweet a letter as you wrote me. . . . I really enjoyed being with Herman this time. . . . We had a lot of heart-to-heart talks and, I believe, know each other a lot better. Knowing is believing, you know." The letter demonstrates the ease with which Johnson got along with George Brown, and the slow and sometimes painful process he encountered in befriending Herman. Over the course of the year, George Brown and Lyndon Johnson became very close, and saw each other often. They got together both in Austin and Washington to talk politics and business and work on building a mutually beneficial relationship.

Their friendship blossoming and their usefulness to each other apparent, Johnson was set to go to work for the Brown brothers again, this time in Puerto Rico. But Johnson soon realized that he didn't have the power to sway federal allocations outside of Texas the way he could inside the state. Two days after Roosevelt authorized the $66.8 million bill, Johnson told the Browns that he had talked with Admiral Ben Moreell, who headed the navy's construction at the time, but had not been able to further the Browns' desires. "I'll do all I can to get you any information on the Puerto Rican project and will let you know when anything breaks. You know how hard it is to get any dope in advance, but I'll have my eyes open. I'll probably wire you if I run into anything which seems likely."

Johnson was unable to work his magic. Despite his appointment to the Naval Affairs Committee, LBJ was not yet influential within the navy. Undaunted, Brown & Root submitted a bid on the Puerto Rican air base, a bid that was lost in the crowd. After the contract was awarded to another competitor, Johnson asked Moreell for an explanation why Brown & Root had not won the contract. He was humbled by the response, which he received from a low-level administrator, that simply stated, "Pursuant to your inquiry relative to the reason why Brown & Root, Inc. . . . were not selected as the contractors for the San Juan Air Base project . . . because they had no experience." What was a natural consideration for the majority of corporations, but had never been an obstacle for Brown & Root before was suddenly a problem. But the firm's faith in Johnson was undiminished.

• • •

His Puerto Rican bid rebuffed, Herman Brown decided to focus on business closer to home—that is, closer to Johnson's power base. Rumors had been circulating for years that the navy was interested in building an air base in Texas. Several different sites had been proposed, but Brown was zeroing in on Corpus Christi where Johnson's friend and former boss, Richard Kleberg, was the congressman. Progress on the site had stalled in Washington. The navy was ambivalent toward the site, unsure whether the base would be developed at all, let alone within the coming years. Herman Brown wanted that contract, even more than he wanted the Mansfield Dam. It was potentially far more lucrative, and with war fast becoming a reality, he knew that an entrée into military contracting would ensure the future of the company. But the situation was politically complicated—almost impossibly so.

The trouble stemmed from the Browns' ongoing support of John Nance Garner, known as "Cactus Jack," Roosevelt's vice president and a fellow Texan. Garner's relationship with Roosevelt had begun to unravel, and by mid-1939, it became apparent that Garner was going to oppose Roosevelt in his 1940 presidential bid. The two had become openly critical of each other, resulting in a deep division within Texas state politics. Johnson had staked his entire political career on Roosevelt, and it was far too late to change course. Most Texans, however, were more loyal to Garner. Herman Brown in particular identified with Garner's hard-line stance against unions. Garner's own fortunes had been built on the back of cheap, unregulated labor, and Brown was becoming increasingly and resolutely anti-union. Houston's congressman,

Albert Thomas, also backed Garner, and in August 1939, stated that "every member of the Texas delegation is for Vice President Garner."

If Johnson was going to be able to help the Browns secure the Corpus Christi contract, which at this point was on life support, he would need the brothers to withdraw their support of Garner. Then, Johnson could claim responsibility for shifting the corporate politics in Houston from Garner to Roosevelt, and gain leverage with the president, ultimately using his influence to win the navy contracts for the Browns.

This was an extremely risky proposition for the Browns. Garner, after all, was the vice president, and Lyndon Johnson was merely a freshman congressman, albeit with some limited entrée to the president. In order for the gamble to pay off, Johnson would have to be able to parlay the support of the Browns for Roosevelt into political favoritism. It was a long shot, to be sure, but Herman Brown was growing increasingly comfortable with Johnson's ability to manipulate the system. George Brown sensed that Lyndon needed the Brown brothers to do something drastic, but was too shy to ask. He wrote to Lyndon in October 1939, "I have been sitting here all week waiting to hear from you. . . . I felt that you had something on your mind last week but did not get around to getting it off." That was the opening that Johnson was looking for. From that point on, Johnson, who had single-handedly saved the Browns from financial ruin, would never again be shy in asking Brown & Root for help. And Brown & Root would never be shy in offering it.

With Herman Brown and Lyndon Johnson, the normal power structure between a politician and businessman was inverted. It should have been that Johnson was the independent thinker, calling shots on behalf of his constituents, and not letting the overbearing influence of one prominent business-man dictate his actions. Instead, it was Herman Brown that held all the sway, directing not just Johnson, but countless politicians over the years. This inverted relationship at Brown & Root carries forward to today. While supporting the army in Bosnia, military officials became so confused about their relationship with the contractor, Brown & Root, that they were actually afraid of upsetting Brown & Root by placing too many constraints on the company. One commander even re-ferred to the company as the "customer" of the army, illustrat-ing the ability of Brown & Root, for decades, to flip the normal vendor-customer relationship on its head.

Exercising his dominance over local politicians, Herman Brown immediately instructed the malleable Albert Thomas to stop backing Garner and start backing Roosevelt. Thomas had a reputation for following Brown's orders to the letter, and four months after Thomas had announced his strong support for Garner, his vote swung the other way.

The move started a domino effect in Washington. Showing his appreciation for what Johnson had done for him in Texas, the state that would be most difficult for him to win in the pri-maries, Roosevelt appointed a good friend of Johnson and the Browns as undersecretary of the Interior. The recipient of this position? None other than Alvin Wirtz, who was still acting counsel for Brown & Root. Wirtz had originally been opposed to Roosevelt's politics, particularly the New Deal or Roosevelt's controversial court-packing plan of years before. But since he had Lyndon Johnson acting as his go-between, arranging proj-ects and cultivating relationships as was the case with the Mansfield Dam, Wirtz had warmed to Roosevelt. Wirtz's job, aside from working under Harold Ickes at the Department of the Interior, was to lead Roosevelt's campaign in Texas against Garner. In an indirect way, the move was also a nod to Herman Brown, who now had another powerful ally in Washington.

In addition to this generous move by Roosevelt, the navy was instructed to consult with Johnson on all contracts being awarded in the state of Texas. Suddenly, Brown & Root was seriously considered for naval contracts, the first of which was the Corpus Christi Naval Air Station, which had become a much higher priority of the navy. It was quickly pushed onto the preferred list of navy projects in February 1940, months after it had been considered a lost cause by Kleberg and the Browns.

At this point, things will begin to sound eerily familiar to anyone who has followed the events surrounding Halliburton in the wake of the Iraq invasion in 2003. The contract for the Corpus Christi Naval Air Station was deemed a "cost-plus" contract, meaning that the contractor would recoup all expenses plus a built-in, guaranteed profit based on a prenegotiated percentage. Normally, that profit can range from 2 percent to 10 percent, depending on the nature of the work and the structure of incentive clauses. The problem with contracts of this nature, as will be discussed in later chapters, is that a contractor has an incentive to increase the expense of the job, thereby increasing its profit. Great for the contractor, not so great for the taxpayer.

In addition, it was decided that the contract would not be put out for competitive bidding. Instead, it was to be negotiated at the navy's discretion. In a scenario that would play itself out again and again throughout the company's history, Brown & Root was the only firm seriously negotiating with the navy for the contract, which it ultimately was awarded. In a matter of months, Brown & Root had gone from being a company that was too inexperienced to build a naval air base in Puerto Rico to being the sole contractor under consideration for this particular job. Things were changing very quickly now. The urgency of the Corpus Christi site had been ratcheted up from "not emergent" to high priority. And it would be big—both in pure dimension and in cost. The original price tag for the job was $23,381,000, and Brown & Root would take a 5 percent profit on top of that. Of all the air bases that the navy was planning at the time, the Corpus Christi site would be almost twice as large as any other. And its funding was fast-tracked, while the others were put on hold until defense appropriations were approved. Almost miraculously, plans for the base had already been drawn up and work had begun by the time news of its existence hit public awareness. Other contractors never even had a chance. Johnson had done it again.

The issue of Brown & Root's inexperience had not gone away, however. Even though they had been awarded the contract, the government felt more comfortable having another, more experienced contractor in on the job, if in name only. Brown & Root was informed that it would need to cut in Henry J. Kaiser, another road builder turned New Deal capitalist. Kaiser had taken a remarkably similar path to riches as Herman Brown—from building roads to bridges to dams and defense contracting. At the time, Kaiser was a much more recognizable name than Herman Brown, and Herman knew that Kaiser was about to get something for nothing. To minimize the impact Kaiser would have on Brown & Root's profits, Herman sent George, the consummate salesman, to Washington to negotiate the deal. Kaiser knew that the Browns needed him more than he needed them, and as such, asked for a healthy 75 percent of the project.

George Brown, countered with 25 percent, which Kaiser found insulting. Brown turned to leave the room. Kaiser said, "Well, what are you going to do?" Brown replied, "I already told you what I'm going to do." Kaiser acquiesced, took his 25 percent, and did virtually nothing to earn it. He set up a company called the Columbia Inspection Company for the express purpose of working on the Corpus Christi job.

The Browns invited another partner into the deal as well: Bellows Construction. Herman Brown knew something that the navy didn't—neither Kaiser nor Brown & Root knew how to build an air base of this magnitude. Like the Mansfield Dam before it, the Browns sought a partner with expertise, and Bellows agreed. "We needed someone who had done buildings," said George Brown. "We hadn't done many." With the construction team in place, work began on the base on July 26, 1940.

• • •

Once started, the project began to grow in size and cost almost immediately. First there was an increase of more than $6 million to the price tag. Then another $13 million. Then another $2 million. With the costs mushrooming and the workforce—at peak 9,300—expanding, Brown & Root found itself in a powerful position in Texas with the ability to dole out subcontracts and jobs to their friends and associates. Alvin Wirtz asked that his brother's firm be considered for the architectural design of the buildings on the base. The Browns were known to regularly hand out jobs to friends of the family, a serious snub to the union activists that regularly disrupted work on Brown & Root sites. As the job grew, contractors from around the country wanted in, but found the door firmly shut. Tommy Corcoran said that James Forrestal, the undersecretary of the navy, "twisted a hell of a lot of tails" to keep the job the exclusive purview of "Lyndon's friends." By the time the project was complete, the total cost was $125 million, more than five times the original value of the contract, and the largest and most profitable work the Browns had ever done.

Looking back on its work for the navy in Corpus Christi, George Brown reflected that it was "the only contract [Johnson] ever played any role in." He admitted that Johnson had recommended Brown & Root to Admiral Moreell, who had ultimately awarded the contract. He went on to say that "getting the Corpus Christi contract was the hardest selling work I ever did. The navy told us it just didn't think we could do the job." The navy was at least partly correct in their original assessment. For $29 million, Brown & Root could not, and did not, do the job. They did it for $125 million.

George Brown's statement that Corpus Christi was the only job that Johnson helped with was, of course, untrue. The Mansfield Dam was almost entirely Johnson's doing. And subsequent work would be too, as the relationship between Johnson and the Browns continued to grow. Johnson's own comments to Ronnie Dugger, years later, directly conflict with Brown's recollection. Johnson went so far as to claim that "I never recommended them for a contract in my life. They never asked me to do anything for 'em. Nothing in the record will show it."

Dugger, who was far more lenient in reporting Johnson's compromised relationship with the Browns than Caro, clarified in his biography of Johnson "this was a most deceptive response. In the first place, it would be a mistake to believe that the way these things must happen in the life of a skillful politician, the businessman comes in and says, 'Congressman, there's a wad of dough to be made. . . . Get me a contract and I'll take care of you.' Rather, the politician and the business-man are friends; they have dinner together; they are mutually aware there is money to be made. . . . Who gets the contract? A great deal depends on who knows what first; then there are the bureaucrats who make the discretionary decisions. Infor-mation is provided to the businessman; perhaps an aide sees a bureaucrat. Nothing official or formal, but when the politi-cian needs help, he has a friend."

Dugger's comments reflect the subtle and discreet nature of political influence peddling, and his words are all the more rel-evant today. It bears mentioning that Brown & Root did good work on the air base although it cost a great deal more than originally anticipated. The company had completed 60 percent of the base in just eight months, allowing for cadets to begin training at the base ahead of schedule. In January 1943, the company received a coveted award from the navy, the Army-Navy Production Award, known as the Army-Navy "E," for "those plants and organizations which showed excellence in producing ships, weapons, and equipment for the navy." While their methods of attaining contracts may have been suspect, the work they did once the contracts were in hand was undeni-ably solid. As such, their contract work with the navy was just getting started.

• • •

Through his relationship with Lyndon Johnson, Herman Brown had learned again and again the value of key politi-cians when it came to scoring lucrative government work. But Brown's efforts to manipulate politicians did not begin and end with Johnson. Albert Thomas, the young congressman from Houston that had already been instrumental in getting Brown the Corpus Christi contract, would prove even more valuable than Johnson during World War II. From a pure bottom line perspective, it was Thomas, not Johnson, who introduced Herman Brown to the most profitable business yet: shipbuilding.

The federal government had originally rejected Thomas' attempt to bring a naval air base to the Houston area. All the same, the eager representative did his share in making certain that the work being done in Corpus Christi, which lay outside his district, would ultimately be done by Brown & Root, a company already based in his district. Thomas wouldn't quit with building air bases. He continued to pursue other defense work in his district as well, lobbying the government for contracts of every kind. In March 1941, a small boatmaker in Houston won a $2 million contract to build four Patrol Craft subchasers for the navy. The job was meager, in relative terms, but the company, Platzer Boat Works, quickly found itself in over its head. With bankers threatening to withdraw their funds, Platzer was in danger of insolvency, with the four subchasers incomplete.

Thomas devised a solution. Knowing the navy was in a bind, needing the boats urgently, he recommended Brown & Root to Admiral Sam Robertson, head of the navy's Bureau of Ships. Soon, the phone rang at Brown & Root, and a navy official asked if the company could help Platzer out. Of course, Brown & Root had no experience building ships. But the opportunity was too good to pass up. Herman Brown knew that the navy was ramping up production of ships dramatically, and immediately saw the small contract as a way to get into shipbuilding in a big way. As he had learned with the Corpus Christi project, the military was far more interested in having their deadlines met than with controlling costs. Once a contract was won, increasing the costs to the military was a foregone conclusion. The Browns decided to take the job, but they didn't want to get Brown & Root involved because of the inherent risks of the business. Instead, they started the Brown Shipbuilding company.

"We didn't know the stern from the aft—I mean the bow—of the boat," confessed George Brown years later. Again, inexperience didn't matter. Herman Brown had been shuffling hundreds of thousands of dollars through Johnson and into the Democratic Party's coffers for the better part of a year now. He had helped substantially in getting Roosevelt reelected, and packing the House of Representatives with Roosevelt loyalists. He was repaying his considerable debt to Johnson, and everyone in Washington knew it. That the Browns were approached to get into the navy shipbuilding business was not because of their expertise—it was because Herman Brown's money had put more politicians in office in Texas than the Democratic National Committee.

The Browns quickly turned around Platzer's dying operation. They hired men from every field imaginable: oilmen, farmers, welders, road builders—anyone with two hands. Only 5 percent of Brown Shipbuilding's original employees had any experience in shipbuilding. The navy gave them a contract extension in September 1941 for eight more subchasers and an additional $5 million. Herman Brown's latest gamble was beginning to pay off as the Two-Ocean Navy Bill signed by Roosevelt in the summer of 1940 kept new orders rolling in. Thomas kept the pressure on the navy, writing them "We are hopeful that additional orders will be forthcoming, and we have good reasons for believing the [Brown Shipbuilding] shipyard will be a permanent industry, continuing its operations after the war."

By 1943, shipbuilding was the biggest business in Houston, and Brown & Root employed more than 15,000 men. By February 1942, three months after the Japanese bombed Pearl Harbor, Brown Shipbuilding's first boat, PC-565, slid down the ways and into the Gulf Coast. On watching the spectacle, George Brown remarked, "I was praying she wouldn't turn wrong side up." The boat would go on to be the first PC to down a German submarine. The Browns, without an ounce of shipbuilding experience, were doing the unimaginable: building boats that outfoxed the German military machine.

Brown Shipbuilding was fast and efficient, and the navy knew it. In January 1942, the company scored a contract for 18 Destroyer Escorts for $3.3 million each. The navy contracted for the brothers to build another shipyard, for another $6 million, and leased it to the Browns for one dollar a year. A few months later, the navy ordered 32 landing craft infantries for $17 million. The money was pouring in, and the ships were sliding out to sea. *Time* magazine, in early 1943, called the Browns "Texas Wonder Boys," and noted that "Destroyer Escorts were plopping into the water so fast it startled even veteran Navy men, and average building time was being slashed two-thirds . . . the infant company's backlog is now over $300,000,000—more orders on hand than giant 38-year old Bethlehem Steel had three years ago."

The Browns had proven again that given the chance to build in any industry, they would get the job done quickly. By October 1943, Brown Shipbuilding employed a jaw-dropping 23,000 people, just two years after its formation. Between 1941 and 1945, the company built 359 ships in all, and won contracts exceeding

$500 million. How did this company, which didn't even exist before 1941, do it? Part of the answer lies in Herman Brown's hiring and employment policies, which were staunchly anti-union.

• • •

Union problems had bubbled up throughout Brown & Root's history. There were problems on the Mansfield Dam, then bigger problems at Corpus Christi. The more employees the company took on, the bigger the problems became. By the time Brown Shipbuilding was employing its peak number of employees, Brown's "open shop" philosophy was hitting a wall, and his workers were getting fed up.

Reports of unsatisfactory working conditions at Brown Shipbuilding had begun to surface the first year of its existence. Albert Thomas was kept busy reassuring officials at the Office of Production Management that nothing would come between Brown Shipbuilding getting boats in the water on time. But the navy investigated the problem, and the War Manpower Commission issued a report blasting Brown Shipbuilding. "Turnover has lately become a serious problem at both yards . . . long hours, excessive commuting distances, lack of nearby housing, and poor lunchroom facilities," were blamed for the discontent. "An unnecessarily severe policy of refusing to rehire any worker who was discharged by any foreman or official of the company and failure of the firm to attempt to hold workers who express a desire to quit also is a contributing factor."

The report only caused Herman Brown to dig his heels in deeper. He had worked hard his whole life, and could not be persuaded to allow workers to artificially limit their loads, for the same pay. It particularly offended Brown for this issue to be surfacing during wartime when patriotism alone should be carrying the day. He wrote an article in the company newspaper entitled "Slugger or Slacker." In it he opined, "Slacker is a rough word . . . we still think it's exactly the right word to apply to some of the men working here in the yards. No, they aren't shirking service in the armed forces, and they aren't draft dodgers; they're WORK-dodgers. And any man who imagines that our war effort doesn't call for the best he's got, every hour of the day he spends at the yards, is a slacker. . . . Look yourself over carefully—are you a producer, or a slacker?"

Brown's tough words backfired. Nine different labor unions wrote to Brown Shipbuilding demanding that employees at the company be allowed to seek collective representation. The letters were ignored, sparking the involvement of the National Labor Relations Board (NLRB). The NLRB set a hearing on the matter, at which Alvin Wirtz argued on behalf of Brown Shipbuilding that the NLRB had no jurisdiction, an argument that was summarily dismissed by the NLRB. Elections were held, unions were formed, and Brown continued to defy them. "It has never been necessary for any employee in any enterprise with which I have been associated to designate a union as his exclusive bargaining agency in order to get a square deal," he told his employees. The unions struck, and picketed in front of the Brown Shipbuilding facilities. But many workers crossed the line and continued to work, in part fueled by the patriotic war rhetoric of Herman Brown.

Lyndon Johnson, whose liberal politics had been forged by the New Deal, supported his friends with vehemence. He sponsored a "work or fight" bill in the House Naval Committee that would allow the draft board to receive the names of absentees from navy contractors. The names would be thrown to the top of the draft pool. It was an outrageous proposal, meant to scare the unionists back to work. Johnson was saying, in essence, that if you weren't willing to work, "the draft board will get you if you don't watch out." There's no telling what would have happened if Johnson's proposed legislation had been enacted, but military officials were having none of it. It would have brought with it an army full of bitter, unmotivated soldiers already with a predilection for loafing or malingering.

The New Deal government was solidly behind the right of workers to organize, but that didn't mean anything to Johnson, who continued to vote against labor laws. The central issue facing the federal government on this issue was crucial to Brown & Root and Brown Shipbuilding, and their ability to win future contracts. If the government were to be either neutral or against the unions, it automatically gave "open shop" companies like Brown & Root a very real advantage. Open shop companies would consistently be able to underbid those with unions. During the war, the federal government had little choice but to shift to a muted stance against unions, which were considered to be subversive to the war effort. This enabled companies like Brown & Root, which had resisted unions from the start, to profit at the expense of union companies.

After the war, Herman Brown continued to lobby hard for union-busting laws in Texas. The infamous "Right to Work" laws of Texas were largely Brown's doing, as he prodded the Texas legislature to set new rules for unions. The company led a vicious battle against the Texas AFL-CIO in the late 1940s, suing every chapter in sight for damages incurred from picketing its plants. Nat Wells, the lawyer that represented one of the craftsmen unions, had this to say of Herman Brown. "I say it's unfair to get the most public work of any contractor in the state, and on every hour of that work for every man . . . taking fifty cents an hour and adding it to his own millions. . . . You know, I'm pretty tired of that socialized millionaire, who is sucking at the public teat, if you please, who has made his millions from your pocket and mine in tax money, starting with a dam down here by Austin, most of the highway work in the state, political connections that gets him lots of federal work; that's your money and my money, our tax money . . ."

The Browns remained defiant. In most cases, they were able to stall the NLRB for long enough to complete the job in question, rendering the labor complaints moot. They were accused of intimidating, threatening, and firing unionizers from several different jobs. While the labor disputes and disruptions were a nuisance, Brown & Root bulled its way through every case, clinging to its ideals of an open shop. In rare cases, the company was forced to make compromises, but the ethos of "right to work" laws stayed strong within the company for years to come. Bill Trott, a Brown & Root road crew employee from 1951 to 1992, put it this way, "I don't know of anybody that ever worked for me that wanted to be part of union. I remember a bumper sticker I once saw in Louisiana. It said, 'Vote against the right-to-work law'. . . silliest thing I ever saw."

Both Howco and Brown & Root managed to profit from wartime, though in vastly different ways. Erle Halliburton kept his head down during World War II, refocusing his business on furthering the oil-field services business. Herman Brown threw himself and his company headlong into world events, capitalizing on the desperation of the military during war. Though the Browns may have exploited the system more effectively than Halliburton, the company's success would not come without scrutiny. Having identified themselves so closely with Lyndon Johnson, and by fighting some very public battles with labor organizations, Brown & Root raised its profile during the war, and thus made itself a political target. As a result, the company would live with a reputation for political influence peddling right up until the modern day, and its relationship with Johnson would bring an official investigation of its political contributions that would nearly ruin it.

5

Collateral Damage:
The Leland Olds Story

Brown & Root's success did not come without casualties. Though in the 1940s, Brown & Root was still 60 years away from actually losing employees in war zones like Afghanistan and Iraq, the company left a different kind of victim in the wake of its tremendous surge in political power in the post-World War II era: political casualties. There had already been C.N. Avery and James Buchanan's widow back in Austin, both of whom lost out on the opportunity to succeed Buchanan in Congress when Lyndon Johnson decided to run. Those victims were more incidental in nature: it wasn't personal, they just happened to be in the way of Johnson and Brown's uncontained ambitions. Most people who fell by the wayside as the Johnson/Brown machine plowed its way to Washington got back up and led normal lives. Leland Olds was not so lucky.

From early on Olds, who would eventually rise to become the chairman of the Federal Power Commission (FPC) under Roosevelt and then Truman, was on a philosophical collision course with the Brown brothers. A voracious academic, Olds decided at a young age to dedicate his life to balancing out the disparity of wealth in the United States. In particular, Olds had seen the horrifying effects of industrialization on working families in Holyoke, Massachusetts, while a college student in nearby Amherst in the early 1900s and vowed to "have some effect toward mitigating the evil of poverty." After college, Olds set out to find the most meaningful profession in pursuit of his goal. Idealistic, but aware of his own limitations, he brought his passion to the slums of South Boston.

Like many who enter the field of social work, Olds was quickly disillusioned by the inherent shortcomings of the system. He wasn't learning anything about the root causes of economic disparity. He was simply witnessing, somewhat helplessly, the tragedy of its effects. He turned to religion as a possible answer, and became a minister in a congregationalist church in Brooklyn. But again, Olds met with an institution that had already accepted defeat in the worsening battle against poverty. As the son of a mathematics professor and a former mathematics honor student himself, Olds took a job with the Industrial Relations Commission during World War I. He was charged with combing through reams of data in an attempt to determine how wages should be set during wartime. What he found was the disheartening reality that while productivity in America continued to rise, wages did not. The average worker was not sharing in the success of American business, and labor unions were being suppressed, sometimes brutally, by powerful industrial companies with the government on their side. He decided at that point that the only solution to this complex and deepening problem was a fundamental shift in the role that government played in regulating labor disputes. Either by owning the sprawling monopolies—like railroads and utilities—or by backing labor, the government must intervene.

It was a philosophy that Olds had evolved through his work as a social worker, minister, and government employee. His brilliance and compassion made him utterly qualified to reach the conclusion. But it placed him diametrically opposite Herman Brown and his "right to work" philosophy. Though he didn't know it yet, and wouldn't until it was too late, the anti-labor forces were gaining political clout that would ultimately vanquish any hope Leland Olds had of making a difference.

Though his ideas were vaguely socialistic, Olds believed that the capitalistic society could work to defeat poverty within the constructs of democracy, he just wasn't sure how. So he went to work learning more about the power industry, how rates were set, how wages were set, and how it could be done better. He did this work on his own, even while on vacation, poring over volumes of texts at his local library in Chicago. He crunched numbers and created new formulas. He did it because he still wanted to be an instrument of change that would allow more impoverished and rural citizens to afford electricity. In the course of his research, he learned that by lowering rates, public utilities could actually increase their profits by expanding their customer base. He wrote thousands of articles, hoping that his words could counter the juggernaut that was American industry in the golden age of the 1920s.

Bringing power to impoverished families became an obsession for Olds. He felt strongly that power would, at the very least, mitigate what he felt was the "evil of poverty." When

Franklin D. Roosevelt (FDR), then governor of New York, called on Olds to share his views on the subject in 1929, he was armed with statistics and research that impressed the sympathetic governor. He offered Olds a job as the executive secretary of the New York State Power Authority, and his ideas were immediately put into action by the agency. By increasing its authority over setting rates, the Power Authority strong-armed reluctant utilities into lowering rates, and as Olds had predicted, their profits increased. His work was finally starting to make a difference, and he had found his calling in government service.

In 1939, after his relationship with FDR had blossomed into a mutual respect and admiration, Olds came to Washington and was appointed the head of the FPC by Roosevelt. Over the previous decade, he had tempered his more radical ideas of a complete government overhaul, and his belief in Roosevelt had engendered a new philosophy that government regulation could work to reverse the negative effects of rampant industrialization. He now knew for certain that change could take place, and as chairman of the FPC, he was in a position to make it happen.

Over the next five years, through the trials of World War II, Olds turned around the fledgling government agency, instilling passion and purpose in its work. He treated his subordinates with paternal respect, and infected the FPC with enthusiasm. He often worked through the night, consuming massive amounts of raw data. He earned the reputation of a fair arbiter in the ongoing battles between labor and industry. He realized and accepted that a healthy utility was better than a broken utility. The utility had a right to a fair profit, and he helped them to realize those profits by lowering rates and extending their service. By the end of his first five-year term at the helm of the FPC, Olds had gained the respect of both the industry and the New Dealers—no small task. Meanwhile, it was business as usual at Brown & Root.

· · ·

Throughout the war, though many labor issues persisted, most of the conflicts took a back seat to the military effort. Just as the Browns had seen on many occasions, workers were torn between a strong tendency to want to support their country in the war and wanting to earn decent wages. In many cases, patriotism won out, paving the way for unfettered industry in the years after the war. Government and industry had gone into business together to fight the war. The result was an astonishing blurring of the boundaries between public and private constituencies. By the end of the war, the government owned as much as 25 percent of America's industry. Between the New Deal and the war, the government had acquired extraordinary control over what had been private industry in years past, particularly in the energy sector. That meant that when the war was over, the instant availability of military surplus goods would create a wild investment opportunity.

By 1941, Secretary of the Interior Harold Ickes was calling for an overland pipeline to counter the vulnerability of the tanker system. Ickes believed that as hostilities between America and Germany intensified, the Germans would go after the tankers in an attempt to disrupt the country's energy supply. Though it seemed an obvious move, the Supplies Priorities and Allocation Board (SPAB) rejected Ickes' request, because it would require the diversion of important resources, like steel and labor, away from higher priority munitions and airplanes projects. Ickes joined forces with 11 private oil companies to help him plead his case. Convincing the oil industry to join in the fight wasn't difficult when the executives considered what a government funded pipeline to the East would do for their business. But the SPAB was steadfast and refused request after request to build the pipeline.

It wasn't until February 1942 that the SPAB relented. German submarines downed 12 American tankers off the East Coast that month alone. By March, the Germans were notching up three tankers a day, as oil spread like a slick, black blanket over the surface of the Atlantic Ocean. Oil supplies to the East Coast had been cut to just 70,000 barrels a day from 1.5 million before the war. By the summer, work began on the two longest pipelines in the country, reaching about 1,500 miles each. The Big Inch was 24 inches in diameter, and the Little Big Inch, 20 inches. The construction, done on a cost-plus basis, cost the federal government—the consortium of private industry that was so eager to have the pipeline built withdrew its financial commitment when it became clear the government would have to build the pipelines regardless of their involvement—$138.5 million in total, and delivered more than 366,000,000 barrels of oil to the East by August 1945. Ickes had been right, and the Inch lines staved off a massive energy crisis in the East.

● ● ●

The end of the war touched off a mad scramble to gain control of the Big Inch and Little Big Inch pipelines, two of the most valuable government assets being unloaded back into the private sector. The fight for the valuable lines, which would give control of a considerable amount of the petroleum supply to the East, was waged by a variety of interests. The winners would need to employ "political entrepreneurship," the best term yet to describe the type of business Brown & Root was now in. For the government's part, there was a need to avoid creating new industrial monopolies in allocating war surplus assets, and the Inch lines had considerable potential for doing so. Ignoring the power of the oil and gas industry would eventually prove too much for the disorganized and overmatched government agencies put in place to sell off war assets. And when the Brown brothers were thrown into the mix, the fight was all but over.

Oil companies with their experience building pipelines, naturally wanted to gain control of the project, but they were not the only interested parties. The natural gas industry, at this time in its infancy, also felt that the lines could be converted into natural gas conduits, providing a cheap and efficient source of fuel to the East that competed favorably with coal. The coal and railroad industries (which transported the majority of the coal), sensing the threat to their established customer base in the East, fought hard to keep the Inch lines in the control of the government and out of the hands of oil and gas interests. The stage was set for a mighty battle.

E. Holley Poe, who had spent most of his professional life as a representative of the natural gas industry, began to string together a group of men who would fight for control of the Inch lines. His history of work with the American Gas Association and later the in the Petroleum Administration for War (PAW), put him in an excellent position to follow the intent of the government in disbursing the Inch lines. Poe also had a seat on the Committee on Postwar Disposal of Pipe Lines, a position that afforded him a measure of direct control over the future of the Inch lines. As such, Poe began lobbying on behalf of the natural gas industry, claiming that the East Coast was in dire need of the fuel to offset the shortages of coal in the region. Less expensive and more efficient than coal, Poe's argument for natural gas met with limited agreement. But Poe had an ulterior motive. He had been scheming all along to put together his own bid for the Inch lines, though he had not alerted anyone in the various government agencies upon which he sat of his plans. Instead, Poe simultaneously influenced the agency's decisions while crafting a consortium to bid on the lines.

The War Assets Administration (WAA) felt strongly, though, that the Inch lines should be sold to the oil companies, since it would require no substantive changes to the pipeline itself. Converting the pipelines to natural gas would be costly, and in the case of a future military conflict, would render the lines useless for petroleum distribution. When the auction for the Inch lines was set, it was clear that oil companies would be given priority. Poe was losing his battle, and even in his position on the Committee on Postwar Disposal of Pipe Lines, was unable to curb the momentum toward the oil companies. But Poe was going to submit a bid anyway, because with the right men behind him—powerful and politically influential men like Herman and George Brown—he might be able to persuade the government to reconsider its position.

Poe went to work putting together a dream team of investors. He scooped up Charles Francis, a partner in Houston law firm Vinson, Elkins, Weems and Francis, and counsel to Brown & Root. From there it was an easy step to secure the financial muscle the team would need. Francis got Herman and George

Brown to come on board. Brown & Root had worked on some of the construction of the Inch lines originally, and as the main financial backer of the team, George Brown took over Poe's operation and dominated the bidding process. The Browns also brought with them the undying support of Lyndon Johnson, and a host of other politicians that could play a key role in submitting a successful bid.

The group, now called the Texas Eastern Transmission Company, submitted its bid along with 16 other interested parties. But the bidding process was severely flawed. There was no standard on which the bids were to be judged, nor was there any standard bidding format. Some bids were heavy on cash up front, others on ongoing payments, and still others were being funded by debt. The WAA was in over their heads and had no idea how to get the most money for the Inch lines. Meanwhile, Texas Eastern continued to meet with influencers in Washington, pleading the case of the natural gas industry. Francis met with General John O'Brien, of the WAA, and assured him that Texas Eastern would convert the lines back to oil distribution in the case of a national emergency. Then Francis met with H.S. Smith of the House Surplus Property Investigating Committee and pleaded for him to "immediately commence an investigation of the proceedings that had been followed in offering these lines for sale [and] . . . pointed out that there were no standards for bidding, no good faith deposits required, and that the whole matter had been handled in a very unbusinesslike manner."

As Francis was relentlessly pushing Texas Eastern's agenda, the nascent company got a break. While Texas Eastern was working all fronts, trying to convince the government of the need for natural gas in the East, the coal miners went on strike. The government forced the workers back to the mines, but the damage had been done. The strike laid bare the vulnerability of the East Coast to the coal monopolies and made a strong case for delivering natural gas as an alternative energy source to the East. The strike occurred while the House Surplus Property Investigating Committee, at Francis' request, was looking into the bidding process on the Inch lines. The chairman of the WAA, Robert Littlejohn, rejected all the original bids on the lines. He created a standard bid submission form and announced a new bidding process that would not give favor to the oil companies. Instead, the Inch lines would go to the highest bidder, period.

The WAA had followed Francis' recommendations to the letter, and the result was a new level playing field on which Texas Eastern knew it could compete and win. George Brown and his crew began lining up the money needed to back a successful bid. The company issued 150,000 shares of stock at $1.00 a share, enough to cover the good faith deposit required for bidding. Herman and George were each in for a 14.25 percent stake, and lent money to others wanting to subscribe to the initial offering, in exchange for their voting rights. Mainly through friends and business associates, Texas Eastern marshaled enough financial backing to cover what would eventually be a $143,127,000 bid for the Inch lines. The night before the bid was to be submitted, one of Texas Eastern's directors slept with the bid under his pillow. After he deposited the bid in the WAA's post office box, he sat guard to ensure that no competitor would see the bid. On February 10, 1947, more than a year after the process had begun, Texas Eastern emerged as the highest bidder, and was awarded ownership of the Big Inch, and Little Big Inch pipelines to the East.

• • •

exas Eastern immediately began paying enormous dividends to the Browns. An initial public offering (IPO) of stock in the young company was tendered at $9.50 a share. The original investors had put in $150,000 of their own money, which, after the IPO had become worth $9,975,000. The Brown brothers alone netted $2.7 million from the IPO. Media reports characterized the sale to Texas Eastern as unfair profits made from what was originally taxpayer money that was used to build the pipelines. The House Surplus Property Committee commenced an investigation looking at the use of political influence during the bidding process. But the sale was final, and the House committee dropped the investigation, though it is not known why.

With the bidding out of the way, it was time for Texas Eastern to start making money on its core business, transporting natural gas to the East. Operating in the natural gas industry, though, was different than any kind of business in which the Browns had previously been engaged. The natural gas industry was heavily regulated by the FPC. Competition, pricing, and the right to build pipelines and pipeline extension all fell under the purview of the FPC. Enter Leland Olds.

As chairman of the FPC, Olds would be keeping a close eye on the business of Texas Eastern. Herman Brown loathed government regulation and felt that it gutted capitalism of its naturally competitive elements. But there were no competitive elements in the natural gas business, particularly in the Northeast, because Texas Eastern was the only company with access to the market. The Browns thought the WAA was handing them a virtual monopoly on gas to the East. Olds had other ideas.

Olds was considered very even-handed when setting prices for the gas industry. He had allowed for a 9.5 percent profit for natural gas distributors, seen as generous by industry analysts. Obviously, Texas Eastern wanted to set its own prices, especially as demand for natural gas began to take off with the coal shortages in the East. But even with the restrictions that the FPC placed on Texas Eastern, the company's IPO had been oversubscribed and brought a windfall of profits to the original investors. In other words, the stock market thought that Texas Eastern was going to clean up.

The Browns knew that if the natural gas industry were to be deregulated, they would be able to charge twice, maybe three times the prices the FPC had imposed. Their return on investment would skyrocket, and the Browns would become the next generation of industrialists, like Rockefeller before them. The company began a frenzied lobbying push to deregulate the industry. Senator Robert S. Kerr, a republican from Oklahoma, conceived of a bill in 1948 that would end the FPC's grip on the industry. Olds wasn't having any of it. His testimony against the bill led to President Truman's veto. The natural gas interests were up in arms. The Browns pleaded with Johnson that Olds had to be stopped. That he was single-handedly socializing the country. And in truth, he was costing them hundreds of millions.

Olds' term at the helm of the FPC was up for renomination in 1949, and the Browns smelled their opportunity. They insisted that Johnson defeat Olds and end his regulatory regime. The oil interests throughout Texas also wanted badly to see Olds defeated, as his policies often curtailed their own capitalistic instincts. Johnson, now a senator, knew that he would need the support of the oil industry if he was ever to make a run for president. So, at the behest of the Browns, Lyndon Johnson was going to have to take down a fellow New Dealer and man of great integrity.

He was going to have to destroy Leland Olds.

• • •

Perhaps the most striking thing about the coming battle between Lyndon Johnson and Leland Olds, besides the overwhelming odds against Olds, was the fact that both men came from such similar backgrounds. Both men knew poverty first hand, and fought to improve the plight of the poor. Both men were handpicked by Roosevelt during the New Deal, and worked to further the ideals Roosevelt embodied during his presidency. Both men believed in rural electrification, and worked, by different means, to bring power to the least fortunate citizens of America. They were friends, colleagues, and kindred souls. But now, Leland Olds was standing in the way of Lyndon Johnson's friends who were increasing their already formidable fortunes.

Though he likely didn't need it, Johnson was constantly reminded by his Texas friends of the need to remove Leland Olds. In a letter from Francis to Johnson dated April 13, 1949, Francis implored Johnson to work on behalf of the oil and gas interests. He complained that "even the most brazen criminals" could get a "square deal" in this country, and "it would seem to me that the oil and gas industry is entitled to parity treatment with criminals." He concluded the letter, "I trust that this major problem will have your immediate attention."

The first thing that Johnson did was angle for the chairmanship of the subcommittee that would be evaluating Olds' renomination. It wasn't exactly a coveted position, so Johnson had no problem securing the post. He then arranged hearings to be held on the renomination—hearings that would entail witnesses and evidence for and against Leland Olds. Only Johnson had a plan. Leland Olds was expecting a rather routine hearing, like the one he endured five years prior, ending in unanimous support of his confirmation. The only hurdle Olds had encountered during the previous hearing was some tepid accusations that he had communist leanings during the 1920s. None of the charges were taken seriously, and Olds was cleared for another five years.

Johnson was going to play the communist card again, but this time he was going to back it up. In the five years since the end of World War II, the fear of communism was starting to take hold in earnest. Though it was still years before Joseph McCarthy would give his first speech, the undercurrent of anticommunism was swelling. Johnson assembled a legal team that began researching Olds' history, looking for anything that could indicate a sympathy toward communism. Alvin Wirtz, the Browns' right-hand man, headed up the research arm of Johnson's operation. The group first looked to Olds' record as chairman of the FPC, scouring documents for any hint of socialist tendencies, anything that could be construed as less than capitalist. They could find nothing. Olds' record was spotless and stunningly fair. If anything, Johnson's research in that area proved why Leland Olds should be confirmed.

Johnson's team needed a new approach. They began poring over Leland Olds' now 20-year-old articles he had written for the Federated Press. Many of the articles espoused somewhat radical ideas, but nothing that could be mistaken for communist support. But among the subscribers to the Federated

Press wire service was the *Daily Worker,* a communist newspaper that closely followed labor issues, something Olds wrote about often. Johnson made photocopies of scores of articles and loaded them onto Brown & Root's DC-3, flew them to Austin, and began painting Olds red.

Johnson and Wirtz worked over their evidence the way a district attorney would prepare to discredit a witness. Of the 1800 articles that Leland Olds had written for Federated Press, only 54 of them were to make it into the hearings. And of those, incomplete thoughts, out-of-context phrases, and incriminating fragments of Olds' writing were parsed out. Johnson picked out witnesses to give testimony during the hearings. Alvin Wirtz was aided in this regard by Ed Clark, who not incidentally owned 40,000 shares of Texas Eastern stock. Clark knew that Johnson was on nothing more than a witch hunt. "He [Johnson] would call early in the morning— 'Communists! Communists!' Bullshit! Communists had nothing to do with this, and he knew it, and I knew he knew it," Clark said. But no matter how much this course of action disgusted Clark, he understood that this was business.

It was only a few weeks before the hearings before Olds had an idea what was coming. He had expected some questions about communism, but as had happened five years prior, he expected the charges to be dismissed as laughable. But when Johnson changed the makeup of the committee, excusing admirers of Olds and replacing them with anticommunist hardliners, it became clear to Olds that he was heading into an ambush. Without proper time to prepare, Olds arrived at the hearing with his wife, an FPC aide, and only a cursory response to the anticipated charges of communist leanings.

• • •

The hearings began and Johnson went right for the jugular. His first witness was Congressman John Lyle of Corpus Christi, where many of the natural gas resources in the country originated. Lyle began, "I am here to oppose Mr. Olds because he has—through a long and prolific career—attacked the church. He has attacked our schools; he has ridiculed symbols of patriotism and loyalty such as the Fourth of July; he has advocated public ownership; he has reserved his applause for Lenin and Lenin's system . . ." Lyle used the photocopies of Olds' articles, some two decades old, to prove that Leland Olds was a communist and subversive force to government. The articles were pulled out of the *Daily Worker,* not one of the 79 other publications that also picked up Federated Press articles. There was nobody in the room willing to stand up for Leland Olds, because Johnson had seen to that. The ideas that Lyle presented were wildly out of context, and some outright fabricated. The hunt was on.

Olds had a statement prepared that would refute many of the allegations Lyle was making against him. In fact, Olds was ready to talk about the way his ideas had evolved from early in his career, and how his record at the FPC demonstrated that. When Olds began to read his statement, however, committee members, shocked by what they had just heard from Lyle, cut him off. Johnson would not allow Olds to read his statement in full, and so for hours on end, his statement sat unread while he fielded angry assaults by the stacked committee. Johnson himself came after Olds, insisting on yes or no answers like an attorney treating a hostile witness.

For two days the committee embarrassed, humiliated, and harassed Olds. Johnson noted that Olds had once been a member of the American Labor Party, a group that, after Olds had left, became a communist organization. Johnson seized on the fact that Olds could not remember when he left the group, something he had done 10 years earlier. He became openly hostile toward Olds, and continually inhibited Olds' ability to defend himself effectively. When witnesses were called in defense of Olds, Johnson hurried them through their testimony, looking at his watch, and cutting them off as soon as their time had expired. One of the witnesses against Olds, William N. Bonner, an attorney from Houston that had interests in the natural gas industry, called Olds a "traitor to our country, a crackpot, and a jackass wholly unfit to make rules." Another witness, Texas attorney Hayden Head, actually argued that because Olds was so intelligent, he was a danger to the American way.

The media began to catch on to what was happening during the hearings. The *Washington Post,* the *Nation,* and the *New Republic* all came to the defense of Olds, and excoriated the tactics being used by the Johnson-led committee. It didn't matter though. It was too late for Leland Olds.

The committee voted 10 to 2 against Olds' confirmation, but the Senate still needed to vote. During the committee's proceedings, Johnson had been sure to call on his fellow senators to let them know how things were going. Some senators came to Olds' defense, but the seeds had been sown by Johnson, and when the senate voted, Olds garnered only 15 votes in his favor, 53 against. Johnson returned to Houston on the Brown & Root plane and went immediately to the Herman Brown's suite in the Lamar Hotel, Suite 8F. He was met with a hero's welcome by the Brown brothers and the rest of their crowd. He went hunting with the Browns at their hunting camp, called Falfurrias. Frank "Posh" Oltorf, Brown & Root's longtime lobbyist, would have this to say about Johnson's victory in Washington. "Even after everything Lyndon had done—even after the Taft-Harley and the way he fought Truman on the FEPC and all that—they [independent oilmen] had still been suspicious. They still thought he was too radical. But now he had tangibly put something in their pockets. Somebody who put money in their pockets couldn't be a radical. They weren't suspicious anymore." Herman Brown had placed his bets with Johnson long ago. Now all of his buddies would as well.

• • •

Leland Olds and his family were already teetering on the brink of poverty, and when he lost his job at the FPC, he needed work badly. President Truman managed to set him up in the Water Resources Policy Commission, but after Truman left office in 1953, Olds had nowhere to go. He started a consulting firm and gave various public speeches, but sadly Leland Olds would find himself impoverished forever after. His wife took the hearings especially hard though. She took her contempt for Lyndon Johnson to the grave.

Olds' replacement at the FPC was Mon Wallgren, a man that *Fortune* magazine characterized as "quite possibly the least effective chairman, or even member, the FPC has ever had. . . . A lazy fellow [and] too preoccupied with politicking to pay proper attention to FPC business." Olds watched as the regulations he had worked so hard to enact were systematically weakened or repealed with Wallgren at the helm.

But things between Texas Eastern and the FPC did not get much better. Wallgren's time at the helm threw the agency into disarray, leading to a disorganized and unmotivated group of commissioners. Policy was doled out inconsistently, and industry never knew what to expect from FPC rulings. Ironically, regulation of natural gas prices actually became far more rigid beginning in 1954, and Texas Eastern would again find itself in a mighty battle with FPC commissioners. Those battles would continue until the days of deregulation in the 1970s. After going through all that trouble of not only ousting Leland Olds, but destroying his life and reputation while they were at it, the Browns were no better off.

Fortunately for Texas Eastern, the demand for natural gas had absolutely taken off. The company could not supply it fast enough, as coal prices continued to rise, and the benefits of natural gas became apparent to consumers. Texas Eastern built new pipelines into New York, New England, and adjacent to their existing Inch lines, just to get more gas into the regions they served. The company, for a brief time, enjoyed a monopoly on supplying Texas natural gas to the East, but soon, with the market burgeoning, competitors rendered the natural gas industry into an oligopoly, regulated by the FPC. Prices did creep up from year to year, increasing from 4.9 cents per million cubic feet in 1945 to 10.4 cents in 1955, mostly driven by demand alone, and still far less expensive than the manufactured gas produced by coal. Gradually, the manufactured gas industry was supplanted by natural gas, as competitors and pipelines sprang up throughout the Northeast.

The Brown brothers, while doing well in natural gas, hedged their bets on the heavily regulated business. As expected, Brown & Root won contract after contract from Texas Eastern to rebuild the Inch pipelines as well as build new ones. This was an eventuality that Herman and George Brown counted on when agreeing to bid on the Inch lines in the first place. Again, with little experience working on pipelines, Brown & Root gained valuable experience and profit from Texas Eastern's expansion into new markets. Brown & Root worked on 88 different jobs for Texas Eastern, ranging from new pipelines to compressor stations. Their revenues from Texas Eastern alone between 1947 and 1984 was $1.3 billion.

As contracting partners, this was a conflict of interest. In a 1950s letter from Charles Francis, now Texas Eastern's general counsel, to then president of the company Dick Carpenter, Francis laid out the issue. "Both the Federal Power Commission and the Securities Exchange Commission regard Herman and George Brown as controlling partners [of Texas Eastern]. We have always denied this but such is a matter open to debate. In rate cases, the Commission Staff takes the viewpoint that all contracts with controlling partners or directors are presumed to be unfair and inequitable and the burden of proof rests upon Texas Eastern to prove the fairness. . . . Hence, it is essential for our next rate case that these contracts be carefully scrutinized, legally approved and adopted by the Board of Directors, without the vote of Messrs. Herman and George Brown. Even with these safety provisions, the difficulties in a rate case in matters of this kind are very great . . ." The company knew what they were doing was wrong and unfair to Texas Eastern shareholders, but there were a number of legal avenues they pursued to make it look right. Regardless, Brown & Root continued to scoop up contract after contract from Texas Eastern, becoming the natural gas company's primary contractor.

Over the ensuing decades, Texas Eastern would diversify into everything from refined petroleum products, coal slurry, and natural gas importing, development, and production. They would build pipelines all over the world, enter the gas exploration frenzy in the North Sea, and even get heavy into Houston real estate development in the late 1960s (the construction of all of which was handled by Brown & Root). The company bought 32 blocks of downtown Houston, much of it run down slums, and planned a grand Houston Center, "the biggest privately owned real estate development project ever." Texas Eastern had visions of elevated walkways, people movers, and underground garages. But by 1989, when Texas Eastern was sold to Panhandle Eastern Corp. (for $2.5 billion in stock), Houston Center consisted of only three office buildings and a Four Seasons hotel. Many of the blocks originally purchased for $50 million, remain undeveloped to this day.

The story of Texas Eastern is, in a nutshell, characteristic of the lengths the Brown brothers would go to increase their power and profit. They had become professional influence peddlers, perfecting the art like no one before them. Looking for the big score, the Browns parlayed political muscle into instant profits upon purchasing the Inch lines. They then battled regulatory agencies, fought off charges of conflict of interest, and worked their political contacts to obtain favorable rates. After having made so much money from the government during the New Deal, then again during World War II, the company continued to trade on publicly owned surplus goods after the war. All the while, the Browns fought labor, taxation, and government regulation, all the same things that had built their fortunes to begin with.

The fact that Leland Olds was a casualty of the Brown machine is ironic for many reasons. Most importantly, Olds was molded by the same force that made Lyndon Johnson— Roosevelt's New Deal. He fought for many of the same things that Johnson believed in. And he very well may have been better for the Browns many business concerns than his successor at the FPC. But Johnson didn't consider any of that when he took up the battle to unseat Olds. Johnson had only one thing on his mind: the Browns' money. Working for the Browns became Johnson's overriding concern, and for good reason. The Browns were working for Johnson, too.

From the time that Johnson became a congressman in 1937, through his successful Senate run in 1948, he collected hundreds of thousands of dollars, maybe millions, from the Browns and their friends. While the extent of the relationship was apparent to some close observers in and around Texas, the rest of the country had no idea how deep the ties between Johnson and the Browns went. With so much money at stake at every stroke of a pen in Washington, the Browns' investments in Johnson were well worth it. Johnson would eventually become part of one of the most powerful circles of influence in all of the nation, the Suite 8F crowd. This group of Houston businessmen and politicians met regularly at Herman Brown's suite in the Lamar Hotel in downtown Houston. Ideas were exchanged, plans were hatched, and money changed hands. Though times were different then, echos of the Suite 8F crowd still exists today, only with different players and even higher stakes.

Ultimately, even in the corrupt and free-wheeling political environment of Houston in the 1940s and 1950s, something had to give. Johnson and the Browns were unabashedly brazen about their mutual interests. Before and especially after the Leland Olds episode, journalists and regulatory agencies began looking more closely at the relationship between the Texan cronies, resulting in an investigation that would nearly end the careers of both.

6

Our Man in Office

"I have some money that I want to know what to do with . . . I was wondering . . . just who should be getting it, and I will be collecting more from time to time." This generous offer was made by George Brown to Lyndon Johnson in January 1960. This transcript of a phone call, placed after more than two decades of what ultimately amounted to illegal campaign contributions to Johnson and his colleagues, demonstrates just how committed the Browns were to their favorite politician. Even after millions of dollars had been raised on Johnson's behalf, the Browns were still willing and able to give.

The Browns understood something about the politics of their day that few of their competitors recognized. To really get your money's worth out of a politician, you have to go all out. Lumping money into a crowded pot gets you nowhere. To really get things done in Washington, you can't just support your politician—you have to *own* your politician. "They would contribute substantially as hell if their friend, somebody who had helped them, had a political campaign," recalled Ed Clark, longtime Brown & Root attorney. Johnson knew that without Herman Brown's money, he would never achieve the one thing he had always dreamed of: becoming president of the United States. Johnson knew this because Brown continually reminded him of the power of his money by meeting Johnson's every financial need. And Brown insisted that Johnson provide a return on his investment by keeping the contracts coming. In fact, taking one look at his voting record on issues like labor laws, corporate taxes, and government regulation made it relatively easy to see that Johnson was working for Brown & Root, not the people of his district or the state. Another indicator was the history of giant and costly public works programs that Johnson had fought to bring to Texas, which inevitably included Brown & Root as the contractor.

Though the world could see what Johnson was doing for Brown & Root, it was considerably more difficult to see what Brown & Root was doing for Johnson. People familiar with the relationship suspected that money must be changing hands. But few in the laissez-faire political environment of Texas cared enough to follow up on it. It was accepted as the way business was done. Mostly though, Texans just wanted to get in on the action. Other politicians in the state came to know that Lyndon Johnson was the man to see to get some of Herman Brown's money. Businessmen in the state knew that the way to get political influence was through Herman Brown. If anything was getting done in 1940s Texas, it was going to have to go through either Johnson or Brown, the most powerful team in the state.

• • •

Herman Brown missed out on the opportunity to fund Johnson's first campaign for Congress in 1937, but he would make up for it quickly in subsequent years. After Johnson won the congressional seat in the Tenth District, he immediately went to work for the Browns, securing them work on the Mansfield Dam, then ramming through successive increases in the contract. The Browns were, of course, very appreciative and eager to show their newly elected representative some gratitude. When Johnson ran for reelection in 1938, Herman Brown persuaded his subcontractors, lawyers, suppliers, workers . . . anyone making money from the Brown & Root machine to support, both financially and electively, the candidate. Lyndon Johnson had as much money as he could spend at his disposal. And he never had a problem getting reelected to Congress again after that.

In addition to the money that Herman Brown contributed to Johnson for his congressional reelection, Brown donated heavily to Johnson's allies throughout the country. In October 1940, after a whirlwind month of arm-twisting and political back-scratching, Lyndon Johnson won an informal role advising the Democratic Congressional Campaign Committee. The position gave Johnson a new national profile, and put him in a position to help Democratic candidates for Congress all over the country. He immediately called on Brown & Root. George Brown had instructed Johnson never to be timid about asking for favors. Timidity would never again constrain Lyndon Johnson.

Campaign contributions from corporations were illegal in 1940, meaning that the money would have to come from various individuals working for or associated with Brown & Root, each contributing a maximum of $5,000. It was a way around the law; often, the money took a circuitous route through various contributors, but it all originated from Brown & Root. It was just as illegal, but far more difficult for the authorities to track. On the face of it, the contributions looked like individual donations.

The money began to pour in just five days after Johnson had secured his post on the Committee. In one week, Johnson had marshaled $30,000 from Brown & Root for the Committee, more than the Democratic National Committee itself could drum up. Each contribution included a letter from the donor, specifically designating the candidate for which the money was to be used. Those candidates were handpicked by Johnson himself, many of whom were already actively soliciting Johnson's help. Letters poured in from desperate Democrats locked in mortal battle with their GOP opponents. Johnson made sure to let each of the lucky candidates know that it was he, not the Committee, who was responsible for their good fortune. Suddenly, dozens of congressional hopefuls found themselves owing Lyndon Johnson, and indirectly Brown & Root, favors. Herman Brown knew that the more powerful Lyndon Johnson became, the more powerful he would be as well.

The 1940 election was an overwhelming success for the Democrats. Dozens of congressmen owed their seat in the House to Johnson, and President Roosevelt himself was eternally grateful for the role Johnson had played in securing a Roosevelt-friendly House. Those elections vaulted Johnson into a new role of national power, with Herman Brown lurking in the shadows behind him. As Caro bluntly puts it, "[Johnson's] power base wasn't his congressional district, it was Herman Brown's bank account."

The Browns, having benefited from owning a congressman, knew that aligning with a U.S. senator would be infinitely more advantageous. The Browns had already begun pushing Johnson toward a run. As early as May 1939, George Brown was planting the seed in Johnson's ambitious brain, writing him, "I have thought about you often out here and don't know whether or not you have made up your mind about what future course you want to take, but some day in the next few years one of the old ones [senators] is going to pass on, and if you have decided to go that route I think it would be 'gret' to do it."

• • •

In April 1941, one of the "old ones" did pass on. Morris Sheppard, a Texas senator for 27 years, died of a stroke in his sleep. Johnson knew that it was early for a Senate run. Like his congressional campaign four years earlier, his name was virtually unknown outside of his district. He would be starting all over again, and it would be a long, expensive campaign. But Johnson had something that no other potential candidate in Texas had. He had Brown & Root's money.

Winning the open Senate seat was going to be expensive. Johnson needed to plaster his name from county to county, buy radio ads, newspaper ads, and hold public-speaking engagements all over the state. It was going to be one of the most costly Senate campaigns to date. Yet, Brown & Root was undaunted. In May 1941, less than a month after Sheppard had passed away, Brown & Root called together dozens of their business partners and subcontractors at a luncheon in Houston. These were Texas-based companies who had been profiting from Brown &

Root's lucrative contracts for years. They were indebted to Brown & Root, some of them even dependent on them. And the orders they were given were clear: support the Johnson Senate campaign with everything you can. "I did everything I could to help get him elected," said George Brown. "Went to rallies and helped get people to speak for him. Organized everybody we could to get a segment—all through the business segment, labor segment, to be for him."

The Browns began systematically contributing money to the campaign, collecting more than $100,000 for Johnson in less than one month. In theory, the contributions were illegal—according to the Federal Corrupt Practices Act—but there were any number of ways around the law. At the time, the limit on spending in a Senate campaign was $25,000, none of which could come from a corporation. Of course, Johnson was not the only candidate who brazenly disregarded this law, which was poorly enforced. Bags of cash, envelopes stuffed with $100 bills, accounting sleight-of-hand; all conceivable techniques of hiding the destination of the Browns' money were employed. Where the Browns got sloppy, or perhaps just greedy, was in looking for ways to mask the corporate contributions as tax-deductible business expenses. Legal fees, excessive bonuses (some as high as $40,000), and "rental fees" were some of the ways that Herman Brown tried to limit the expense of his political contributions. Herman Brown knew that he had to continue supporting Johnson with company money. He just didn't want it to impact the bottom line quite so much.

In some cases, the money took roundabout routes in getting to Johnson, a sort of political money-laundering scheme. Lawyers would take bonuses from the Browns, pay the money to someone else in their law firm, take it back in cash, and give it away to the campaign. Some of the money was used to pay campaign expenses directly, never having gone through the campaign headquarters. Radio ads, transportation costs, printing fees, all were routinely paid for by unknown Johnson supporters. And it was more than just money that Brown & Root contributed. Johnson's rallies were peopled with enthusiastic Brown & Root employees, adding their vocal talents to the cause. At this time, Herman Brown's influence over other politicians and businessmen in Texas was growing considerably. Brown had become the center of a growing sphere of influence in the state, the Suite 8F crowd—a group of business and political elites who met regularly in Herman Brown's suite in the Lamar Hotel in Houston. The group began to recognize its collective power over Texas politics in the early 1940s, and as such was often able to close ranks and support united causes. Among the informally initiated were Houston's leaders in banking, insurance, law, oil, construction, and media. It was becoming a true force in Texas, and Herman Brown was at the center of it. With his forceful temperament and growing fortunes, Brown was able to sway the political beliefs of his wealthy colleagues, giving Johnson wide support from the business community.

Brown kept the money flowing throughout the Senate campaign. When Johnson was showing weakness in the polls, Brown again called on his subcontractors, some of whom were reluctant to spend even more money on what was beginning to look like a losing cause. But Brown put the screws to them. "Now listen, we've made you a lot of money," he would tell them. As things grew increasingly desperate for the Johnson campaign, the money spigot was opened yet wider. Votes were openly purchased in certain districts of the state—it is worth mentioning that certain counties had always put their votes up for sale, and Johnson was not the only Texas politician employing this technique. Time became a factor, and Herman Brown lost patience with some of the covert methods he had used to funnel money to Johnson. He gave $5,000 of his own money directly to Johnson, and began shuffling more through his subcontractors. Though it will never be known how much money Brown & Root contributed to Lyndon Johnson's 1941 Senate campaign, the experts believe it was upwards of $200,000. Some people believe that Johnson spent $500,000 on that campaign after all was said and done.

Despite having an unlimited amount of Brown & Root's funds at his disposal, waging the most expensive campaign in the history of Texas politics to date, and calling in favor after favor from Herman Brown, Johnson lost the election to Pappy O'Daniel. Johnson, the Browns, and half the business community in Texas were shocked and devastated by the loss. But losing the election would be nothing compared to what would come after. The Wild West atmosphere and free-wheeling spending of the election had raised a red flag in Washington. The Internal Revenue Service was going to take a closer look.

• • •

Ironically, if Lyndon Johnson had won the 1941 Senate seat in Texas, life for Brown & Root would have continued much as it had over the previous decade. Johnson likely would have alerted the Browns of contracts coming from the federal government and fought to squeeze every dollar he could out of each contract for his most trusted supporters. Instead, because Johnson did not win, Brown & Root faced trouble from the federal government. Because Johnson was not Brown & Root's newly appointed senator from Texas, he would have a very hard time fixing the problem.

A full year had passed since the madness of the 1941 Senate race, and Lyndon Johnson had settled, grudgingly, back into his role as congressman. Though he still had strong connections in the White House, Johnson knew that he had missed out on an opportunity to gain even more influence in Washington. That was leverage he would sorely miss when in July 1942, the Internal Revenue Service (IRS) noticed some anomalies in Brown & Root's books and began an investigation. It is arguable whether the investigation would have been pursued if Johnson had been senator, even with the serious suspicions of the IRS and the enormous amounts of money involved. But with Johnson emotionally struggling to recover from a devastating loss, the investigation steamed ahead.

The IRS was focusing on the large and ambiguous attorney's fees and employee bonuses that Brown & Root had used to disguise their campaign contributions, thereby enabling them to write them off their taxes. It was essentially a tax evasion investigation and the IRS didn't know the true destination of the money. The Brown brothers knew the destination of the money, and so did Lyndon Johnson. If the IRS were to continue digging, they would eventually find their way to the Johnson Senate campaign, and Brown & Root would be facing criminal charges for attempting to defraud the government. Worse, Johnson's political career would go down in flames. A fine they could handle, but neither Johnson nor the Browns could sustain a criminal conviction. The investigation had to be stopped.

Brown & Root called on Alvin Wirtz to represent them, but they knew that it was really Johnson who would make this go away. Never before had the interests of both the Browns and Johnson been so perfectly aligned. And never before had the stakes been this high. Johnson crafted a plan to halt the investigation by enlisting the support of the president. Johnson and Herman Brown had confidence in Roosevelt's support given the role both Brown & Root and Johnson had played in securing a Democratic House. And they hoped this confidence was well placed because the president was probably the only chance they had.

Johnson told the president that there was a politically motivated investigation into the Browns' business in Texas, and that it was intended to end Texas' support of the New Deal. Brown & Root had been great financial backers of New Deal candidates in Texas and, without their financial backing, the New Dealers would take a hit. The allegations of a political witch-hunt weren't true, but it didn't matter. It was the kind of argument that would strike the right chord with the president, who as Johnson and Herman Brown anticipated, discussed the matter with the folks at the IRS leaving Brown & Root confident that this was the last they would hear of the matter.

It wasn't going to be that easy though. The IRS had seen enough already to believe that this was indeed a very serious issue. They were going to proceed with the investigation. Johnson, regrouping now, began going up the chain of command at the IRS. He met with Commissioner Guy T. Helvering, but Helvering had his hands tied. Helvering told Johnson that the Secretary of the Treasury himself, Henry Morgenthau Jr., was behind the investigation now, and he was not the kind of man that would bend to political tail twisting.

Johnson called on James Rowe, who had been his liaison to the White House during the 1941 Senate campaign, to get Roosevelt to turn Morgenthau back. But nothing would work. Rowe's attempts at stalling the investigation were met with Morgenthau smelling blood and turning up the heat. By winter in 1942, the case was starting to come together. IRS agents were interviewing people throughout Texas, setting up shop in Brown & Root's accounting department, and subpoenaing bank records and check stubs. Bonuses were found worth more than $150,000 that they believed had in some way gotten into the Johnson campaign coffers and had been written off as tax deductions. Brown & Root subsidiaries, like the Victoria Gravel Company, which was paying exorbitant attorney fees to lawyers who in turn paid off Johnson's campaign expenses, were unearthed. Many of the bonuses began as checks, but by the time the money arrived at campaign headquarters, it was all cash. A typical scam was for an employee or subcontractor to receive a $5,000 payment, cash it, stuff $100 bills into an envelope and mail it straight to the Johnson campaign.

Finally, the investigation reached the very top of the company. By the summer of 1943, IRS agents began interviewing Brown & Root executives. Many were defiant, denying any allegations of impropriety. George Brown played innocent. "We have certainly not directed anybody to give campaign funds. We knew it was not legal to give any political funds, and if anybody working for Brown & Root gave any political funds, it was without our knowledge. Certainly I don't think it has been charged to Brown & Root. If it has, it certainly shouldn't have been." Herman Brown, as straightforward as ever, admitted he had paid only the standard $5,000 personal contribution into the campaign.

Meanwhile, Wirtz and Johnson continued to seek audience with Roosevelt to plead their case for having the investigation terminated. Every attempt to intervene, however, was met with not only resistance, but a redoubling of the IRS's efforts. By the fall of 1943, panic was beginning to set in at the Brown & Root camp. Morgenthau had opened the investigation up to outside individuals, meaning Johnson officials and possibly even Johnson himself could become targets of interviews and further investigation. Agents began to close in on the Johnson camp, identifying a campaign employee named Wilton Woods who had taken a $7,500 payment from Brown & Root, and, they believed, handed it over to the Johnson campaign. Though Woods originally gave testimony that fed the IRS agents' suspicions, upon arriving in Washington, DC, in January 1944, he and his attorney—Everett Looney, part of the Suite 8F crowd—declined to comment on all questions posed.

It was all getting too dangerous for Johnson, and he urgently phoned the president to request a meeting after the Woods interview. The IRS had already determined that Brown & Root owed over $1 million in back taxes, but they were growing increasingly convinced that the company also had partaken in criminal wrongdoing. Finally, on January 13, Johnson was given an audience with the president. Immediately following that meeting, Roosevelt ordered a full report from the IRS on the status of the investigation. The report gave clear evidence of fraud and tax evasion, and even had admissions on the part of some participants of their role.

The next day, a new agent was assigned to the Brown & Root investigation, one who had not been involved in any way up to that point. After three days of familiarizing himself with the investigation, the new agent decided that there was insufficient evidence to bring criminal charges against Brown & Root, particularly in light of the role the company played during the war. He recommended a 50 percent penalty, amounting to $549,972. The original team of agents, who had been working on the case for 18 months, were told to drop it when they asked to continue the investigation. After all was said and done, the fine was in fact lowered to $372,000, and that was the last anyone heard of the Brown & Root IRS investigation.

That the case was dropped, in part, on the basis of Brown & Root's participation in the war was, of course, laughable. The war business had come to Brown & Root through Johnson's manipulation of the political system. And it had made Herman and George Brown fantastically wealthy. In researching this mess, I got the impression that had the Browns been making ships that aided in the war effort, or just building roads or dams at home, it wouldn't have mattered to them, as long as they were making ever-higher profits. The work that made them millionaires was the same reason the company was spared prosecution on potentially illegal campaign contributions and defrauding the government. The power of Brown & Root's political investments had indeed come full circle.

• • •

After what they had just been through, you would think that the Brothers Brown would reconsider their political spending habits. Not only had their candidate lost after they had broken every rule of campaign financing and spent hundreds of thousands of their own money, but they had nearly been found guilty of actual crimes, crimes that require jail time. It appeared that the time had come to cool off the relationship a little bit, and that maybe Brown & Root should get back to the business of competing on the basis of its actual merits rather than relying too much on a single political figure. These would have been logical things to conclude. But the truth was that Brown & Root *needed* politicians to succeed. And Lyndon Johnson *needed* Brown & Root. The two were inextricably linked, and backing out was no longer an option.

The IRS investigation of the 1941 Senate campaign had gone unnoted by the media and the public, but the Texas political scene was growing ever more familiar with Johnson's coziness with Brown & Root. In 1946, during a reelection campaign for congress, Johnson's opponent, Hardy Hollers, said what was on many people's minds. He called Johnson "an errand boy for war-rich contractors." It was the exact kind of tough political talk that senators and congressmen are today employing in calling for a congressional investigation of Halliburton's business in Iraq. Hollers went on to say, "If the United States Attorney was on the job, Lyndon Johnson would be in the federal penitentiary instead of in the Congress." Though Hollers had no political experience, the words resonated with Texans, who had grown weary of corrupt politicians, but knew little else. Johnson was reelected, as almost all Texas congressmen were at that time (until they died), but the race was closer than expected, proving that Hollers had struck a chord.

But what could Johnson and the Browns do about it? Severing ties was out of the question. There was only one direction to move in, and that was forward, deepening the relationship and furthering both of their aims. That opportunity was presented when Johnson chose to run for Senate again, this time in 1948. The Browns promised to fund the campaign as richly as the first, maybe more. Any money that Johnson needed, he was to have. Because this time, the Browns couldn't lose. And neither could Johnson.

Johnson had made it into the second primary. Upon reaching the second primary against Coke Stevenson, the well-liked former governor of Texas, Johnson was way behind in the race, and some in the Johnson camp felt he should concede the race to Stevenson. But it was far too late for quitting. Brown & Root had again funded the campaign up to that point beyond all reasonable limits, and along the way Johnson had waged a smear campaign against Stevenson that had backfired. The campaign was so dirty—with Johnson once again linking his adversary, this time Stevenson, to communist groups—that the Browns feared retaliation from Stevenson if he were to be elected to the Senate. They felt certain that an investigation into their funding of the Johnson campaign would be launched, and that Stevenson would shut them out of Washington, DC, closing all the doors that Johnson had previously opened. It was entirely possible that if Johnson were to lose again, both Johnson and Brown & Root would be finished. According to Ed Clark, Brown & Root's attorney, "They [Brown & Root] were regulated in a thousand ways, and Stevenson would have run them out of Washington. He would say, if anyone wanted to give them a contract, 'They're personally objectionable to me.' The Browns had to win this. They *had* to win this. Stevenson was a man of vengeance, and he would have run them out of Washington. Johnson—if he lost, he was going back to being nobody. *They* were going back to being nobody."

The future of Brown & Root was once again in doubt, and once again it was all in the hands of the lanky politician from the Texas Hill Country. Again money flowed, but this time in absurd quantities. Desperation was driving the campaign, and according to Caro's account, men carrying grocery bags full of hundred dollar bills ($25,000, $40,000, even $50,000) walked from business to business collecting cash donations for Johnson. There were stories of Johnson's men misplacing sacks with $40,000 inside, or leaving money in a shirt pocket. One thing that the Browns had learned from the last Senate race was that questionable campaign donations were a cash-only business.

Johnson was flown all over the state in Brown & Root's plane. The money paid for helicopters to get to smaller towns. He bought media placements and radio spots. Brown & Root called in their subcontractors again, as in the last election, and began applying steady pressure. According to former U.S. Senator Ralph Yarborough, "They were spending money like mad. They were spending money like Texas had never seen. And they did it not only so big but so openly . . . they were utterly brash. And they were brash about how they spent it, and they were utterly ruthless. Brown & Root would do anything." And they did.

Historical documents have shown that much of the money the Browns contributed was used to buy votes in South Texas. Ed Clark flew on Brown & Root planes down to "Mexican Country," where votes could be bought, to do business with the county judges. But even with that advantage, and with election day fast approaching, Johnson still didn't have enough votes. After the election, on August 28, 1948, Johnson knew he didn't have enough to win, so he started working the phones, telling people to "find" more votes as the returns continued to trickle in. They did, and Johnson began to catch up, even as many as six days after the polls had closed. Finally, it appeared that

Johnson had won the primary by a total of 87 votes, earning Johnson the nickname, "Landslide Lyndon."

The drama was not over. Because so many votes had shown up after the election, the Stevenson camp disputed the results in court. The matter was referred to the Texas State Democratic Executive Committee, which would hold a vote at the State Democratic Convention in Fort Worth on who had won the election. Like the popular vote before it, the Executive Committee vote was going to be extremely close. Johnson called Herman Brown.

Brown, ironically, hated politicians, but this was no time to let his principles get in the way. Brown came to the convention and worked the crowd for Johnson. He flew people in from around the state to vote on Johnson's behalf. "That night in Fort Worth, Herman Brown called in all his chits," says Caro. "It was necessary that he call them in, he told the recipients of his calls, because if Lyndon Johnson didn't win in the Executive Committee tomorrow, there might not be any more contracts—or subcontracts. The full, immense, weight of the economic power of Brown & Root was thrown behind Lyndon Johnson that night." It worked. Johnson won the Executive Committee vote by one, 29 to 28. On January 3, 1949, Lyndon Johnson became a U.S. senator for the state of Texas.

From his first congressional reelection campaign, through his successful Senate campaign, Brown & Root had supplied the money and the muscle behind Lyndon Johnson's career. Now that they had gotten him to his highest post yet, they were expecting great things. And they would get them, though George Brown would later play down the benefits of Johnson's Senate tenure. "In a material way there was no way for him to help us because we had to be low bidder on everything that we got from the government. So the only thing he could do at all would be to give us information that might become available to him as to what appropriations they were thinking about." But Brown & Root's relationship with Johnson had gotten them more than just the lucrative contracts from government agencies. It had earned them the respect and loyalty of the entire Houston business community. There was a rising force in Houston politics, at the center of which was Herman Brown. This force was known simply as Suite 8F.

• • •

During the 1930s and 1940s, a rare and unique group of obscenely wealthy and successful men were in the process of forming one of the most powerful informal special interest groups in history. Though rich and influential businessmen are common in any city, the cohesive group that jelled in Houston in the middle of the twentieth century was exceptional by any measure. The Suite 8F crowd would collectively control the development of Houston and have a far-reaching impact on legislation throughout the state and the country. Combining sheer wealth, a common will, and a broad range of political influence, Suite 8F was nothing less than the reigning governing body of Texas for the better part of three decades.

Herman Brown's suite at the Lamar Hotel in downtown Houston became the regular meeting place for a cast of characters that included, aside from both Brown brothers; Jesse H. Jones, a legendary millionaire that came to be known as "Mr. Houston," who built his fortune on everything from lumber trade to banking to newspaper ownership, and ultimately held several high-ranking posts in national politics including chairman of the Reconstruction Finance Corporation and Secretary of Commerce; Gus Wortham, the founder of the American General Insurance Company and real estate magnate who would serve as the civic leader of the group; James A. Elkins Sr., a judge and cofounder of the massive law firm Vinson and Elkins, who also founded Houston's largest bank, First City Bancorporation, and funded Wortham's American General Insurance early on; and James Abercrombie, known simply as Mr. Jim, who founded Cameron Iron Works, one of the top oil tools manufacturers in the world.

Though that core group served as the guiding force of Suite 8F, the group would have many peripheral members who came and went depending on whether their power was waning or on the rise. Alvin Wirtz, Ed Clark, and former long-time Texas Governor William P. Hobby all spent considerable time with the boys in Suite 8F. John Connally, another former Texas governor, partner at Vinson and Elkins, and Secretary of the Navy, also ran with the Suite 8F crowd. And of course, Lyndon Johnson, the man whose hands held the Browns' future, was a regular guest at Suite 8F gatherings. Anyone who meant anything to Texas state politics put in their time at Suite 8F. It was a rite of passage, and Herman Brown was the gatekeeper.

In the beginning, Suite 8F was simply a social gathering place, where friends of the Browns could congregate to have a drink, talk about business and politics, and unwind after long days of work. Gradually, the room began to take on much more importance, however, as deals that shaped the financial and political landscape of Texas were made. Houston historians Joseph Pratt and Christopher Castaneda described the common goals of the group as working toward a "healthy business climate, characterized by a minimum of government regulations, a weak labor movement, a tax system favorable to business investment, the use of government subsidies and supports where needed to spur development, and a conservative approach to the expansion of government social services."

The inherent irony in the purpose of the group was that they at once tried to limit the impact of politics on their respective businesses, while using those same politicians and legislation to further their aims. Political candidates in Texas would literally interview at Suite 8F in order to secure the collective support of the group. If successful in gaining the backing of Suite 8F, elective success virtually always followed. Spurning 8F was political suicide. Journalist Harry Hurt wrote that the group met "to relax—drink and play poker—but also to talk politics, exchange ideas, make business decisions, and choose the candidates they would support for public office . . . Their blessing was the blessing of 'The Establishment.' Their rule was virtually unchallenged and—they would emphasize—very 'civic-minded' gerontocracy."

Former Mayor of Houston Roy Hofheinz learned the raw power of this "civic-minded gerontocracy" when he was hand-picked by the group to run for office. After supporting Oscar Holcombe as mayor for 10 straight terms, Suite 8F grew tired of Holcombe's desire to step up social programs in the city. The group abruptly switched camps, throwing their support behind Hofheinz, who promised to be a more business-friendly leader. In 1953, riding a wave of support from Suite 8F, Hofheinz unseated Holcombe.

During his second term, Hofheinz backed a drive to raise property assessments in Houston, a move that angered the members of the 8F elite. All of the Suite 8F crowd owned real estate in Houston, and the move by Hofheinz was seen as ungrateful and in direct conflict with the group's financial interests. Immediately, Suite 8F, having already proven to Holcombe how crucial their support was by unseating him in 1953, asked Holcombe to come back as mayor and promised their support. In response, Hofheinz told both Houston newspapers that in 1952 he had met with the Suite 8F crowd, in anticipation of his 1953 run for mayor. He said that he was told by Herman Brown that Suite 8F had decided to unseat Holcombe. Hofheinz was assured that he would have the group's support "and all you have to do is call them down the middle." With this act, Hofheinz essentially hung himself politically. In 1955, Holcombe beat Hofheinz with 57 percent of the vote, and Suite 8F demonstrated once again where the real power base of Houston resided.

• • •

The business interests of the Suite 8F crowd overlapped to an absurd degree. They served on the boards of each others' companies. They merged and acquired companies with each other. In one instance, the Browns owned a controlling share in Houston's First National Bank. In the 1950s, they were looking for a merger partner, as their investment had fallen on hard times. They started negotiations with Jesse H. Jones, also known as "Uncle Jesse" and "Jesus H. Jones," who owned the National Bank of Commerce. Jesse lived upstairs from the Suite 8F, in the penthouse suite at the Lamar Hotel. Jesse was older, and even more powerful than the Browns, and he was a tough sell on the bank. He dragged negotiations out, angling for a better price. Finally, the two thought they had sealed a deal, but at the last minute, Jones wanted to renegotiate. George Brown, who had been handling the negotiations, simply drove down the street to City National Bank, owned by James Elkins, and cut a deal with him, creating the largest bank in Houston.

Gus Wortham, who occupied Suite 7F in the Lamar Hotel, funded his American General Insurance Company with money from Judge Elkins and Jesse Jones. The company, in turn, supplied insurance for his friends' businesses, including a supply of workman's insurance for the Mansfield Dam, which was built by Brown & Root. He later led the Houston Chamber of Commerce, the organization that would ultimately supplant Suite 8F as the guiding hand of the Houston business community. Vinson and Elkins supplied Brown & Root with legal advice to supplement that of Ed Clark and Alvin Wirtz. Charles Francis, the man that was so crucial in securing Brown & Root's interests in the Big Inch and Little Big Inch pipelines, later became a partner in Vinson and Elkins. The incestuous nature of the Suite 8F crowd was their strength, and made the group a force that dominated Houston's development throughout the 1940s and 1950s.

Though the impact of Suite 8F could be felt nationwide—it was Suite 8F, anchored by Herman Brown, that was behind the strident anti-union laws that were passed during the post World War II era—the full weight of the group was felt in and around Houston. In the late 1950s, the Suite 8F crowd decided it was time that Houston get a new, state-of-the-art jet airport to supplement the smaller Hobby Airport. The aim of the group, as always, was to build Houston into a world-class city, where big business could get done. A major new airport would go a long way toward achieving that aim. Besides, all of the

Suite 8F members were frequent travelers, and they had lost patience with Hobby Airport, then called Houston Municipal, and the fog delays that plagued air travel south of the city.

Acting more like the Texas Legislature than a group of self-interested businessmen, the group commissioned studies of potential sites for new airports, despite the fact that Hobby Airport had recently been renovated. They went ahead and quietly purchased land north of the city, and created the Jetero Ranch Company as their corporate body. All of this was done before there was any official proposal for a new airport in Houston. So confident was the Suite 8F crowed that it could make a new airport happen, they didn't bother to alert anyone else in Houston. They then met with Mayor Holcombe, whom they had installed as mayor two years earlier. At the meeting, the mayor was informed that Suite 8F—not formally, of course, but the members of Suite 8F—had purchased the land with borrowed money and would hold on to it until the city was ready to build the airport. Holcombe, not surprisingly, supported the idea.

Holcombe arranged to have the city buy the land from Jetero for $1.9 million, and fund the purchase and the subsequent airport construction through the issuance of bonds. But Holcombe left office shortly after and his replacement, Louis Cutrer, was skeptical of Suite 8F's motives. "You're not going to tell me that that bunch of high rollers isn't in this for the money," he said. "They're looking for a profit on this." Cutrer tried to hold up the deal while the Browns tried to spin the airport deal to the public as a "civic service." Public support for the project waned, and Cutrer asked for an extension on the purchase plan that Holcombe had arranged. Ultimately, it was a futile resistance for Cutrer, and he was forced to make a humiliating public apology to the group for doubting their intentions. The airport purchase went forward as Suite 8F had planned, and Houston Intercontinental Airport opened in 1969. Now Bush Intercontinential Airport, it remains the main terminal serving the Houston area today.

• • •

Recognizing the power of Suite 8F, senators, congressmen, and businessmen from all over the country regularly visited when in Houston. But the power of Suite 8F was not the actual room in the Lamar Hotel, but the collection of men who occupied it. And the group moved together, in varying combinations of people, from place to place around the state and country. Each year the group could be found, together, at the Kentucky Derby (many of the members invested in race horses). They joined the same social clubs. And they vacationed together, usually at the Palomas Ranch, close to Falfurrias, Texas. The Browns shared the 40,000 acre ranch there with Abercrombie, where the men would retreat to hunt, play cards, and drink.

The group also frequented the Browns' ranch in Fort Clark, Texas, a sprawling estate purchased from Army surplus land in West Texas. The Browns would invite senators and congressmen to the ranch for the weekend, dispatching one of their fleet of DC-3s to scoop them up from their respective districts and deposit them on Herman Brown's home turf. As one DC-3 pilot recalls, "If it wasn't hunting season, why, it was always political season. That is to say we'd go by Austin and pick up a group of congressmen or senators or something and go out and spend the weekend at Fort Clark and they'd have their big political powwows." In 1957, Lyndon Johnson wrote Herman Brown in his typical over-the-top manner, to let him know, "I want to go on record that last week at Fort Clark was one of the most enjoyable weeks I have ever spent in my life."

Fort Clark was a man's world, where senators could get falling-down drunk, men could play with guns, and no one would fear the consequences of their actions. Even the journalists who were often invited to join in the festivities would not dare write about their time at Fort Clark. After one visit to Fort Clark, Herman Brown's son-in-law, Ralph O'Connor, was appalled by some of the behavior these stately men were exhibiting. Brown pulled him aside, and said, "It's very easy for people to, without knowing it, to say things, to say so-and-so was drunk, sloppy drunk. That's why these people come down here. He's a very important man. He's got to let off steam. I don't want you to say anything."

Closer to Washington, DC, the Browns also owned a ranch in Middleburg, Virginia, where they could court senators and congressmen without flying them all the way out to West Texas. Known simply as "Huntland," the 450-acre farm gained brief notoriety when in 1955, Lyndon Johnson suffered a heart attack there during a visit. Johnson went to great lengths to conceal his trips to the Browns' ranches, often telling his secretary not to contact him unless it was an emergency, and never to let a caller know of his whereabouts.

As the Suite 8F crowd grew in national power through the 1950s, they became a very real force in Washington. Lyndon Johnson was a senator. Alvin Wirtz, who died while attending a University of Texas football game with Herman Brown in 1951, was Under Secretary of the Department of the Interior. Jesse Jones held positions as federal loan administrator, chairman of the Reconstruction Finance Corporation, and secretary of commerce. And George Brown himself served as a member of several high-profile presidential commissions.

The Presidential Materials Policy Commission, which later came to be known as the Paley Commission, was organized by Harry Truman to study the issue of natural resources in America. The group consisted of five men, and the report they produced in June 1952, entitled "Resources for Freedom," caused a stir. The report recommended, among other things, government support of drilling and exploration. Brown & Root had been doing considerable work in offshore drilling at the time, and the Paley Commission findings not surprisingly benefited that business.

George Brown, who evolved into the role of Brown & Root's liaison to the White House, went on to serve on several other commissions. He was appointed by Eisenhower to advise the Joint Congressional Committee on Atomic Energy. Eisenhower again tapped Brown to join a commission to study conservation of land and water in Texas. In 1959, Brown was appointed to the Commerce Department's Business Advisory Council. And then in the 1960s, with his old friend Lyndon Johnson in the White House, Brown was appointed to the Space Council that studied issues regarding NASA. Brown was the only businessman on the Space Council, and played a major role in convincing NASA to build its Manned Spacecraft Center in Houston. Brown & Root subsequently won the contract to build the Center.

The obvious and open manner in which Suite 8F in general, and the Browns in particular, influenced politicians at every level was appalling to many. But there was very little that anyone could do about it. As it has been for centuries, the nature of this kind of political influence is very difficult to pin down.

Friends like the Suite 8F crowd did business behind closed doors, leaving no trail behind them. Alvin Wirtz, known for burning his correspondences and instructing their recipients to do the same, set the tone for this group. They must have known what they were doing was wrong, which is why they went to great lengths to conceal their motives. For the keen observer, however, the common will of these men and their intent was plain to see. The deals, the political manipulation, the illegal campaign financing, it was all apparent to anyone willing to admit it to themselves. But often, the truth is the hardest thing to believe, and most citizens, given the choice, preferred to believe that their democracy was intact and their individual needs meant something to their elected representatives. The truth was far from it.

PART III

From Vietnam to Iraq

7

Vietnam and
Project Rathole

s striking as the similarities between modern-day Kellogg
Brown & Root (KBR) and the company's distant past are,
there is no escaping the fact that history is indeed repeating itself when we look at the role the company played during the
Vietnam War and compare it to KBR's work in Iraq today.
From the unpopularity of the wars themselves to the role that
powerful vice presidents played in securing massive construction contracts for the company, the parallels of the Vietnam
and Iraq Wars are stunning.

During World War II, self-interest actions by companies like
Brown & Root were excused by the media and the public because of the overwhelming need for American support of the
war. The words "war profiteering" were never used in those
days. Anything less than unmitigated support of America's
troops and the companies that supplied them was deemed

unpatriotic. Brown & Root emerged fat with profits—at the end of the 1960s, the company was the largest engineering and construction firm in the country—and it had gained an unsavory national reputation as an influence-peddling war profiteer.

The years of Vietnam would bring great change to Brown & Root, just as they did for the rest of the country. As the political landscape shifted beneath their feet, the company would endure the loss of their founder, Herman Brown; the heartbreaking sale of the company to Halliburton in 1962, a nasty public battle over a major scientific project for the National Science Foundation, and yet another politically charged bid to win a massive contract to build NASA's Manned Space Center in Houston. Although the monetary gains were great, the company suffered its greatest loss: its independence and relative innocence. Though Brown & Root was far from without sin leading up to the Vietnam era, they exited the turbulent times publicly tainted by their relationship to then President Lyndon Johnson. What had been a bunch of Texas good old boys scratching each others' backs became a national political grudge match between the Republicans and the Democrats as Johnson rose in power during the 1960s. Defending their actions became a full-time job for the Brown brothers from Belton. And the brashness of years past melted into a more complex and sensitive understanding by Brown & Root of the nation's political zeitgeist.

• • •

During the 1950s, as Brown & Root was basking in the glow of their new senator, Lyndon Johnson, Howco was undergoing a major expansion overseas. The company, by then well entrenched in the global oil well services business, began to acquire its way around the world. With its hydraulic fracturing division growing into one of the largest parts of its business, the company leveraged its continuing success by moving into new markets in Saudi Arabia, Peru, Columbia, Indonesia, Mexico, Italy, Cuba, Libya, and Iran. From 1951 to 1957, the company's foreign revenues increased from $7 million to $32 million, and its overall revenue grew from $94.5 million to $194.1 million. The post-war boom was treating the folks at Howco very well as the demand for oil exploded.

But the good times would not last. By the mid-1950s, demand for oil had begun to wane and recession set in. Oil consumption was dropping at a rate of about 7 percent a year, the first such downward trend since the outbreak of World War II. Erle Halliburton's health was also in full retreat, and in 1957, the man who as a pauper promised to make a million, died a multimillionaire, leaving behind a company valued at $200 million with 10,000 employees.

In response to its declining revenue, Howco went on a spending spree in an attempt to diversify the company and safeguard it against fluctuations in the global oil industry. It acquired Welex Jet Services Inc., for just over 359,000 shares of stock in the fall of 1957. In 1958, Howco picked up the Dallas-based Otis Engineering Company, a maker of well-control equipment. Two years later, the company officially changed its name to Halliburton Company, and began the process of courting another Texas-based company that had grown up during the Great Depression—Brown & Root. Though the purchase of Brown & Root in 1962 would leave many financial analysts scratching their heads given the disparate core competencies of the two—and some are still scratching today—the purchase of the Brown brothers' business carried Halliburton through turbulent times.

• • •

During the late 1950s, the Browns were experiencing growing pains of their own, though not of the financial kind. By 1957, at the height of Johnson's power in Washington, Brown & Root's revenues were $262 million. They had profited from military contracts, including two major contracts to build air bases in France and Spain. The combined values for the French and Spanish contracts, between 1953 and 1961, totaled $472 million. They also built a major naval air base in Guam between 1946 and 1957 that brought in $81 million. All of the faith that the Browns had put in Johnson and all the money they had kicked into his campaigns, were paying off.

Johnson's ambitions would take a toll on his personal relationship with Herman Brown and reveal both men's true feelings about the other. By the late 1950s, Johnson, whose ultimate goal had always been to become president, felt that he had gained enough power and prominence to make a run at the Democratic nomination. Herman Brown was perfectly comfortable with Johnson as Senate majority leader, and felt that Johnson's plan to run for president was ill-advised, with a slim chance for success. As he had done prior to all of his previous campaigns, Johnson met with the Browns, this time flanked by the powerful Suite 8F crowd, at the ranch at Falfurrias. Johnson opened his presentation by saying, "I want to tell all of you fellows something. I'm thinking about running for president, and if I do, it's going to cost all of you a lot of money. So I want you to think about it." Herman Brown didn't need to think about it, and blasted back at Johnson, calling his idea "the biggest mistake you've ever made."

Johnson continued to plead his case to the men, going so far as to count out the delegate votes he thought he could win. But Brown wasn't having any of it. He interrupted Johnson and told the men it was time to go hunting. This was one political discussion Herman Brown didn't want to have. Even after everything they had been through together, it seemed that Brown still didn't trust Johnson. In Herman Brown's eyes, Johnson was still just a politician, and as such, a means to an end. It became clear to Johnson, just as it had 30 years prior when Brown squeezed newly elected Congressman Johnson on the Marshall Ford Dam, that Brown was using him. Brown feared that as a presidential candidate, Johnson would have to bow to disparate interest groups, and as a result, dilute his solid support of the Browns. He was right. As Johnson campaigned, the distance between him and front-runner John F. Kennedy increased. In response, Johnson jettisoned his support of a national right-to-work law, a broader version of the antilabor legislation that Brown had rammed through the Texas Legislature years earlier and staunchly supported on a national scale. It was the first time that Johnson had let his political ambitions override his need for Herman Brown's support.

Despite the widening riff between Johnson and Herman Brown, the presidential hopeful continued to lean on the Browns financially and grew even closer to George Brown, who had longed served as a buffer between his fiery, distrustful brother and his good friend Johnson. When Johnson needed $60,000 to pay for a televised debate against Kennedy, Brown ponied up the cash. Though Herman Brown vehemently opposed Johnson's presidential bid, the campaign financing from

Brown & Root came through as it had in the past. After all, it was too late for the Browns to withdraw their support now. As Senate majority leader and presidential candidate, Johnson's political power had exceeded the Browns' financial largesse. The tables had finally turned for Johnson. And despite Herman's objections, it was not lost on him that having a card-carrying member of the Suite 8F crowd in the Oval Office would have to be good for business.

But he didn't win. Johnson fell hopelessly behind in the polls, and essentially conceding defeat, agreed to become Kennedy's running mate. Herman Brown was incensed. In his mind, the only thing the vice presidency could give Johnson was a higher public profile and less power, two things that Herman Brown had no use for. George agreed. "I just thought it was wasting his time as Vice President when he could be Senate Majority Leader," said George Brown. "I knew he'd be awfully restless as Vice President." Further enraging Brown was the fact that Johnson had not consulted with him in advance of this decision. August Belmont, who was in Suite 8F with Herman Brown when the news came over the radio, recalled it this way: "Herman Brown, who had sort of a face the color of those red flowers anyway, he jumped up from his seat and said, 'Who told him he could do that?' and ran out of the room."

Houston historian and University of Houston professor, Joseph Pratt told me that Johnson's decision to accept the vice presidency ended his relationship with Herman Brown. "Symbolically the break comes in 1960 when Johnson decides that he can't run for president and Herman Brown is pissed," says Pratt. "George Brown was deeply involved in the decision, but Herman had an older, harder, tougher edge. Once Johnson became vice president he moved out of the Browns sphere."

The move was a watershed moment for the politician where he felt he no longer needed Herman Brown's stamp of approval, that he had essentially outgrown his main benefactor and had catered to his needs for the last time. It was clear that the relationship between Johnson and Herman Brown could not survive mutually exclusive decisions. As long as their interests were aligned, they were close friends, but the moment Johnson spurned his patron, the friendship was revealed for what it was: a business relationship.

. . .

Herman Brown passed away five days after his 70th birthday, the victim of a ruptured aneurysm, in November 1962. Lyndon Johnson eulogized Brown at the funeral and called him "a builder of his community, his country, and his world." In preparation for Herman's death—his health had been failing for years—Herman and George had donated their stock to the Brown Foundation, the charitable arm of the Brown empire that had overseen the brothers' extensive philanthropy for over a decade. Before the donation in 1962, the Brown brothers owned 95 percent of the stock in the still-private company, all of which was turned over to the foundation.

In the months leading up to Herman's death, the Brown brothers had been involved in merger talks with Halliburton. Though it seemed a strange fit, the Browns wanted to sell the company, and they didn't want to sell it to a competitor. Halliburton certainly seemed a likely candidate. For one thing, Halliburton was an oil field services company and had no experience with the type of heavy construction in which Brown & Root had become a world leader. Brown & Root had done some pipeline work, built some offshore drilling platforms, and owned some petrochemical plants, but beyond that had no experience in the nuts and bolts of the oil business.

Yet, there were some similarities between the two companies. Halliburton and Brown & Root were both built on the backs of hard-nosed, gritty Texans who had come from nothing. They both were steadfastly open shops that loathed labor unions. And since Halliburton had moved its headquarters from Duncan, Oklahoma, to Dallas in the late 1950s, they were relatively close in proximity. The major difference between the companies was that Halliburton focused on research and development, serving one market well with new technology. Brown & Root was a far more political animal, content to win the big contracts through insider maneuvering, then throw men at it until it was done. Perhaps it was those wildly divergent styles that made them complimentary, but few in the business press at the time saw the connection.

Neither, perhaps, did Herman Brown. Though it was the Browns who initially approached Halliburton's board with the idea of a merger long before Herman Brown passed away, the deal was later called off. It is thought that Herman Brown was not comfortable with the acquisition. One month after Herman's death, George Brown was president of Brown & Root and the acquisition was back on. As the lead negotiator of the transaction, George Brown shepherded the deal through relatively quickly. Halliburton bought 95 percent of the stock in Brown & Root from the Brown Foundation for a price of $36,750,000. Halliburton used an $18 million loan and $15,295,000 of its own cash, plus 70,000 shares of its own stock to fund the deal. The final terms of the deal were announced on Christmas Eve 1962. As part of the negotiation, Halliburton

also acquired several other Brown properties, including High-
lands Insurance Company, Southwestern Pipe, and Joe D.
Hughes trucking company. George Brown was named to the
board of Halliburton.

It is hard to imagine a deal of this nature being consum-
mated while both Erle Halliburton and Herman Brown were
alive. Erle Halliburton detested the politics that the Browns had
so thoroughly embraced and Herman Brown had great trouble
turning over the reins of his beloved Brown & Root. But with
both men out of the picture, the deal took place in mere weeks.
George Brown no doubt took comfort in the fact that Halliburton had a history of granting autonomy and independence to
its acquisitions. Indeed Brown & Root maintained this attitude
until the late 1990s, when then-CEO Dick Cheney sought to
consolidate Halliburton into a more cohesive and streamlined
company. But for the 30 years after the merger, business at
Brown & Root went on as if Halliburton had never acquired the
company, and Herman Brown had never died.

• • •

Prior to Herman Brown's death, Brown & Root had begun
negotiations for a bizarre new contract being let by the National Science Foundation. This negotiation brought with it
the stark realization that with Johnson as the vice president,
and later president, Brown & Root was no longer able to fly
under the radar.

The idea, borne out of the 10-year-old National Science
Foundation, a government agency that was supposed to be
protected from the normal bureaucratic politics of the day,
was to drill an impossibly deep hole through the core of the

earth and pierce the mantle that lay six miles below the surface. Even as the United States was gearing up for sending a man into outer space, the race was on to delve further into inner space. The Russians were planning a similar experiment, lending a certain competitive urgency to the U.S. project. Scientists believed that by sampling the various layers of earth en route to the mantle, including the mantle itself, they could learn the mysteries of how the earth was formed. A Yugoslavian professor named Andrija Mohorovicic had discovered a transitional layer of earth between the outer crust and the mantle, which came to be known as the "Moho." It was thought that this layer held valuable data that justified the expenditure of the project, dubbed Project Mohole. In 1961, the four-year project that was expected to cost $15 million began testing off the coast of California.

The plan was fantastically ambitious. Offshore oil rigs had proven that they could drill in ocean waters hundreds of feet deep to find oil that lay just under the surface. But the areas where the earth's crust is thinnest, thus making the long drill possible, lay under miles of ocean water; and the distance to be drilled once terra firma had been reached, was beyond anything the oil industry could imagine. Nothing of the sort had ever been attempted, and that interested Brown & Root—the company that repeatedly gravitated toward massive projects in which they had no experience.

After the testing phase of Project Mohole was completed in 1961, the National Science Foundation recommended that one primary contractor be selected to complete Phase II of the project: the design and building of a rig that could complete the mission. There was no single company that had the capabilities the drilling would demand. Oil companies had some of the expertise and a great deal of self-interest, both of which would be needed to achieve the goals of Mohole. Though the National Science Foundation was wary of oil interests clouding the scientific motives of the job, they had to admit that oil companies seemed like a logical choice for the job. In July 1961, the National Science Foundation invited the business community to submit proposals, stating that preference would be given to those contractors submitting bids with no fees attached. They received 10 responses, four from oil companies; some with detailed information on how the job would be done. Socony Mobil, allied with General Motors, Texas Instruments, and Standard Oil of California, spent $150,000 researching and developing their bid.

Brown & Root's proposal was not among the original bids. The company had missed the initial briefing session in July for those interested in bidding, and they had failed to communicate with the National Science Foundation at any stage prior to the bidding deadline. But when the National Science Foundation officials opened the bids in September 1961, there was the Brown & Root proposal, a last-minute surprise submission that shocked the staff. Brown & Root had no scientific work on its resume, only one PhD on staff, no partners in their proposal, and a handful of shallow-water drilling operations to its credit. Its proposal was full of general marketing materials and short on details directly pertaining to Mohole. And it asked for a fee. When the National Science Foundation rated the proposals, Brown & Root's ranked fifth, far behind that of Socony Mobil, which the National Science Foundation panel called "in a class by itself; outstanding as to every important aspect."

The groups with the top five submissions were asked to revisit their bids and strengthen them in any way they saw fit for the final competition. In the meantime, the National Science Foundation was busy getting its ballooning budget approved by the House Appropriations Subcommittee. The chair of the committee was none other than Texas Congressman Albert Thomas, a member of the Suite 8F crowd and long-time beneficiary of Brown & Roots' political largesse. Thomas was the man who played a key role in securing the Corpus Christi contract for Brown & Root prior to World War II. He was also the man who had proven to be the largest obstacle to National Science Foundation funding in the past. As the director of the National Science Foundation, Dr. Alan T. Waterman, was delivering his budget justification speech to the committee, he mentioned, casually, that Brown & Root was one of the finalists for Project Mohole. That was all Thomas needed to hear. He called the budget "a work of art."

With Thomas' stamp of approval, Brown & Root won the contract over its higher-ranking competitors, and despite asking for a $1.8 million fee. Originally, competitors were told that submissions that did not include a fee would be given priority. The National Science Foundation wanted a contractor who was interested in the scientific aims of the project and would do the job at cost. But when Dr. Waterman was asked by the press why he chose Brown & Root and their $1.8 million fee, he gave this baffling explanation: "Perhaps we were wrong, but we felt that it was more businesslike to pay a fee." It was a total reversal from the National Science Foundation's earlier stance, and it left the other competitors completely dumbfounded.

The other justification that the National Science Foundation gave for granting the contract to Brown & Root was their expertise in project management, which to that point was unassailable. Brown & Root had garnered a reputation for being able to get a job done, no matter what it was, on time. It is true that many Brown & Root projects saw their budgets soar to unforeseen heights. But the job got done, and for many of Brown & Root's customers, particularly the military, that was more important than controlling costs. The National Science Foundation, however, was not that kind of customer.

Even before submitting an overall plan for the project to the National Science Foundation, Brown & Root began ratcheting up the costs. Project Mohole was originally expected to cost $15 million, but by the first year of Brown & Root's involvement, the budget had bloated to $47 million, then $68 million the following year. As the company's budget increases met with resistance from the National Science Foundation, the priority status that the Mohole had been promised began to fall. The manager Brown & Root had assigned to the job was abruptly removed and reassigned to lead the NASA Manned Spacecraft Center project. In its first year with the contract, Brown & Root assigned four different lead managers to Project Mohole, and the pace of work was far slower than expected.

Then the technical difficulties began. Brown & Root planned to build the drilling platform on top of two 500-foot submarines that would support its weight. The scientists from American Miscellaneous Society (AMSOC), an affiliate of the National Science Foundation that had been advising Brown & Root during the planning phase, strongly opposed the idea and rejected it as being too difficult and too costly. They espoused a plan that used two surface ships to support the platform. The two groups bickered incessantly and publicly, and ultimately, Brown & Root took the unprecedented step of discharging the AMSOC advisors in May 1963.

To top off the growing mess, congressmen began questioning the origins of the contract, alleging that political favoritism had played a role. As the budget ballooned and discord between Brown & Root and National Science Foundation reached a fever pitch, lawmakers questioned whether it was prudent to spend $125 million (the ultimate budget for Project Mohole) to basically drill a hole in the ground. But every criticism was met with a stern defense from Albert Thomas, who managed to protect and save the program for years while the technical glitches were supposedly getting worked out. After Thomas' death in February 1966, there was no one left to defend Brown & Root's project, and the congressmen attacked what they were now calling "Project Rathole."

One of the most vehement opponents of Project Mohole was a young Illinois congressman by the name of Donald Rumsfeld, who alleged that political contributions had played a role in the Mohole contract. Rumsfeld, debating in the House the summer of 1966, after five years of delays and added costs on Mohole, pointed out that the House had rejected further funding of the proposal once already, but its efforts to stop Project Mohole were rebuffed when President Johnson, in 1965, asked the Senate to restore the project. It was obvious, said Rumsfeld, that between Lyndon Johnson and Albert Thomas, Project Mohole was being kept alive through artificial means in an effort to benefit big Democratic backers like the Browns. He pointed out that the Browns had donated $25,000 to the Presidents Club, a major fund-raising arm of the Democratic Party, and alleged that the donations and the still-lingering contract had everything to do with one another. "Perhaps this is all another preposterous coincidence," he said, but there were "too many preposterous coincidences." I doubt that Rumsfeld even knew at the time how far back the mutual back-scratching between the Browns and Johnson went.

The Browns and Johnson were not surprisingly, if disingenuously, indignant. "You can expect to have periodic charges of this kind until November," said Johnson of Rumsfeld's comments, referring to upcoming elections. "They usually come from the party that has been rather strongly rejected by the people," Johnson said, reminding the public of the previous elections in 1964, when he beat Republican candidate Barry Goldwater in a landslide victory. Contributions, he concluded, "do not influence the awards." It was too late, however. Rumsfeld's accusations had hit their mark, and the Senate voted down the continued funding of Project Mohole.

The irony is that Donald Rumsfeld as Secretary of Defense in 2004 finds himself on the other side of the debate, as a member of an administration that has had to repeatedly defend its choice of Kellogg Brown & Root as its primary contractor in Iraq. Today, the role that Donald Rumsfeld played during the Mohole debacle is being reprised by Henry Waxman, a Democratic Representative from California. In the current flap over Kellogg Brown & Root's contracts in Iraq, Waxman has sought to uncover more about the nature of Halliburton's work in Iraq, it's ongoing relationship to Dick Cheney, and the possibility of political favoritism. And he has been asking many of those questions to the current Secretary of Defense Donald Rumsfeld. Like an unshakeable case of déjà vu, Brown & Root has been kicked around like a political football for decades, first by the Republicans in the 1960s and 1970s, then by Democrats in the 2000s. You would have thought the two parties could have seen eye-to-eye at some point in between and put a stop to the company's relentless politicking. But there was too much money to be made and too many campaigns to fund. Halliburton always had friends in Washington.

• • •

Part of the reason that Brown & Root failed to come through on Project Mohole was that the company was distracted. What had been seen as a patriotic mission to help America beat the Russians in the race to inner space was supplanted by the even more patriotic mission of helping America beat Russia to the moon. There were no concerns, just as there never had been, that the company was biting off more than it could chew. Frankly, there was no reason for the company to hold back during the early 1960s. With Johnson in the White House, Albert Thomas holding the purse strings for government agencies (as the chair of the House Appropriations Committee), and George Brown acting on several business advisory councils and presidential commissions, the iron was hot. An article in *Life* magazine captured the growing national awareness of Johnson's relationship with Brown & Root when it lampooned a conversation between John F. Kennedy and Lyndon Baines Johnson. Kennedy says to Lyndon after the 1960 election, "Now, Lyndon, I guess we can dig that tunnel to the Vatican," to which Johnson replies, "Okay, so long as Brown & Root get the contract."

After 40 years of setting up a favorable political environment both locally and nationally, the Browns put their varied talents and strengths on display when it went after the high-profile contract for NASA's Manned Spacecraft Center. Brown & Root's dream team for securing the NASA contract started with, as usual, Lyndon Johnson, the vice president of the United States in 1961 and the chairman of the National Aeronautics and Space Council, advising the president on space-race issues. Johnson also had been the chairman of the Senate's Space Committee in the 1950s, while he was Senate Majority Leader. In the spring of 1961, Johnson had appointed George Brown to be the only civilian member of the Space Council, a committee that advised the administration of NASA-related decisions. Albert Thomas was already the chairman of the House Appropriations Committee, which held considerable influence over NASA's budget. And finally, James Webb, the director of NASA beginning in February 1961, was a very close friend of Lyndon Johnson. In some ways, Brown & Root had won the contract for the Manned Spacecraft Center before the center was even conceived. "Albert and Lyndon worked as a team," said George Brown.

The first order of business was to convince NASA to locate its center in Houston. Competition had been keen among several different states, including President Kennedy's home state of Massachusetts. But Brown & Root's influence was even greater than that of the president in this case. NASA knew that if Houston was passed up again as it had been in 1958 for the Goddard Space Flight Center (Maryland), Albert Thomas would wield his power over NASA's budget. That alone would have been enough for NASA to choose Houston as the site.

Meanwhile, George Brown was convincing the Space Council of Houston's viability as a site. He arranged for his friend Morgan Davis, the chairman of oil giant Humble Oil & Refining, to donate a thousand acres to Rice University, Albert Thomas' alma mater (and George Brown's as well). Rice would then offer the land up to NASA and work closely with the organization in cultivating a space program that would attract the necessary scientific talent to the Houston area. Brown was the chairman of the Rice board and as such enlisted the Rice faculty's support for the plan.

Between Johnson, Thomas, and Brown, NASA Director James Webb didn't stand a chance. He selected Houston as the site for the center in September 1961, months before would-be competitors could even submit a bid. It was a full-court press from day one, and Webb, not even a year on the job (a job he owed to Johnson to begin with) made the only politically viable choice he could.

Now that the Manned Spacecraft Center was to be based in Houston, the next order of business for Brown & Root was to win the building contract. The Army Corps of Engineers quickly whittled a list of 175 architectural and engineering firms down to one it felt was the most suitable. The winner? Brown & Root, a contractor without strengths in either architecture or engineering. There were the requisite outcries of political favoritism from the spurned competitors, but since none of the competitors really believed that anybody *but* Brown & Root was going to build the Manned Spacecraft Center, the contract award hardly came as a surprise. Brown & Root picked up $2.3 million on the architecture contract, but tacked on dozens of millions more over the years as its joint venture work with Northrop Corporation continued to service the center, later named the Johnson Manned Spacecraft Center.

The Johnson Center is one of the last monuments to Brown & Root's dominance in the United States—it is the symbol of the Browns' ability to manipulate the political system to their benefit. There were many symbols dotting the domestic landscape: the Mansfield Dam; Corpus Christi Air Base; and the

Inch pipe lines to name a few. But as Vietnam clouded the political environment, Brown & Root would get pulled overseas and into a new line of work that would forever change the nature of the company.

• • •

The contracts for both Project Mohole and the Johnson Manned Spacecraft Center would be dwarfed by what was to come in Vietnam. In a stunning parallel, both Johnson and George W. Bush would escalate the wars that defined their presidencies based on questionable evidence. And both escalations would result in a bonanza of contracts for Brown & Root. While George W. Bush struggles with the political fallout of the war on terrorism and claims that Iraq was prepared to use weapons of mass destruction, he might do well to learn from a fellow Texan's presidency 40 years earlier, when Lyndon B. Johnson escalated the Vietnam War by blowing the Gulf of Tonkin incident out of proportion, or from his own father's memoir, *A World Transformed* where the former president explained his reticence to invade Iraq during the Persian Gulf War, writing: ". . . we had been self-consciously trying to set a pattern for handling aggression in the post–Cold War world. Going in and occupying Iraq, thus unilaterally exceeding the United Nations' mandate, would have destroyed the precedent of international response to aggression that we hoped to establish. Had we gone the invasion route, the United States could conceivably still be an occupying power in a bitterly hostile land. It would have been a dramatically different—and perhaps barren—outcome." Johnson, who became president in 1963 after Kennedy's assassination and who was elected with broad support in 1964, used the Gulf of Tonkin incident, a minor fracas in retrospect, to justify the sending of ground troops into Vietnam. The result of that move was the need for billions of dollars worth of bases, airstrips, ports, and bridges. Enter Brown & Root.

In 1965, a year after Johnson stepped up America's participation in Vietnam, Brown & Root joined three other construction and project management behemoths, Raymond International, Morris-Knudsen, and J.A. Jones to form one of the largest civilian-based military construction conglomerates in history. The group, which came to be known collectively as RMK-BRJ, went on to do more than $2 billion worth of work in Vietnam, of which Brown & Root took a 20 percent cut. The contract was cost plus 1.7 percent, meaning that the consortium would be reimbursed all costs, plus an additional 1.7 percent profit, a method of contracting that encourages the contractor to markedly increase costs, thereby increasing their profit. The world would be reintroduced to this concept nearly 40 years later when Kellogg Brown & Root won the same type of contract in Iraq.

RMK-BRJ literally changed the face of Vietnam, clearing out wide swaths of jungle for airplane landing strips, dredging channels for ships, and building American bases from Da Nang to Saigon. As part of the single most lucrative contract the company had ever entered into, Brown & Root was in Vietnam from 1965 to 1972 pulling down $380 million in revenue in the process. But the gains had a cost.

The Vietnam contract had Brown & Root written all over it. Similar to the priorities in Iraq in 2003, the emphasis was on speed, not cost. RMK-BRJ was building everything from roads to entire cities for the American military. Because of the rapid buildup of troops in Vietnam—up to 165,000 in 1966 from just a few dozen thousand prior to Johnson's escalation—the army found it impossible to move men and supplies around the country. Ports were backed up for weeks and in some cases roads didn't even exist. RMK-BRJ built two 10,000-foot jet runways and two deep-water piers in Da Nang; a permanent jet runway in Chulai; two jet runways in Phanrang; ammunition and fuel storage facilities; barracks; helicopter landing pads; pipelines; hospitals; communications facilities; and warehouses. In short, the construction conglomerate built everything the American military needed in Vietnam. They did 97 percent of the construction work in the country during the seven years they operated there. The remaining 3 percent went to local Vietnamese contractors.

They were moving enough dirt to dig the Suez Canal and paving enough roads to surface the Jersey Turnpike every 30 days. They had a small army of their own in the country, 51,000 at the height of operations in 1967, the largest employer in Vietnam. Twenty-three employees died and more than a hundred were wounded. But their efforts were not in vain. The supply problems dissipated. The ports opened up. Vietnam became a modern country practically overnight. Then it got ugly.

Even as early as 1966, reports started reaching back to the homeland that the United States was pouring money into a sieve called Vietnam. One study by the *New York Times* found that nearly 40 percent of the billions being spend in Vietnam was being stolen, used in bribes, or outright wasted at the rate of half a million dollars a day. RMK-BRJ came under fire for not kiting costs and wasting upward of $5 million in its first year in the country. Its workers were manipulating currency and selling goods on the black market. Dozens of employees were sent home as punishment. By 1968, when most of the country had grown weary of the war, Senator Abraham A. Ribicoff, Democrat from Connecticut, filed a report with the Senate's Permanent Subcommittee on Investigations alleging kickbacks in the construction consortiums in Vietnam claiming that millions were being "squandered because of inefficiency, dishonesty, corruption, and foolishness." He ordered an immediate General Accounting Office investigation into RMK-BRJ.

The GAO investigation, completed in 1967, charged RMK-BRJ with losing $120 million during its first five years in Vietnam. It said that "normal management controls were virtually abandoned," and that millions were lost due to lax security. After decades of receiving accolades from government agencies and the military, Brown & Root was coming under fire for wastefulness and inefficiency. The Pentagon actually acknowledged some of the blame in 1966, admitting that it had misled the contractor, low-balling the estimated costs of the construction. By 1968, Johnson's last year as president, RMK-BRJ was significantly scaling back its operation to about 15,000 employees. The public impression was that Brown & Root was part of a war-profiteering machine that monopolized work in Vietnam, mistreated workers, and wasted millions of taxpayers' dollars. But it would get even worse.

Brown & Root became the symbol of war-profiteering to opponents of the war. And as the antiwar protests ramped up throughout the 1960s, George Brown became the face of the war profiteer. In 1971, the protests reached a fever pitch, and Brown found himself the target of a particularly hateful outburst. He was to be honored by the University of Texas as a distinguished alumnus, despite having only attended the school temporarily. Students rallied and protested his appearance. During the ceremony, students rushed on stage and handed Brown a "special award," a picture of the infamous tiger cages, horribly inhumane prison cells built by the French government 75 years earlier to hold prisoners. RMK-BRJ was hired by the military to build new, more humane prison cells to replace the tiger cages. Forty years later, Kellogg Brown & Root would again be called to build prisons for another unpopular war when the army contracted the company to build the terrorist prison in Guantanamo Bay, Cuba, after the September 11, 2001, attacks, a place where detainees have been held for more than two years. Brown's association with the tiger cages was unfair, given that his company was merely hired to replace them. But subtle distinction was not a luxury that protestors of the day indulged in.

What was truly unfair was categorizing George Brown as a war profiteer since he had repeatedly advised Johnson against the escalation in Vietnam, believing that the war would destroy Brown and Johnson both. But Johnson didn't listen and the war raged on into the 1970s. Brown was dogged by protestors everywhere he went, despite the fact that he was removed from Brown & Root's day-to-day activities. Even Brown's alma mater, Rice University, could not stem the tide of protestors when Brown visited the campus. It was a stark contrast to the repeated applause Brown received for his company's work during World War II.

The controversy and criticism was a small price to pay, however, for a company that had vaulted suddenly to the top of its industry. Mohole, NASA, and Vietnam had done for Brown & Root (which was part of Halliburton, but still operated independently) what the Mansfield Dam and World War II couldn't:

It made them the largest construction company in the United States. In 1947, Brown & Root was the forty-seventh largest construction company in the country. By 1965, they were number two, and by 1969, number one, with sales of $1.6 billion. Most of the momentum took place while Johnson was president, a coincidence that was not lost on the competition. The rapid rise brought on a fit of jealousy from Brown & Root's biggest rival, Bechtel of San Francisco. "Brown & Root . . . had gotten most of the choice projects during LBJ's administration, from constructing the Space Center in Houston to building the infrastructure for the Vietnam War. Bechtel, by contrast, had come away with only comparative crumbs." Bechtel found itself in a position to protest Kellogg Brown & Root's ties to the government again in 2003 when the Iraq contracts were awarded. Bechtel pulled out of the running for certain contracts because the company felt the structure of the bidding favored Kellogg Brown & Root.

The 1960s and 1970s saw the end of the Brown brothers' involvement in their beloved company's affairs. It also saw an unrelenting tide of political controversy beset the company and hound it right into the 1980s. Amazingly, throughout it all, the company achieved stunning financial success. As the events of the Iraq War will attest, controversy and bad publicity do not necessarily mean sagging profits. In fact, it has been quite the opposite for Brown & Root. The more controversy, the more profit. The Bush administration has been able to deflect these controversies repeatedly with a well-timed statue-toppling or dramatic landing on an aircraft carrier. In the meantime, Halliburton and Kellogg Brown & Root are keeping the meter running in Iraq, with the value of their contract now reaching $2 billion and counting.

8

Empty Pockets

In the late 1970s and throughout the 1980s, things started to unravel for Brown & Root, as the company found itself besieged first by misfortune, then scandal, then tragedy, then the bizarre, and finally the economy. Lyndon Johnson died in 1973 and George Brown retired in 1975, beginning a precipitous, if somewhat delayed, decline for Brown & Root. Though the company had ramped up its business dramatically throughout and subsequent to the Johnson presidency, it was not prepared to lose its political power base and its best salesman in the space of just two years. The decline in revenues that would result culminated in a truly dark decade during the 1980s for Brown & Root, as well as its parent company Halliburton. In the first five years of the 1980s, Brown & Root's workforce was cut from 80,000 to 20,000, as it struggled with a lingering recession, a bust cycle in the oil business, and a washout of its government contracting business.

If anything, what happened in the 1980s taught the company that it needed to get back to its basic business model: win government business and use political contacts to do it. With so much of its political capital wrapped up in three men— Herman and George Brown and Lyndon Johnson—it is easy to see why the company experienced such a vacuum after all three were removed from the business. The vacuum nearly sucked the life out of the company during the 1980s. It wasn't until the early 1990s that Halliburton and Brown & Root would master the game again by scoring one of the biggest military outsourcing contracts in American history.

• • •

Brown & Root hadn't planned on swearing off politicians, it just happened that way. In fact, when Lyndon Johnson died in 1973, Brown & Root was already working on their next move. The company had staked a claim in a man who had come to represent the next generation of Texas politics, a man that had served as Johnson's campaign director for decades, as governor of Texas for most of the 1960s, and had become Richard Nixon's most trusted advisor. In February 1969, months after he had left the governorship of the state, Brown & Root named John Connally to its board of directors. The man who had been riding in the front seat of John F. Kennedy's car in November 1963 and took a bullet in the chest, now represented Brown & Root's future in Washington.

Connally was working for Vinson & Elkins in the early 1970s as well, the powerful law firm founded by James Elkins, a member of the Suite 8F crowd. Since Nixon's narrow 1968 victory, he served as an advisor and was eventually appointed secretary of the treasury in 1971. There was a great deal of talk about how Connally would mount a run for the presidency in 1976, possibly even switching parties—up to that point, Texas had been a one-party Democratic state, but Connally would change all of that forever. It seemed for a time that Brown & Root would pick up seamlessly from Johnson's abrupt departure from the White House in 1968. In 1972, Connally even arranged for President Nixon to attend a barbecue at his ranch in Texas, at which all of the usual Suite 8F suspects would have a chance to gain favor with the president. Connally was growing in power by the day, and although he could never be as dedicated to Brown & Root as Lyndon Johnson, he was a man intimately familiar with the company's modus operandi, and would certainly be attentive to the company's needs.

On June 17, 1972, five men were arrested trying to bug the offices of the Democratic National Committee at the Watergate Hotel in Washington, DC. At first it seemed the scandal that ensued over the next two years would have no impact on Brown & Root, but when Nixon's Vice President Spiro Agnew announced his resignation in 1973 amidst the growing scandal, Nixon let it be known that Connally would be his choice to succeed Agnew as vice president. For a moment, it looked like Brown & Root would have another pet politician as the sitting vice president. It wasn't to be. Connally took heavy fire from Democrats on his decision to switch to the Republican Party, and quickly became a political liability for Nixon. Though he vowed to support a run for president by Connally in 1976, Nixon chose Gerald Ford to be vice president instead.

Ultimately, it was all academic. Nixon resigned in disgrace the following year, sinking many of his political allies, including Connally, along with him. Though Connally would mount bids for the Republican nomination in both 1976 and 1980, he was never again taken seriously after Watergate. Brown & Root's horse had exited the race, brought down by one of the strangest political controversies in American history. Things would become even worse, however, and stranger.

• • •

At the time that George Brown officially resigned his chairmanship in 1975, Brown & Root was the top engineering and construction firm in the nation, pulling down over $5 billion in contracts and accounting for, at times, as much as 75 percent of Halliburton's overall revenues. After leaving Vietnam in 1972, the company was still enjoying some residual contracts that George Brown had engineered before he left. And with the guidance of its new parent company, an oil-field services giant, Brown & Root ventured heavily into the world of offshore drilling, building massive platforms and drilling rigs for major oil and gas companies.

The workforce at the company increased from 10,000 in 1960 to 66,500 in 1975. The company's growth and profitability were astounding, though, as it turns out, not entirely legitimate. The company came under fire for its offshore drilling business practices in 1977 when a federal grand jury indicted Brown & Root for collusion and price fixing with competitor J. Ray McDermott. George Brown, by then retired, recalled little during his testimony. It was alleged that the companies were parsing out the work to each other. The company that had agreed not to get a specific job would submit an obscenely high bid, which their partner would easily underbid (but still submitting an exceedingly profitable bid). Both companies admitted no guilt, pleading no contest and were fined $1 million each by the Department of Justice. Brown & Root paid some $90 million in civil suits as well. Halliburton's CEO at the time, John Harbin, said of the suits: "We're still doing business with these big customers, and our records don't show any guilt. There are three sides to everything—ours, theirs, and the government's." The fines and subsequent lawsuits were the beginning of a long slide from grace for Brown & Root, which over the ensuing years would tumble from the top of the construction world into relative obscurity.

• • •

Concurrent with the devastating criminal and civil suits over price fixing, Brown & Root endured the tragic and bizarre deaths of five of its top executives in just two years, all coming immediately after the resignation of George Brown in 1975. First, in January of 1976, a charter plane attempting to land at an airport in Anchorage, Alaska, where Brown & Root had been doing work on offshore drilling platforms, crashed, killing Senior Group Vice President G.A. Dobelman; Warren T. Moore and Wolf Pabst, president and vice president of subsidiary Alaska Constructors; and Vic Abadie Jr., a manager of Brown & Root's San Francisco offices. The plane had landed a full mile and a half short of the runway. Two Brown & Root executives managed to survive the crash, including W. Bernard Pieper, who walked away from the crash relatively unharmed and later became president of the company.

Almost exactly a year later, the company endured the death of its president, Foster Parker, in January 1977. On January 8, Parker walked into a hardware store in downtown Houston and purchased a .357 Magnum and a box of ammunition. A week later, Brown & Root was subpoenaed by the Federal Grand Jury investigating the alleged J. Ray McDermott price-fixing scheme. A week after that, Parker was found dead in his bedroom, a bullet wound to his right temple.

The apparent suicide of Brown & Root's president, a man hand-picked by George Brown himself, had the entire Houston community dumbfounded. The case was riddled by unanswered questions. There had been death threats made against company executives in the weeks preceding Parker's death, but police decided to rule the death a suicide after they learned Parker had bought the gun himself weeks prior. But the clerk at the store said that Parker had originally intended to buy a shotgun for home protection, but later settled on the magnum. A shotgun would have been strange choice for a man intending to kill himself. In addition, company officials declined to say when exactly they had been informed of the Federal subpoena, though they admitted that it was before January 14, when they announced it to the public. None of it made sense. On one hand there seemed to be enough evidence to pursue the case as a potential homicide, since there were death threats and no suicide note. On the other hand, Parker had likely known about the coming indictment, which at that time, threatened to completely ruin the company. That would support the case for suicide.

The police ultimately ruled the death a suicide, which left those who knew Parker scratching their heads. Aside from being troubled by the impending legal battle the company was facing, no one could imagine why Parker would take his own life. Regardless, the vacuum created by the plane crash, Parker's death, and Brown's retirement left Brown & Root management in disarray. And Connally's abrupt tumble out of national politics sent the company into a new world without an ally in Washington. Things worsened in 1978 when the price-fixing suit was settled, exacting heavy penalties of nearly $100 million. It also resulted in six top executives pleading no contest to conspiracy and mail fraud. The outcome was a management team that had effectively been gutted and a company that was temporarily without leadership or direction.

• • •

By the end of the 1970s, Brown & Root was the largest engineering and construction firm in the nation, with more than 80,000 employees, but nothing seemed to be going its way. In 1977, the company had won an $800 million contract with the Iranian government to build two naval bases along the Gulf of Oman. The company had set up an Iranian office to oversee the work, but in 1979, before construction had begun in earnest, the Ayatollah Khomeini unseated the Shah of Iran, and the United States ordered an evacuation of Americans in the area. Brown & Root had to walk away from the project, one of the most lucrative it had won in years, and left $23 million on the table. Combined with rising oil prices and a severe reduction in offshore drilling due to growing environmental concerns, Brown & Root was in for a shaky decade under the Reagan administration.

In just one year, from 1979 to 1980, Brown & Root's revenues plummeted by more than half. The company began a long and painful process of restructuring, laying off thousands of employees each year until 1984, when Brown & Root was a shell of the company it used to be, employing only 20,000 and closing up many of its offices around the world. Since George Brown's retirement in 1975, there had not been a chairman at Brown & Root, and the position would not be filled again until 1982. Without Brown, the company had trouble winning new construction projects, and it began to focus on smaller, less profitable projects.

The company started work on nuclear power plants, and thought the emerging industry could return them to glory. But disaster, and lawsuits once again undermined Brown & Root's progress. In the midst of $5.5 billion contract with the Houston Lighting & Power Company in the early 1980s, Brown & Root was sued for mismanagement of the project. The Houston utilities company was seeking a whopping $6.3 billion in damages, a sum that once again threatened the very existence of the company. In 1985, Brown & Root settled the case with $750 million in cash, but between the bad publicity and the growing public opposition to nuclear plants following the Three Mile Island incident, yet another avenue of revenue was effectively closed off for Brown & Root.

George Brown passed away in January 1983, leaving his company in dire straits. Brown & Root was under fire from unhappy customers, and suffered from a dearth of quality leadership and big projects. By 1986, when oil prices were dropping rapidly, the company was losing money at the rate of $6 million a month. Equipment went unused. New contracts remained unattainable. Although all heavy construction firms experienced serious downturns in their business during the 1980s, no company was hurt as badly as Brown & Root. It slipped from first to eighth in the rankings of engineering and construction firms. It had very little government contract work to speak of and its national profile was quickly disappearing.

Brown & Root's parent company couldn't help them either. Halliburton was also experiencing a simultaneous downturn in revenues throughout the 1980s, as the oil glut from OPEC reduced drilling in the United States from more than 4,000 rigs to just over 600. Like its fiercely independent subsidiary, Brown & Root, Halliburton reduced its head count from 115,000 in 1981, to 68,000 in 1984 as the price of oil plummeted from $32 a barrel to $12. The situation for Halliburton was as bad as it had ever been, and there was only one thing that was going to pull the company out of its seemingly endless decline: war.

• • •

By the summer of 1990, Saddam Hussein had begun amassing Iraqi troops at the border of Iraq and Kuwait in anticipation of an invasion. His justification for the impending war was that Kuwait was waging economic warfare against Iraq by flooding the world markets with cheap oil. He also accused the Kuwaitis of stealing Iraqi oil from the Rumaylah oil field near the border and vowed to "annex" Kuwait as a result. By August, the United States had embargoed all trade with Iraq and warned that military action against Kuwait by Iraq would result in U.S. action against Iraq. American workers were ordered to leave the area, but a couple dozen Halliburton workers were trapped inside Iraq. The workers in Kuwait and Iraq were detained by Hussein's forces, brought to Baghdad, and not released for several months. Halliburton was in the middle of another raging conflict, and this time its own employees were in danger. Hussein released the prisoners in December 1990 in an attempt to discourage American participation in the conflict. It didn't work.

On January 12, 1991, Congress authorized President Bush to engage Iraq in war, and just five days later, Operation Desert Storm commenced in Kuwait. As with the more recent war in the Gulf, it didn't take long for the United States to claim victory—it was all over by the end of February—but the clean up would last longer, and was far more expensive than the military action itself. In a senseless act of desperation and defeat, Iraqi troops set fire to more than 700 Kuwaiti oil wells throughout the country, resulting in a constant fog of thick, black smoke that turned the day into night and literally set the countryside ablaze. Few will forget the images of the plumes of smoke, anchored by jets of flame dotting the landscape. The Iraqi troops had booby-trapped the wells with C4 explosives, and detonated them upon their withdrawal from the country. It was thought the mess would take no less than five years to clean up, as lakes of oil surrounding each well blazed out of control, making it nearly impossible to approach the burning wells, let alone extinguish them.

With the Kuwaiti government in exile, the task of capping the fires was an exercise in confusion. Seven million barrels of oil a day were being wasted by the fires, and Kuwait was blanketed by the smoke that created an 800-mile long plume. Kuwaiti officials, exiled everywhere from Saudi Arabia to the United States, scrambled to assemble a team to fight the blazes. Four teams of wild well fighters emerged from the chaos: Red Adair, Boots & Coots, and Wild Well Control (all from Houston), and Safety Boss, a Canadian company. Bechtel was contracted to provide logistical support for the operation.

Halliburton would take losses of $29 million associated with its loss of work in the area due to the war, but with the fighting now over, Halliburton would be right back in the thick of it, angling its way into the cleanup and rebuilding effort that was expected to cost around $200 billion over the next 10 years. The company got on board with the wild well fighting companies and sent 60 men to help. Meanwhile, Brown & Root won an additional $3 million contract to assess the damage that the invasion had done to Kuwait's buildings, a contract that was increased seven times over by the end of their involvement. A Texan was president of the United States, waged a war, and Brown & Root was back in the government and defense contracting business.

Regardless of the extent of Halliburton's involvement, the company had popped back onto the government's radar screen. Now back in the good graces of the federal government and the military, Halliburton was not going to squander the opportunity. Brown & Root won contracts to extract army troops from Saudi Arabia after their services were no longer needed in the Gulf region and ship ammunition from the Middle East to locations around the world. The company was back in the army logistics business in earnest for the first time since Vietnam. The rebirth of the military outsourcing business would blossom to unforeseen heights immediately following the Gulf War.

9

The Big Score

Military outsourcing is nothing new. Private firms have been aiding in war efforts since long before Brown & Root won its first navy shipbuilding contract. The hiring of mercenary forces literally dates back to the beginning of recorded history when the Bible tells the story of how the Egyptians employed the services of outside armies to drive out the Israelites. Throughout time, where there has been war, there have been soldiers for hire. But the nature of military outsourcing, now more commonly known as *privatization*, has changed dramatically in just the last decade.

Here in the United States, privatization took on a whole new meaning after the end of the Cold War, when Americans were promised the famous "Peacetime Dividend" as a result of the reduction in military spending. At first, the military was expected to do less with less. That resulted in the massive reduction in the number of active troops—reduced by a third since

1989—and severe cutbacks in government spending toward the military. But since the end of the Cold War and since the reduction in force, the United States has been engaged in a succession of smaller, shorter, but fiercely contested wars around the world. Kuwait, Somalia, Haiti, Bosnia, Kosovo, Afghanistan, and Iraq are but a few of the conflicts that have required the participation of war machines, ammunition, and most importantly, troops.

The trend toward a smaller military, begun by President Reagan in the 1980s, and continued throughout the 1990s, put the federal government in an awkward position. It appeared that there was going to be just as much for the military to do, just fewer people to do it. This combination of a reduced military and continued conflict gave rise to an unprecedented new industry of private military firms. The firms would assist the military in everything from weapons procurement and training, weapons maintenance, training of troops (both foreign and domestic), and logistics. On the surface, the trend appealed to America's capitalistic sensibilities. It seemed reasonable that a privatized military would be more nimble, efficient, and cost effective if open competition was cultivated. Competition would cut down on the burgeoning bureaucracy of the government and create a growing new industry in the United States that would even help fuel the economy. It had worked in other industries, to varying degrees, so why not the military?

But the military is not like other industries. The distinction between public and private markets is simple and stark. The government, or the public sector, is expected to act on behalf of its citizens, spending their tax money to better their lives. The private sector is motivated solely by profit. In the case of waging war, an action taken to ostensibly improve the lives of citizens, it would seem that the government should remain the sole dispenser of funds, and the military should remain the sole recipient. Peter Singer, author of the definitive work on the subject of military outsourcing, *Corporate Warriors: The Rise of the Privatized Military Industry,* puts it like this: "In fact, providing for national, and hence their citizens', security was one of the most essential tasks of a government. Indeed it defined what a government was supposed to be. The result is that the military has been the one area where there has never been a question of states outsourcing or privatizing. Even the most radical libertarian thinkers, who tend to think that everything should be left to the market, made an exception of the military. All viewed national defense as something best carried out by a tax-financed government force."

In the 11 years since the first Gulf War, the number of private contractors used in and around the battlefield has increased ten-fold. It has been estimated that for every 10 soldiers in Iraq, there is one private contractor. The increase has been nothing less than astounding, and it has caused the country to redefine its beliefs about everything from free-market dynamics to war profiteering. Though there are some highly controversial outfits, like Military Professional Resources Incorporated (MPRI), which offers training in warfare tactics and personnel, companies like Halliburton, which became the fifth largest defense contractor in the nation during the 1990s, have played an even more critical role in this trend.

• • •

The story behind America's Super Contract begins back in 1992, when in the wake of the first Gulf War, the Department of Defense, headed by Dick Cheney, was impressed with the work Halliburton did during its time in Kuwait. Halliburton and Brown & Root not only helped put out oil-well fires during the summer of 1992, but won large contracts to help rebuild Kuwait in the aftermath of the Iraqi invasion. Sensing the need to bolster its forces in the event of further conflicts of a similar nature, the Pentagon asked private contractors to bid on a $3.9 million contract to develop a classified report demonstrating how a private firm could provide logistical support to the army in the case of further military action. The report was to look at 13 different "hot spots" around the world, and detail how services as varied as building bases to feeding the troops would be accomplished. The contractor that would potentially provide the services detailed in the report would be required to support the deployment of 20,000 troops over 180 days. It was a massive contingency plan, the first of its kind for the American military.

Thirty-seven companies solicited for the contract, and Brown & Root beat them all out. The company was paid another $5 million later that same year to extend the plan to other locations and increase the detail of the report. The report was a furthering of the Logistics Civil Augmentation Program (LOGCAP), a program the army had been using since the mid-1980s. But this time the Pentagon wanted to see what it would look like if just one contractor handled all of the contingencies, rather than spreading the wealth around to different contractors in different locations. There was understandable doubt as to whether one private firm could absorb the myriad requests of the army around the world. Hence, the need to produce Brown & Root's report, which remains classified to this day.

The Brown & Root report convinced Cheney that it was indeed possible to create one umbrella LOGCAP contract and award it to a single firm. The contract that was developed out of Brown & Root's report is now known simply as LOGCAP and has been called the "mother of all service contracts." It has been used in every American deployment since its awarding in 1992, at a value of several billion dollars and counting. And the lucky recipient of the first, five-year LOGCAP contract was the very same company hired to draw up the plan in the first place: Brown & Root.

The LOGCAP contract pulled Brown & Root out of its late 1980s doldrums and boosted the bottom line of Halliburton throughout the 1990s. The contract is structured as a *cost-plus* contract, or in contract legalese, a *cost-reimbursement, indefinite-delivery/indefinite-quantity* contract. Even a layman can tell that means good things for the contractor. In cases where the government and its contractor will have difficulty estimating the resources needed in fulfillment of a particular contract, cost-plus provides the flexibility to continually add on "task orders," or additional services to the contract on an ongoing basis. Basically, it's a blank check from the government. The contractor makes its money from a built-in profit percentage, anywhere from 1 percent to 9 percent, depending on various incentive clauses. It seems reasonable enough, until we remember Brown & Root's history of ratcheting up costs on government projects. In the case of LOGCAP, as was the case with Brown & Root's involvement in Vietnam, the structure of the contract encourages the contractor to spend excessive amounts of money. When your profit is a percentage of the cost, the more you spend, the more you make.

Before the ink was dry on Brown & Root's first LOGCAP contract, the U.S. Army was deployed to Somalia in December 1992 as part of Operation Restore Hope. Brown & Root employees were there before the army even arrived, and they were the last people to leave. At first, the task orders that Brown & Root won through LOGCAP were substantial, but not outrageous. They made $109.7 million in Somalia. In August 1994, they took in $6.3 million from Operation Support Hope in Rwanda. In September of that same year, Operation Uphold Democracy in Haiti netted the company $150 million. And in October 1994, Operation Vigilant Warrior made them another $5 million.

The contracts to that point were good revenue for Brown & Root, but hardly the type of monster contracts they had been used to in the LBJ days. Still, a far more important trend was developing: The army was growing dependent on Brown & Root. In the spirit of "refuse no job," the company was building the base camps, supplying the troops with food and water, fuel and munitions, cleaning latrines, even washing their clothes. They attended the staff meetings and were kept up to speed on all the activities related to a given mission. They were becoming another unit in the U.S. Army.

There was no question they were doing a quality job. Every military officer, past or present, I spoke with was more than satisfied with Brown & Root's performance. They made life better at the camps, and that made the troops happier. And as many commanding officers told me, a happy army is a motivated army. Few of the army officers had any problem with the fact that there was some waste involved. Bob Borroughs spent 32 years in the army as an aviator and ran the logistics from the army side in Somalia. He worked hand-in-hand with Brown

& Root and believed that the company occasionally took advantage of its preferred contractor status. But he didn't mind. "I had an unlimited budget because of what we were doing there, and I'm sure they overcharged me on some things. But I would have been in real trouble if they hadn't been there."

Brown & Root was back to doing what they did best, providing contractor services to the armed forces under extraordinary circumstances. The army was constantly amazed at their ability to get things done quickly. Often it cost them more than if they had done it themselves, but in the overall war effort, it was worth it. By the time the conflict in Bosnia started in 1995, Brown & Root was ensconced in the military machine, and earning lucrative contracts. It was as if World War II and Brown Shipbuilding were back in business. The army's growing dependency on the company hit home when in 1997 Brown & Root lost the LOGCAP contract in a competitive re-bid to rival Dyncorp. The army found it impossible to remove Brown & Root from their work in the Balkans, by far the most lucrative part of the contract, and as such carved out the work in the area to keep it with Brown & Root. In 2001, Brown & Root won the LOGCAP contract again, this time for twice the normal term length: 10 years.

LOGCAP became part of the popular vocabulary after Halliburton was awarded several contracts in Iraq, which some lawmakers saw as blatant favoritism to the company once headed by Cheney who was CEO from 1995 to 2000. Many of these arguments were undercut by the fact that the task orders awarded to Halliburton, with the exception of Operation Restore Iraqi Oil (RIO), in Iraq fell under the existing LOGCAP contract, competitively bid back in 2001. This was, of course, true. And the fact that Halliburton had already competed for the work in

Iraq took a great deal of the sting out of these charges. But nobody bothered to go back and question the original legitimacy of the LOGCAP contract, circa 1992. If they had, they would have found that LOGCAP should never have been awarded to Brown & Root in the first place.

The question of LOGCAP's legality was first brought to my attention by Steve Schooner, co-director of the Government Procurement Law Program at George Washington University. When I related the story of how Brown & Root was contracted to design LOGCAP originally in 1992, and then was allowed to bid on its own contract, it raised red flags for Schooner. "If that's what really happened, then it's illegal," he told me. Schooner pointed me in the direction of the Code of Federal Regulations, which dictates the terms of all federal procurement. There, buried in countless pages of contractual guidelines, under Chapter 1, section 48, subsection 9.5, are the organizational conflict of interest rules. The idea behind the conflict of interest rules, as stated by the Code of Federal Regulations, is to prevent "the existence of conflicting roles that might bias a contractor's judgment; and prevent unfair competitive advantage." All of this is a fancy way of saying that allowing a contractor to bid on a contract it designed would constitute an unfair advantage.

Maddeningly ambiguous, the Code of Federal Regulations then attempts to clarify the law by providing mock examples using fictional circumstances. Several examples ring true to the LOGCAP scenario, but two examples in particular appear to apply to Brown & Root's case. You need to look through the fictional scenarios to draw the parallel to Brown & Root. The first example (f) reads as follows: "Company A receives a contract to define the detailed performance characteristics an agency will require for purchasing rocket fuels. Company A has not developed the particular fuels. When the definition contract is awarded, it is clear to both parties that the agency will use the performance characteristics arrived at to choose competitively a contractor to develop or produce the fuels. Company A may not be awarded this follow-on contract." The next relevant example reads: "Company A receives a contract to prepare a detailed plan for scientific and technical training of an agency's personnel. It suggests a curriculum that the agency endorses and incorporates in its request for proposals to institutions to establish and conduct the training. Company A may not be awarded a contract to conduct the training."

Brown & Root competed against four other firms for the LOGCAP contract that it had designed. It would be safe to say that the contract was awarded under highly questionable circumstances. Brown & Root clearly had a competitive advantage in addition to proprietary knowledge and should never have been allowed to compete for the contract. As they had done so many times before, the company had worked the system to perfection, and scored a contract that has netted the company more than $2.5 billion since it was first enacted.

Joan Kibler, a spokesperson for the U.S. Army Corps of Engineers, the branch of the army that oversaw LOGCAP for most of the 1990s before they transferred management of the contract to the U.S. Army Material Command, said she had asked around the Corps to find out more about the conflict of interest. "It's an interesting thing you bring up and that really needs to be confirmed. The Pentagon really needs to answer that question." Pentagon officials declined to comment.

10

Backseat Cheney

Richard Bruce Cheney was born on January 30, 1941, the same time that Franklin Delano Roosevelt was beginning his third term as president of the United States. In fact, Cheney shares FDR's birthday, of which his parents, staunch Democrats, were immensely proud. There is an odd symmetry when you consider that despite being a lifelong conservative Republican, Cheney would once again fatten Halliburton at the government trough during his time as CEO, much like FDR had done (via LBJ) for Brown & Root 60 years earlier. The names changed many times over the six decades since the company made its first fortune from the American military during World War II, but the business model had not. During its most successful years, Brown & Root had thrived by using political influence to garner government work, and the late 1990s, the Cheney era, would be no exception.

To the uninitiated, the appointment of Dick Cheney to the chairman, president, and CEO positions at Halliburton in

August 1995, made little sense. Cheney had almost no business experience having been a career politician and bureaucrat. Financial analysts downgraded the stock and the business press openly questioned the decision. Cheney, having been Secretary of Defense under the first Bush administration, was in theory a celebrity appointment, a big name that was supposed to be big news. But for someone that had spent so much time in the Washington spotlight, Cheney was still an unknown quantity, with very little public personality and even less experience in business of any kind, let alone the expertise needed to manage one of the largest oil services companies in the world. Halliburton must have understood Cheney's value though. Clearly the time had come for Halliburton to get back in the business of politics, and with Dick Cheney at the helm, they had all the fire power they would need.

• • •

Born in Nebraska, Cheney moved with his family to Casper, Wyoming, when he was thirteen years old. Casper was a typical oil town, and Cheney would later recall the giant, bright red Halliburton trucks kicking up dust as they rolled through town during his youth. As an oil town, Casper attracted the get-rich-quick folks from the surrounding areas, and money was the overriding concern of the townspeople. Family, sports, and Betty Crocker were the other pursuits of choice, and politics was virtually eschewed. Cheney played outside linebacker at Natrona County High, and dated the most popular girl in school, Mustang Queen Lynne Vincent. By his senior year, Cheney had little direction, and a friend of the family made a phone call to Yale University and asked the school to take Cheney on a full scholarship. Yale accepted Cheney without question, and the quiet kid from Casper was headed for the Ivy League.

Despite his ease in being admitted, Yale proved to be too difficult for Cheney. After completing four semesters of study, Cheney flunked out, and returned to Wyoming to get a job. By 1963, he was building power lines in Rock Springs, Wyoming. He became fully blue collar, joining the International Brotherhood of Electrical Workers. At the time when he should have been graduating from Yale on a full scholarship, he was instead living the life of a simple laborer, rooming with friends and getting arrested for drunk driving (twice). Things didn't start to turn around for him until he married Vincent in 1964, and re-enrolled at the University of Wyoming.

Lynne made it known to Dick that "she wasn't interested in marrying a lineman for the county," and Cheney started to bear down at school. He made straight As and took a job as an intern at the Wyoming legislature. He was exceedingly quiet, given to terse, one-word answers, but he applied himself diligently and devoured information. In 1968, Cheney took a job with a Republican congressman from Wisconsin named Bill Steiger, and began working on a piece of legislation that would eliminate federal funding to college campuses that had been home to antiwar protests. It was in this context, the radical 1960s, that Cheney forged his conservative values, disgusted by the student rallies peopled by uninvolved academics. Cheney himself avoided the draft by enrolling as a student at a Casper Community College after attending the University of Wyoming and claimed a deferral.

When Donald Rumsfeld was appointed director of the Office of Economic Opportunity, Cheney wrote him a letter advising Rumsfeld on how to best handle the job. It was a bold and presumptuous move, but it paid off. Rumsfeld hired Cheney onto his staff, and the two of them moved up through the ranks of government together, Rumsfeld always in front, Cheney, silent and strong, in tow.

Cheney has been described by those who know him as everything from low-key to downright bland, but the confidence he inspired and the loyalty he professed made him an indispensable part of Rumsfeld's rise to power. He was often chastised by Rumsfeld for speaking too quietly or slowly, but his advice was considered to be of great value, and as Rumsfeld navigated the bureaucratic waters of Washington in the early 1970s, Cheney came along for the ride. Eventually, Rumsfeld ended up as Gerald Ford's White House chief of staff, with Cheney as his deputy. During this time, Cheney was assigned a codename by the Secret Service that would perfectly sum up his disposition: Backseat.

Cheney's unique blend of quiet knowledge and anti-charisma earned him the nickname. He has never been comfortable in the spotlight, more content to be the silent strength behind a benefactor. He reads voraciously and studies political and military history. He has a calming effect on those that work with him, a reassurance that comes not through blustery overconfidence, but studied, metered wisdom. When Ford lost to Carter in 1976, Cheney returned to Wyoming and became a junior congressman. The move demonstrated his devotion to the life of a public servant. It would have been easy for Cheney to carve out a lucrative lobbying business in Washington, peddling influence to the highest bidder. Instead, he chose the life of an untested elected official in a district nobody cared about. It wasn't an easy life. Many years of heavy smoking and the stress of running his own office resulted in a heart attack at age thirty-seven, the first of four he would suffer through the present day.

• • •

For 10 years, Cheney worked as a Republican representative for Wyoming, until in 1989, George H.W. Bush tapped him to become his Secretary of Defense. Cheney wasn't Bush's first choice, but after Senator John Tower of Texas failed to win the confirmation, Brent Scowcroft, national security advisor and former Ford aide, recommended Cheney. Cheney breezed through the confirmation process and became the seventeenth secretary of defense.

As defense secretary, Cheney was a worrier. He worried about the Soviet Union, even long after it collapsed (to this day in fact). He worried about nuclear proliferation, and the fate of Russia's arsenal. And long before George W. Bush made his infamous "axis of evil" speech, Cheney pointed out the growing danger of Iran, Iraq, and North Korea. But most of all, Cheney worried about the effect the long-promised peacetime dividend would have on the armed forces. In his first year in office, Cheney reduced military spending by $10 billion. He canceled a number of complicated and expensive weapons systems, and reduced the number of troops from 2.2 million to 1.6 million. Year after year, from 1989 to 1993, the military budget shrank under Cheney.

The army took the biggest hit, sustaining troop reductions of more than 25 percent. Though the Cold War had ended, Cheney must have known that the U.S. troops would be committed to smaller, but possibly more, skirmishes around the world. Already he had overseen the liberation of Kuwait and the invasion of Panama to capture Manuel Noriega. And toward the end of his tenure in 1992, he had committed 26,000 troops to provide security and relief to Somalia. In fact, since the Cold War ended, American troops have been dispatched nearly 40 times around the world as compared to only 10 times over the entire history of the Cold War. The world had become an ostensibly safer place after the collapse of the Soviet Union, but U.S. troops were still in high demand, despite there being far fewer of them.

During the conflict in Kuwait, Cheney was faced with the decision of whether to continue the battle into Iraq and force the surrender and capture of Saddam Hussein. At the time, concerned about troop commitments and the potential of heavy casualties, he decided against it. Troop limitations were hampering the ability of the American military to get the job done. The army depended very little on civilian contractors in the early 1990s, and Cheney was inclined to change that. The idea was to free up the troops to do the fighting while private contractors handled the back-end logistics. It was also a tidy way of handling the public relations nightmare that ensued every time the United States committed troops overseas. More contractors meant fewer troops, and a much more politically palatable troop count. All of these factors resulted in the development of the LOGCAP mega-contract that was awarded to Brown & Root at the end of Cheney's time at the Pentagon. His last day on the job was January 20, 1993, five months after LOGCAP was finalized and awarded.

· · ·

After cleaning out his desk to make way for the Clinton administration in the winter of 1993, Cheney joined the American Enterprise Institute, the neo-conservative think tank, where he and a number of his likeminded politicos spent their time writing and researching various issues of domestic and foreign policy. Among the positions espoused by the group was the elimination of the continued threat posed by Saddam Hussein. They believed that America had the responsibility of removing him from power. The decision not to pursue Hussein into Iraq during the first Gulf War was one that would haunt Cheney until he finally accomplished the goal in 2003.

After leaving office, Cheney also spent some time mulling a presidential run in 1996, setting up a political action committee and visiting 47 states en route to a possible nomination. But in 1995, he announced he would not be running. Speculation on why Cheney declined to run varied from the fact that he didn't have the charisma to sustain a televised campaign to the fact that his youngest daughter, Mary, is a lesbian, and Cheney had upheld a policy banning gays from the military while he was secretary of defense. It was more likely, however, that Cheney's reluctance to run came from a different source. He was faced with a tempting economic opportunity that promised a far easier road.

• • •

The story about how Dick Cheney came to be Halliburton's CEO goes like this: During a fishing trip at the Miramichi River in New Brunswick with a group of high-powered corporate CEOs, the men were discussing the ongoing search for a CEO at Halliburton. Cheney was asleep back at the lodge and, in his absence, the men decided that Cheney would be the man for the job, despite the fact that he had never worked in the oil business. Without Cheney there to protest, he got the job. True or not, the story explains Cheney's baffling appointment to the

CEO position as well as anything. Unlike 15 years earlier when he chose the life of a public servant, this time Cheney chose to embrace a drastic career change. With Cheney as their CEO, Halliburton would have considerable leverage in Washington. The company was in the process of ramping up its government and military contracting work after 10 long years of drought, and Cheney's contacts on Capitol Hill and the Pentagon offered a new level of access.

● ● ●

Up until Cheney's appointment in the fall of 1995, Halliburton's business results had been decent. After a loss of $91 million in 1993, the company had returned to profitability in 1994 with an operating profit of $236 million. With the new revenue coming in from LOGCAP, Halliburton, and its prize subsidiary Brown & Root, were back on track. Though LOGCAP was producing only modest revenues—about $212 million between 1992 and 1995—it was successful in re-integrating Brown & Root into the military machine. Besides, with a monopoly on army logistics in its back pocket, Brown & Root was sure to cash in sooner or later on a major conflict, even with a dove of a president—Bill Clinton.

That opportunity finally presented itself in December 1995, just two months after Cheney took the CEO job, when the United States sent thousands of troops to the Balkans to provide stability to a region that had been uprooted by war. As part of Operation Joint Endeavor, Brown & Root was dispatched to Bosnia and Kosovo to support the army in its operations in the region. The task was massive in scope and size. The company immediately set to work building two camps in the middle of wheat fields, with no existing foundations or infrastructure. In the course of just a few months, Brown & Root created what amounted to two small cities—one in Bosnia, one in Kosovo—capable of housing and feeding 5,000 troops each. Troop limitations imposed by the White House drove the army to rely heavily on LOGCAP and the services Brown & Root could provide. The result was a bonanza for Brown & Root.

From 1995 to 2000, Brown & Root billed the government for more than $2 billion in services. The company did everything from build the camps to deliver the mail, with 24-hour food service and laundering. It provided firefighting services, fuel delivery, sewage construction, hazardous material disposal, and the maintenance and delivery of equipment. In short, Brown & Root became the lifeblood of the U.S. army in the Balkans, an indispensable part of the military machine.

One example of the work Brown & Root did in the Balkans was Camp Bondsteel. The camp was so large that the U.S. General Accounting Office likened it to "a small town." The company built roads, power generation, water and sewage systems, housing, a helicopter airfield, a perimeter fence, guard towers, and a detention center (à la Vietnam). Soldiers at the camp said the only thing missing was the patch on their uniforms that said, "Sponsored by Brown & Root." The camp, still in use today, has communications towers, satellite dishes, and a six-mile perimeter. Bondsteel is the largest and most expensive army base since Vietnam. It also happens to be built in the path of the Albanian-Macedonian-Bulgarian Oil (AMBO) Trans-Balkan pipeline, the pipeline charged with the task of connecting the oil-rich Caspian Sea region to the rest of the world. The initial feasibility project for AMBO was done by Brown & Root.

Brown & Root's cash flow from LOGCAP ballooned under Cheney's tenure, jumping from about $144 million in 1994 to more than $423 million in 1996, and the Balkans was the driving force. By 1999, the army was spending just under $1 billion a year on Brown & Root's work in the Balkans. The company had become so integral to the army's work in the region that in 1997, when the first LOGCAP contract ran out, the army carved out the Balkans region from the follow-on contract, awarded to Brown & Root competitor Dyncorp, and kept it in the hands of Brown & Root. The new contract, a sole-source, noncompetitive contract, was called the Balkans Support Contract, and it remains with Brown & Root to this day. The fact that a Balkans Support Contract even existed, separate and distinct from LOGCAP, underscored a fundamental flaw in the original design of the LOGCAP contract, in that awarding a single contract for all army logistics support created an artificial dependency on that one contractor. Though LOGCAP was originally intended to be competitively awarded in its entirety every five years, the Army found it too disruptive and expensive to remove Brown & Root midstream. The company had become indispensable.

The work in the Balkans was all done under the cost-plus structure of LOGCAP, which guaranteed a 1 percent profit on top of expenses, with the possibility of up to 8 percent in award fees. Between 1995 and 2000, Brown & Root was given the full award fee for five evaluation periods, 99 percent two times, and 98 percent one time. But the cost-plus structure of the contract came back to bite the army and Brown & Root when the General Accounting Office issued a report in September 2000 charging serious cost-control problems in the Balkans.

The main problem with the work in the Balkans was a lack of oversight by the army. From the army's perspective, everything was running smoothly. After all, Brown & Root made their lives considerably easier. By assigning ever-increasing amounts of work to the contractor, the Army was able to reduce force size and concentrate on more important things. And it wasn't their money that was being spent. There was also a fundamental and more systemic problem occurring. The army was unclear about how the LOGCAP contract was to be used. Originally, the contract was "intended to be the option of last resort." The army had come to think of LOGCAP, and subsequently Brown & Root, as another branch of the military, at their beckon call. The results were disastrous, and fantastically expensive.

Critics say Brown & Root benefited from the confusion. The GAO found that the company overstaffed and oversupplied the army, resulting in higher costs and in turn, higher profits. In one instance, Brown & Root was tasked with building a fire-fighting force to staff the camps in Bosnia, Kosovo, and Macedonia. The company submitted a plan for 116 fire-fighting personnel. Army engineers concluded that no more than 66 were needed. But Brown & Root was able to haggle with the Army, finalizing an agreement to staff 77 firefighters and the corresponding amount of trucks and equipment. Despite the difference of opinion on the matter, the army gave in to Brown & Root's requests, showing the rising level of authority the company had in influencing army policy.

Indeed, the army was confused about its authority over its primary contractor. In December 1999, the administrative contracting officer at Camp Monteith in Kosovo, issued a task order to Brown & Root to build a tent for use as the post office at the camp. The government estimated the cost to be $6,000, so the officer placed a $10,000 limit on the cost of the construction, giving Brown & Root ample wiggle room. Upon hearing this, the lead administrative contracting officer at Camp Bondsteel sent an e-mail to his equal at Camp Monteith, telling him that Brown & Root "is the army's customer and that such funding limitations affect the army's relationship with the customer." How the customer-vendor relationship in the Balkans got so turned around is anybody's guess. The army is, of course, the customer in the relationship, not the reverse.

Brown & Root was growing in power by the day in the Balkans, and so was the wastefulness. The company was leasing generators at a cost of $13 million a year to provide 100 percent power redundancy throughout the base camps. Army officials, after the money had already been spent, noted that they didn't need the capacity that Brown & Root was providing, and the excess would cost $85 million over five years. The GAO also estimated that the company had overstaffed 85 percent of the projects in Bosnia and that "half of the crews had at least 40 percent of their members not engaged in work." The cleaning services staff was finishing their work in a fraction of the time they were given, resulting in long breaks several times a day.

The situation in Bosnia was a mess, and it harkened back to the cost overruns of the Vietnam era and RMK-BRJ (Raymond International, Morrison Knudson, Brown & Root, and JA Jones Construction). It also was a foreshadowing to the cost concerns of Kellogg Brown & Root's work in Iraq. It was a pattern the GAO had tried to address in 1997, when it issued a report suggesting ways to improve the management of LOGCAP. But the situation had only worsened. Part of the problem was the challenge of hiring local labor to complete tasks. It was originally thought that this would considerably lower costs in each military deployment, as well as curry favor with the locals. Instead, locals turned out to be difficult to manage and rely on, and worse, they posed a significant security risk.

In Somalia in the early 1990s, Brown & Root relied heavily on local labor, and at one point was the country's largest employer. Bob Borroughs, the army officer in charge of Brown & Root during the brief American occupation there, remembers truckloads of "skinnys," as the American soldiers referred to the locals, showing up whenever a job needed to get done. "One time we told them we had to get a roof put on the customs house, which had been mortared," Borroughs recalls. "The next day, two tractor trailer rigs showed up with a hundred skinnys sitting on top. I don't know how they did it or where they came from, but Brown & Root got whatever we needed."

Where they got the labor was the problem. Borroughs said that one of the first "bad guys" the Americans arrested in Mogadishu, warlord Mohamed Farrah Aidid's "finance guy," was found with "a bunch of Brown & Root checks in his pockets." According to Borroughs, Brown & Root was hiring workers and buying supplies from the government the Americans were there to defeat. If that's the case, Brown & Root was making the troops' life easier at camp by making it harder for the soldiers to defeat the enemy. In addition, there were concerns at the American base camp outside of Mogadishu that the locals that worked inside the camp perimeter, were working as agents of Aidid. In his bestselling book *Black Hawk Down*, Mark Bowden references a Brown & Root employee who was feeding information to Aidid. Dan Schilling, an air force combat controller in Somalia says "We did have real concerns about using locals. The guy could be squeaky clean on paper, but in a country like Somalia, you never know. When trucks full of locals came into camp to clean out the latrines, I usually steered clear of the bathrooms. If you're really determined to get something into the compound, you could do it. No one's going to check out the inside of the sewage truck. If they really wanted to, they could wall off a section, they could put some C4 in there." Borroughs, an unflappable, crusty veteran, who has seen everything in his 32 years of service, took the inherent risks of hiring locals in stride, and told me, without a hint of irony, "sometimes you have to work with the devil to make things work."

General William Nash, the former American commander in Bosnia and U.N. administrator in Kosovo, told me that working with the locals is part of the game in modern day warfare. "Who knew who the bad guys were? There are so many things you don't understand, that's just the ignorance of being the new guy on the block." Nash felt that in Bosnia, like Somalia, things ran as well as they could have, all things considered. "Was there waste in Bosnia? Of course there was. When you come in on the leading edge of an operation, you've got to expect that there will be some degree of less than perfect organization. To some extent, it's the cost of doing business. There were a lot of scams that people could run. The fact that they got over on some portion of the contract, I can't deny. Life is real."

Nash is a realist, if nothing else. And his views of the waste that went on in Bosnia reflect his level-headed understanding of war-time contracting, and a lifetime of military service. But when it comes to Iraq, and Brown & Root's (now known as Kellogg Brown & Root) involvement there, his tone turns much darker. "[Iraq] is different. The contracts that we're concerned with now are the rebuilding of the country, [not war-time work]. Personally I think that these rebuilding contracts smell to high heaven. The whole thing is [fouled] up."

Cheney seemed to take a similarly accepting approach to the overspending issues in Bosnia as Nash. Even as the GAO reports were coming out, Cheney chose not to get involved in the work in Bosnia, declining to visit the camps his company was supporting. He felt that it would represent a conflict if he was to appear too close to the military contracting side of the business, given his history in the department of defense. As CEO of Halliburton, Cheney specialized in delegation, and would often use that fact as a shield from contracting controversy. But a CEO is ultimately responsible for all of the actions of a company, and Cheney's decisions during his time as CEO raised serious questions about his true political beliefs.

● ● ●

"It is a false dichotomy that we have to choose between our commercial and other interests." That quote, delivered by Dick Cheney in a speech given to the Cato Institute in the summer of 1998, succinctly sums up the vice president's business strategy while CEO of Halliburton. Cheney was speaking out against economic sanctions levied primarily by the Clinton administration against countries suspected of terrorist activity. "Our government has become sanctions-happy," Cheney continued. His main gripe was that by sanctioning various countries, known sponsors of terrorism, it hurt Halliburton's business. In particular, Cheney objected to sanctions against Libya and Iran, two countries that Halliburton was already doing brisk business with anyway. In fact, during Cheney's time as CEO, Halliburton was even conducting business with Iraq, the country Cheney had led our troops against as secretary of defense in the first Gulf War, and would again go to battle with in 2003. Under the circumstances, it's hard to imagine a regime with which Dick Cheney wouldn't do business.

Cheney's anti-sanction history is well documented. While a Representative from Wyoming, Cheney twice opposed levying sanctions against the apartheid government of South Africa. He favored carving out a piece of Cuba that could engage in free trade with the United States, like West Berlin. And as CEO of Halliburton, he joined the United States–Engage lobby, a group of trade affiliations lobbying to end sanctions against Libya and Iran. But in looking at Halliburton's business in countries that are under strict American and U.N. sanctions, it's difficult to understand why Cheney even felt the need to lift the sanctions. Business was being done in those countries despite efforts to the contrary.

Severe sanctions have been in effect against Libya since 1986, when Ronald Reagan was in office, and Libya had been implicated in several terrorist attacks against the United States and other nations, including the bombing of Pan Am Flight 103 over Lockerbie, Scotland. The Reagan administration believed that the Libyan government was supporting these acts financially and otherwise. Yet Brown & Root has been working on a project, the size and scope of which boggle the mind, for more than 20 years. The Great Man-Made River Project is a $25 billion project that Colonel Moammar Qaddafi conceived and initiated in the early 1980s. It consists of 2,200 miles of massive underground pipes, 14 feet in diameter, that zigzag underneath the sun-baked sands of the country for the ostensible purpose of transporting water, found deep under the Sahara desert, to regions in need of it. The idea is to bring water to the thirsty nether regions of the country to use for agriculture.

Brown & Root began work on the project in 1984, drawing up feasibility plans and drafting specifications. When stricter sanctions were imposed in 1986, the company simply transferred the work to its British office and kept the follow-on contracts coming to this day. In his speech given to the Cato Institute in 1998, Cheney stated flatly that economic sanctions "almost never work." With companies like his own skirting the sanctions with such ease, it's easy to see why.

Even more troubling, the pipeline may end up carrying more troops than it does water. In 1997, engineers working on the project came forward to say that Libya's explanation of the project was improbable at best. The engineers said that the enormous storage areas being constructed every 50 miles were far too complicated and immense for carrying water. They believed that the facilities were in fact intended to store military equipment, even poison gas. The tunnels are large enough to move military troops, equipment, or even install a rail line. "Qaddafi seems to have taken a leaf out of Kim Il Sung's book and created a potential military arsenal underground," feared one engineer. The tunnels are slated to intersect with Tarhuna mountain, a known chemical and biological weapons plant, and national security experts felt it possible that Qaddafi could use the tunnels to conceal movements of weapons and troops from U.S. satellites.

But Halliburton's business continued in Libya, and the company was still managing the project as of 1997, with CEO Dick Cheney fighting hard to have the official sanctions against Libya removed. The company declined to say whether it was still working on The Great Man-Made River Project today.

• • •

Libya was not the first country on America's list of terrorism sponsors with which Halliburton did business. The company has had an office in Tehran, Iran, since 1975, when it was awarded contracts worth more than $800 million to build a naval base for the Iranian Imperial Army. That business, and other oil-related business, continued for nearly three decades before, just recently, Halliburton agreed to re-evaluate its business with Iran. New York City Comptroller William Thompson, who manages the city's pension funds, was incensed by Halliburton's business in Iran and insisted the company provide a full reckoning of its business deals in the country. Acting on behalf of the police and fire department pension funds, he filed a shareholder proposal asking Halliburton to disclose all details related to its Iranian business. The report that came back was incomplete, according to Thompson, and as of December 2003, Halliburton still had not provided enough information to satisfy the city.

Far more disconcerting though, is the work that the company has done in Iraq, the country against which Dick Cheney waged war twice during his career in public office. Between stints as secretary of defense and vice president, while Cheney was CEO of Halliburton, he helped to rebuild Iraq and enrich Saddam Hussein, circumventing strict sanctions and putting money into the pocket of America's public enemy number one.

In 1996, a U.N. program called Oil for Food was created as a way to provide humanitarian relief to Iraqi citizens while keeping in place the international economic sanctions against Iraq and the Saddam Hussein regime. The idea was to allow Iraq to export its precious oil in exchange for humanitarian aid, everything from first aid and medical supplies to the most basic food and water requirements. There were restrictions on the type of goods that could be imported by Iraq: anything deemed even remotely for military use was strictly prohibited. It seemed that the world had devised a clever way to obtain the much-needed oil of Iraq, without shouldering the burdensome crises of conscience associated with doing business with a brutal, murdering dictator.

Not surprisingly, the Oil for Food program was exploited for personal gain, on both sides of the deal making. The Council for International Justice, in a September 2002 report, estimated that for every $6 billion a year Iraq earned from the Oil for Food program, Saddam Hussein made $2 billion. He used this money for everything from luxury goods to weapons and training for his military. Oil for Food was the main source of income for Iraq, but the system was rife with corruption, skimming schemes, and kickbacks. Worse, the United States was consuming 75 percent of the oil exported from Iraq under the program.

The Oil for Food program was so thoroughly corrupt that it was reduced to a punch line. General Tommy Franks, the U.S. commander of forces in Iraq called it "Oil for Palaces." Saddam Hussein and his sons were growing richer by the day, exploiting the poorly audited program by providing substandard services for its people and pocketing the rest. It is estimated that of the $57 billion the country earned through the Oil for Food program, only $23 billion of it was spent on humanitarian goods. That comes to about $170 per year per person, or less than the United Nations spends on dog food for mine-clearing operations ($400 per dog per year).

It was through this program that Halliburton did business with Iraq between 1998 and 2000. In September 1998,

Halliburton closed on its $7.7 billion stock merger with Dresser Industries, the company that gave George H.W. Bush his first job. The merger made Halliburton the largest oil-field services firm in the world. It also brought with it two foreign subsidiaries that were doing business with Iraq through the controversial Oil for Food program. The two subsidiaries, Dresser-Rand and Ingersoll Dresser Pump Co., signed $73 million worth of contracts for oil production equipment while Cheney was CEO.

Cheney told the press during his 2000 run for vice president that he had a "firm policy" against doing business with Iraq. He admitted to doing business with Iran and Libya, but "Iraq's different," he said. Originally, Cheney denied the business ties to Baghdad outright, telling ABC-TV in the summer of 2000 that "We've not done any business in Iraq since U.N. sanctions were imposed on Iraq in 1990, and I had a standing policy that I wouldn't do that." Executives at both subsidiaries said later that no such policy existed.

Three weeks later, Cheney was forced to admit to the business ties, but claimed ignorance. He told reporters that he was not aware of Dresser's business in Iraq, and that besides, Halliburton had divested itself of both companies by 2000. In the meantime, the companies did another $30 million worth of business in Iraq before they were sold off. But ignorance of the contracts was also ruled out as an excuse, as Cheney was forced into the uncomfortable position of either admitting he didn't know that his company was trading with Saddam Hussein, or that he just didn't care. James Perrella, the former chairman of Ingersoll-Rand, said that Halliburton was simply concerned with whether the business with Iraq was legal, which it was.

Halliburton must have been aware of the inherent dangers of doing business through foreign subsidiaries with sanctioned states. In 1995, just before Cheney came on board, Halliburton was fined $3.8 million for violating sanctions by re-exporting goods through a foreign subsidiary into Libya. So Cheney's claim that he was unaware of the Iraq contracts either makes him a terribly irresponsible CEO or a deceptive politician. Either way, he's not the man I want bending the president's ear on a daily basis. But more importantly, it's difficult to imagine how Cheney justified in his own mind profiting from sales with Saddam Hussein, through a program that was widely known to be a joke. In essence, Cheney had gone to war against Iraq as defense secretary, helped rebuild Iraq's oil business and military as CEO of Halliburton, then went to war again as vice president. Apparently, how evil Saddam Hussein is depends on which side of the business-government continuum you currently sit.

• • •

The Dresser merger, and the subsequent fallout, was the crowning achievement of the Cheney years at Halliburton. But Cheney left Halliburton with a few other legacies as well. Brown & Root had nearly doubled its government contracts, from $1.2 billion in the five years prior to his arrival, to $2.3 billion during his five years as CEO. Halliburton soared from seventy-third to eighteenth on the Pentagon's list of top contractors. Its government contracting business grew 91 percent. In the five years before Cheney took over, Halliburton secured $100 million in government-backed loans from the

U.S. Export-Import Bank. During the five years of Cheney's tenure, that number increased to $1.5 billion. By the time he left in 2000 to become George W. Bush's running mate, the reason that Halliburton had chosen Dick Cheney as its CEO had become clear, though Cheney continued to deny that he had any influence on Halliburton's government business. During a vice presidential debate in 2000, Al Gore's running mate Senator Joseph Lieberman mentioned casually that Cheney had done well financially at Halliburton. Cheney responded by saying, "I can tell you, Joe, the government had absolutely nothing to do with it."

Then how did Cheney do it? The answer, of course, is through the government—by hiring a handful of his pals from the Beltway. David Gribbin, Cheney's former chief of staff, became Halliburton's chief lobbyist in Washington. Admiral Joe Lopez, a former commander of the sixth fleet, was hired to be Kellogg Brown & Root's governmental operations expert. Together, Cheney's team made Halliburton one of the top government contractors in the country. On the surface, it appeared that Cheney had been doing a great job. The stock had increased 157 percent from the time Cheney came on board in the fall of 1995 to the time he announced his resignation in July of 2000, paying regular dividends to stockholders. Things were going so well that Cheney told the *Dallas Morning News* that, though he was helping presidential candidate George W. Bush to find a vice presidential running mate, he was not the man for the job. "I made a long-term commitment to the company and I have absolutely no desire to go back to government," he said in May 2000, two months before he left Halliburton to become Bush's running mate.

When Cheney did leave, he took a golden parachute package, and was forced to cash in his stock options for more than $30 million. He also left in his wake a grand jury investigation into over-billing and a Securities and Exchange Commission (SEC) investigation into Halliburton's accounting practices while Cheney was CEO. Just two months after Cheney left the corner office at Halliburton, a former employee of the company, turned whistle-blower and claimed that Halliburton had over-billed the U.S. government by $6 million and used poor quality materials in its decommissioning of the Fort Ord military base in California. The company settled the case, admitting no wrongdoing, by paying the government $2 million in February 2002. The SEC investigation is ongoing.

But there was more. The company had changed its accounting for revenues during Cheney's tenure, allowing them to postpone revealing big losses on construction projects that had run over budget. It was reporting sales before it had even billed its clients, and kept them on the books for more than a year, even if there were only slim hopes of recovering the money. In making the change, Halliburton failed to inform its stockholders of the new accounting practice for more than a year, as the SEC requires. The company maintains that it followed generally accepted accounting principles. The cost overruns that Halliburton was booking as revenue accounted for 50 percent of the company's operating profit in the fourth quarter of 1998. In May 2002, the company announced that it was under investigation, and Cheney, now safely tucked away in the White House, referred all questions regarding the matter back to Halliburton. The SEC investigation is ongoing, but Halliburton settled 20 shareholder suits related to the matter in June 2003. The accounting firm that Halliburton used was Arthur Andersen, the same company that went down in the Enron debacle. In a promotional video produced by Arthur Andersen in 1996, Cheney had this to say about the firm, "One of the things I like that they do for us is that, in effect, I get good advice, if you will, from their people based upon how we're doing business and how we're operating, over and above the, just sort of the normal by-the-books audit arrangement."

Suddenly it seemed like Cheney hadn't been such a great CEO after all. The stock that Cheney had cashed in on near its peak was plummeting. In the two years since Cheney had left office, the stock had gone from $49 a share (August 2000) to $14.57 (August 2002). One defense that was heard often as the Iraq business, the over-billing, and the aggressive accounting practices came to light after Cheney left Halliburton, was that Cheney was more of a "hands-off" kind of manager, not involved in minor details like pumping up revenues or doing business with Saddam Hussein. But Cheney's history has been one of utter involvement in even the smallest details of his work. He has been known to pepper low-level intelligence personnel at the White House, poring over information and data. Several former coworkers have remarked at how Cheney was an information hound, devouring statistics and working long hours. It's hard to believe that Cheney was so utterly unin-volved in Halliburton's day-to-day business *and* didn't have anything to do with the company's increase in government business. If both were true, what exactly did he spend his time on at Halliburton?

During an address to the Export-Import Bank, in May 1997, Cheney wisecracked that "When I was secretary of defense, my biggest problem was with the Congress of the United States.

Now that I'm chairman and CEO of a Fortune 500 company, my biggest problem is the Congress of the United States." Perhaps no statement from Cheney about his time at the helm of Halliburton better explains why he was brought on board to head up a major international oil conglomerate as that. But as vice president of the United States, Cheney would be in an even better position to help out his former coworkers. In 2001, the 2000 election was finally decided and George W. Bush had won. Halliburton had another vice president in their pocket.

11

Fall from Grace

Bob Grace is not a political man. Since 1976 he has run GSM Consulting, a small engineering consulting firm in Amarillo, Texas, advising oil companies on drilling strategies and well-control methods. It's not glamorous work, and it's not particularly profitable. Grace runs a small office of 10 employees, and still travels personally from site to site most days of the month, plying his trade. He teaches in drilling schools, he manages drilling projects, and works about a half dozen wild-well control jobs a year. Bob Grace doesn't care for politics and doesn't know much about them. He is simply a small business owner scraping by from year to year.

But in the wake of the first Gulf War, Bob Grace became something more than a simple businessman. As he recalls his time in Kuwait, leading an international team that extinguished more than 300 oil-well fires set by Saddam Hussein's retreating troops, his even tone and Texas drawl tighten up a bit, betraying his pride and excitement of his time in the Middle East. Grace worked for nearly nothing in Kuwait, but he is enormously proud of the work he did there, both from a professional and patriotic standpoint. He knows that rebuilding the Kuwaiti oil fields was his crowning professional achievement, but he also feels that it was one of the finest things he accomplished as a human being. "They said it would take five years to put out those fires, but we did it in less than a year," he told me with thinly veiled pride.

But when talk of a U.S. invasion of Baghdad was dominating the headlines as early as the fall of 2002, Bob Grace found himself suddenly unappreciated by the same government that had relied on his expertise 10 years earlier. Despite dozens of phone calls to everyone from the Pentagon to his local representative, he could not extract even the littlest bit of information about how he should offer up his services again in Iraq. He got form letters in response to his inquiries. He was dismissed and disregarded by government agencies. One decade after he had worked nine straight months putting out mighty fires in Kuwait, away from his family, for very little financial gain, he was persona non grata.

As in the first conflict in the Persian Gulf, it was clear that there was going to be a substantial need for oil infrastructure repair after the war. What had changed between the first Gulf War and the second that would leave Bob Grace out in the cold? Put simply, everything. Halliburton, a company that Grace had worked with hundreds of times over during his career—usually as his subcontractor—now dominated the war business. And the Bush/Cheney administration was unrelentingly secretive. The combination of these two facts led Grace to believe that there would be no coalition of businesses rebuilding Iraq's infrastructure after the war. The administration's decision had already been made, six months before the first bombs were dropped in Baghdad. Bob Grace knows now what he couldn't have known in the fall of 2002: "We never had a chance."

• • •

In December 2001, with Cheney in the White House, Kellogg Brown & Root won back the LOGCAP contract it had lost to Dyncorp four years prior. During that four years, KBR held on to the work in Bosnia through the Balkans Support Contract, which, had it remained under the LOGCAP contract, would have constituted the bulk of the revenue generated by LOGCAP during those years. Instead, Dyncorp won a contract that was essentially gutted of its most lucrative work, and KBR never skipped a beat. It was as if KBR had never lost LOGCAP; the 2001 re-compete just made it official again.

The company went to work on the War on Terrorism right away, building one thousand detention cells in Guantanamo Bay, Cuba, for terrorist suspects, at a cost of $52 million. The work had to feel familiar to KBR. It had done the exact same thing some 35 years ago in Vietnam. When troops were deployed to Afghanistan, so was Kellogg Brown & Root. They built U.S. bases in Bagram and Kandahar for $157 million. As it had done in the past, KBR had men on the ground before the first troops even arrived in most locations. They readied the camps, fed the troops, and hauled away the waste. And they did it like the military would have done it: fast, efficient, and effective.

It was good work, solid revenues, but nothing like the windfall the company had experienced in the Balkans. There were some gripes from the media about the company's ties to Cheney and the possibility of political favoritism, but overall the contract was fairly competed and the work being done was above average. What happened next opened the company up to far more warranted scrutiny.

By October 2002, George Bush and Dick Cheney were beating the Iraq war drums in earnest. It was becoming increasingly clear that the United States was going to invade Iraq, regardless of what Saddam Hussein did. On October 10, Bob Grace received a letter from his congressman, Mac Thornberry of the Thirteenth District in Texas, assuring him that "in the event that Saddam Hussein leaves power . . . international partners will work to strengthen a changed Iraq as needed." By December, a colleague of Grace's, also interested in work in Iraq, received a letter from Alan F. Estevez, Assistant Deputy Under Secretary of Defense, indicating that "[t]he Department is aware of a broad range of well fire fighting capabilities and techniques available. However, we believe it is too early to speculate what might happen in the event that war breaks out in the region. If for any reason the U.S. Government is called upon to suppress well fires through contract support, we would do so in accordance with the Competition in Contracting Act and implementing regulations."

But it wasn't too early to speculate after all. In fact, KBR had already developed a contingency plan in the event of oil-well fires, assigned under a task order of LOGCAP. It's not unusual for the Defense Department to keep war plans under wraps prior to military action, so the idea that Grace was shut out of the planning stages was not cause for concern. KBR had obtained one of the highest levels of security clearance leading up to the invasion, and for national security reasons, it was the only company that was working on the contingency plan. But after the invasion began, only a handful of fires were set, which KBR dealt with easily.

Far more difficult to justify was the follow-on contracts that KBR won for repairing and rebuilding the aging Iraqi oil infrastructure. What was a simple task order under LOGCAP—developing a contingency plan for putting out oil-well fires—morphed into an ever-growing contract called Operation Restore Iraqi Oil. The work assigned to KBR under RIO, a piece of business now approaching $2 billion, does not fall under LOGCAP. The nature of work has nothing to do with logistics or supporting army troops. But the contract for restoring the Iraqi oil infrastructure was given to Halliburton, and it was not competitively bid (as Assistant Deputy Under Secretary of Defense Estevez had promised Grace). It was given to Halliburton out of convenience, because they had developed the plan for fighting oil fires (all of which were, by this time, extinguished).

Bob Faletti, a spokesperson with the Army Corps of Engineers, which is the department of the army that is overseeing RIO, explained it to me this way. "When [KBR] finished with that classified document [the oil-well fire contingency], there were three companies that had the capabilities and the security clearances to do the work, because it was still classified. Of the three companies, KBR was one of them. It made sense that you could hire any of those companies and they would do a good job, but you would spend two to four weeks getting the other companies up to speed. So it made sense to award the noncompetitive part of the contract to KBR, because you save time and money."

KBR got the contract because it wrote the plan, in much the same way the company was awarded the original LOGCAP contract because it designed it. The company was in the unique and highly coveted position of drawing up contracts that only it could win. Bob Grace was livid. "The DoD in December assured us that everything would be competitively bid," he recalls. "When the news of the contract came out in March, I contacted the DoD and told them that I felt the thing was wrong. We were told that KBR got the work because they were the only ones who could respond to the contingency plan. That's because they wrote it."

The awarding of the RIO contract to KBR was in apparent violation of the same Code of Federal Regulations Guidelines that should have prevented the company from winning the first LOGCAP contract. But Faletti says that national security concerns overrode the Code of Federal Regulations in this case. "When you compete you have to advertise it and that defeats the classified nature of it, and you have to allow companies time to compete for it," says Faletti. Though the invasion of Iraq and the possibility of there being oil-well fires was hardly a secret, Faletti's point would be valid if not for the fact that the official end of war came on April 15, and as of the end of 2003, the contract for RIO was still in Halliburton's hands, awaiting a competitive re-compete.

The saga of Operation RIO illustrates not only the danger of sole-source contracts like LOGCAP, but the extent to which Halliburton has embedded itself into the U.S. military machine. Peter Singer, author of *Corporate Warriors: The Rise of the Privatized Military Industry* and a Fellow at the Brookings Institution, told me that if Dyncorp had been in possession of LOGCAP at the time of the Iraq War, the oil-well fire fighting plan probably would have been developed by someone else, and Dyncorp certainly wouldn't have been in a position to repair the damage to the Iraqi oil infrastructure. But because it was KBR, exceptions were made. Says Singer, "You often hear the 'we don't have any other choice' excuse. But yes you do, you always have other choices. You have the choice to compete it out, but if you keep awarding it to the same company over and over, why would competitors bother. You can't let the identity of the firm drive the contracting process. The morphing of LOGCAP into something inappropriate in Iraq, where we took a military logistics contract and then morphed it into fire fighting, then oil-well repair, and then oil infrastructure repair, should not have happened. It should not have been added noncompetitively. They clearly could have done that, they had the time to do it. All of that could have been done, but they didn't. Would we be in this mess right now if Dyncorp still had that contract. No. And that inappropriate morphing of the contract has turned out to be worth over $2 billion to the firm." And counting.

Ironically, the competitive re-bid process put the Army Corps of Engineers in a bind. Halliburton is probably the company best suited for this kind of work, regardless of how they obtained the contract. But given the public furor over the non-competitive nature of the original RIO contract, a political and business debate that has raged on for the better part of 2003, the Corps couldn't possibly assign all of the work back to KBR, which was among the competitors in the re-bid. Though KBR has already made a small fortune in Iraq, it is likely to get cut out of many future contracts. "That's my nightmare . . . I'm going to be wrong no matter what I decide," says Faletti, who managed the re-bid process, which ultimately awarded an additional $1.2 billion to KBR to continue repairing the southern oil fields.

• • •

Trying to prove that there was political favoritism involved in the awarding of Iraq contracts to Halliburton is a little like trying to build a murder case without the murder weapon. In cases like this, there is rarely a smoking gun. As Lyndon Johnson's biographer Ronnie Dugger wrote when analyzing Brown & Root's patronage of Johnson in the 1940s and 1950s, skilled politicians like Dick Cheney would know better than to leave traces of their influence lying around for interested parties to find. When Johnson told reporters that he had never recommended Brown & Root for a contract in his life, he was lying. When he backed that statement up by saying, "Nothing in the record will show it," he was telling the truth. It wasn't for years afterward that the truth came out, as often happens, after the consequences of such actions were far past relevancy.

In the case of Cheney's potential influence in the awarding of contracts to Halliburton in the modern era, we need to look instead at motive and opportunity. Why would Dick Cheney want to help his former company by sending a massive reconstruction contract their way? Because he had sold his stock in the company when the Bush team won the White House in 2000, it appears he had little personal financial incentive to intervene. Instead, the reasons may be far more subtle, even human, in nature.

After Cheney left the company to join the Bush campaign in August 2000, Halliburton once again endured a stunning decline of fortune. The main culprit was the 1998 merger with Dresser that saddled the company with asbestos liabilities that ultimately led to the bankruptcy of two Halliburton subsidiaries, including Kellogg Brown & Root. The drama began in 1997, when Dick Cheney and then Dresser CEO

William Bradford began the courtship that resulted in the merger. Cheney and Bradford handled most of the early negotiations personally, and sealed the deal while quail hunting in South Texas a month before the merger was announced.

At the time, Dresser was fighting off a legacy of asbestos lawsuits stemming from a former subsidiary called Harbison-Walker Refractories Company, a division Dresser spun off in 1992. Dresser's products, like bricks and pipe coatings, had contained asbestos, which resulted in a wave of litigation against the company during the 1990s. By 1998, as the Halliburton-Dresser merger was entering its final phase, the stakes were raised. A month before shareholders were to vote on the merger, a letter from Harbison-Walker's new parent company, Global Industrial Technologies, to Dresser's Bradford, indicated that the asbestos liability situation was worsening and the company would look to Dresser for help in settling the claims. This information was not passed along to shareholders prior to their vote to approve the merger. In fact, Halliburton officials claimed that it was not shared with them until after the merger had closed in September 1998, a full five months after the letter was sent.

In presenting the risks of the merger to shareholders, Cheney and the board failed to mention the potential impact of the inherited asbestos liability, despite the fact that the company would be adding 66,000 new claims to its books. By this time, several dozen prominent American companies had already resorted to bankruptcy protection as a result of asbestos litigation. Warranted or not, asbestos claims had become a major force in American business. It wasn't until March 1999 that Halliburton disclosed the asbestos situation to its shareholders in its annual report, but even then the company dismissed the claims as immaterial to its ongoing operations.

In the summer of 2001, a year after Cheney had left the company, it became clear to the public that Harbison-Walker was going bankrupt under the strain of the asbestos claims and that litigants would be going after Halliburton's deeper pockets. Halliburton's stock began to plummet, sliding from $53.93 a share when Cheney cashed out to just $13.20 by July 31, 2002. The number of asbestos claims against the company soared to more than 320,000 by the end of the year. The struggle to resolve these claims dragged on for years. At one point, it seemed that Halliburton might be saved by a piece of legislation wending its way through Congress that would limit corporate payouts in asbestos suits. Halliburton tried to extend the negotiations with its claimants presumably so that it could take advantage of the legislation when it passed, but the judge in the case wasn't buying it. By December 2003, Halliburton was forced to file a prepackaged bankruptcy of its Dresser II Industries and Kellogg Brown & Root subsidiaries, and pay out an eye-popping $4.4 billion settlement to put the asbestos issue behind them for good.

Financial analysts believe that one of two things occurred when Halliburton merged with Dresser. Either Dick Cheney was not aware of the extent of the asbestos liability he was saddling his company with through the merger, or he didn't care. "The job of the CEO is really in my mind to make sure that the company stays out of trouble," says one current Halliburton analyst that declined to be identified. "I think either he wasn't getting the right information from his people or if he was getting the right information, he was ignoring it. It was no secret at that time that Dresser had asbestos liability, but they didn't properly assess it. Either he wasn't doing his job, or if he was, then they were willfully being blind to some facts they had in front of them. If anyone should be pissed off, it should be the shareholders of Halliburton who got saddled with asbestos liability under Cheney's watch. If anybody is ultimately responsible, it has to be the CEO."

A pattern from Cheney's time as CEO begins to emerge in light of these comments. According to public statements made by Cheney:

- He was unaware of Dresser's business in Iraq.
- He was unaware of the accounting changes that took place at the company.
- And he was unaware of the massive asbestos liability that plagued Halliburton after he left.

It's rare, perhaps unprecedented, that a CEO has been so insulated from his own company's business. What's even rarer in these times, when CEO after CEO is indicted, sued, fired, and generally reviled for everything from poor profitability to corporate malfeasance, is that Halliburton shareholders (and the media in general) have given Cheney a free pass.

Even if Cheney was unaware of these various problems, we would have to assume that he was aware that as his company was increasing its percentage of revenues from taxpayer dollars—remember that Halliburton's government business doubled while Cheney was CEO—it had increased the number of tax-sheltered subsidiaries in the Cayman Islands from 9 to 58 during Cheney's watch. The move to protect Halliburton's money from U.S. tax collectors is estimated to cost the IRS $70 billion a year. That's one way to make government smaller.

Cheney's legacy at Halliburton includes an ongoing SEC investigation into the company's accounting, a rash of criticism for its business in countries that sponsor terrorism, bribing an official in Nigeria, and an asbestos suit that devastated the stock and resulted in bankruptcy of two prominent subsidiaries. It's not hard to believe that Cheney feels responsible for the state of his former company and the losses of its shareholders. Wouldn't anyone in that position want to do something to help?

• • •

The media firestorm that erupted over the RIO contracts awarded to KBR put Vice President Dick Cheney in an awkward position. The question of whether Cheney might have been in a position to influence the decision has been raised repeatedly. The most commonly heard defense of Cheney is that he has no financial ties to Halliburton, a sentiment expressed by Cheney himself on more than one occasion. This, however, turns out not to be true.

In a September 14, 2003 interview on *Meet the Press* with Tim Russert, Cheney had this to say about the allegations against him, "Since I've left Halliburton to become George Bush's vice president, I've severed all my ties with the company, gotten rid of all my financial interests. I have no financial interest in Halliburton of any kind and haven't now for over three years." The Congressional Research Service, a nonpartisan agency that investigates political issues at the request of elected officials, says otherwise. Cheney has been receiving a deferred salary from Halliburton in the years since he left the company. In 2001, he received $205,298. In 2002, he took in

$162,392. He is scheduled to receive similar payments through 2005 and has an insurance policy in place to protect the payments in the event that Halliburton should fold. In addition, Cheney still holds 433,333 unexercised stock options in Halliburton, the profits from which he has agreed to donate to charity. Ten days after Cheney denied any financial interest in Halliburton on *Meet the Press,* the Congressional Research Service published a report indicating that "deferred salary or compensation received from a private corporation in the reportable year is considered as among the 'ties' retained in or 'linkages to former employers' that may 'represent a continuing financial interest in those employers, which make them potential conflicts of interest.' "

The report goes on to say that "The general, underlying principle of the conflict of interest laws adopted by Congress, and of the regulations promulgated by the executive branch, embodies the axiom, 'that a public servant owes undivided loyalty to the Government,' and that decisions, advice, and recommendations made by or given to the Government by its officers be made in the *public* interest and not be tainted, even unintentionally, with influence from private or personal financial interests." The language in the report is unambiguous, and it clearly states that Vice President Cheney's relationship with Halliburton constitutes not only a financial interest, but a conflict of interest as well.

Faced with this understanding of the law, Cheney's only remaining defense is that "[a]s vice president, I have absolutely no influence of, involvement of, knowledge of in any way, shape, or form of contracts let by the Corps of Engineers or anybody else in the federal government." In theory, this is true, and sounds an awful lot like the excuses he gave following

Halliburton's accounting and asbestos problems. But given Cheney's utter involvement in the planning stages of the Iraq war, his history and contacts within the Department of Defense, his appetite for information, and his attention to detail, it is very hard to believe that he was unaware that Halliburton would be playing a major role in the rebuilding of Iraq, a fact that was known to others in the Pentagon as early as six months prior to the invasion. Why more wasn't done to at least give the appearance of open competition in the awarding of Iraq contracts is anyone's guess.

To make matters worse, Cheney is still in touch with the executives at Halliburton. One financial analyst that covers the company but declined to be identified said "Cheney is very loved within Halliburton. He's seen as almost like the Godfather. Executives have told me, 'yes, I still have contact with Dick Cheney. He calls me up once in a while just to see how things are going and find out what's going on in the energy business.'" Comments like these don't bolster Cheney's case that he has severed all ties with the company. And phone calls like the ones the financial analyst referred to certainly give Cheney the opportunity to meddle in the contract award process, even if it's just giving the company a heads-up on work coming down the road, an act that would instantly skew the playing field.

• • •

What followed the awarding of the RIO work was nothing short of a media and political firestorm. Newspapers, magazines, Internet sites, even the late night talk show hosts used the Halliburton story as grist for everything from in-depth analysis to offhand one-liners to *New Yorker* cartoons. Halliburton once again became the symbol for everything that was wrong with an unpopular war, much as it had 40 years prior in Vietnam. But Halliburton became more than just a rallying cry from the anti-war crowd, it became a political football of epic proportions, a tangible, easy-to-understand one-word denouncement of what Democrats had been trying to sell the American voters for three years: the Bush administration was too personally tied to corporate interests to make objective decisions.

The leader of the Democratic opposition to Halliburton is Henry Waxman, a representative from California. Over the course of 2003, Waxman fired off dozens of letters to everyone from Secretary of Defense Donald Rumsfeld to Secretary of the Army Les Browlee. He contacted the Office of Management and Budget, the Comptroller General, the U.S. Army Corps of Engineers, and the Export-Import Bank. His main concern was why the government was issuing no-bid contracts to a company that had clear ties to Vice President Dick Cheney, as well as a history of doing business with terrorist states, and a habit of overcharging the government.

Though politically motivated, it all sounded reasonable enough. The information Waxman sought involved taxpayer money, and as such, should be publicly available. But what Waxman found out was that it wasn't just the Bob Graces of the world that were being shut out of the Iraq contract process, it was the Congress of the United States, and the American population in general. Mike Yeager, a spokesperson for Congressman Waxman, told me that at every turn, Waxman's requests for information were denied. "We hope to understand the contracting process and the practices that are going on and the problem that we've confronted with the administration is the practice of reflexive secrecy, something you see it in all aspects of this administration. They have a standard of secrecy. Members of Congress have an inherent right to information on contracts, because the process is vulnerable to abuse, and we have not been able to get the most basic information."

Without the release of basic documents, even months after the official end of hostilities in Iraq and long after national security concerns had abated, Congressman Waxman was left to draw his own conclusions. Waxman's office felt, like many others in Congress, that once the war had begun, the need for operational security surrounding the contract process should have been lifted and competitive bidding should have begun. They couldn't understand why it hadn't played out that way. When I asked Yeager whether he felt that political favoritism had played a role, he demurred, explaining that without the information Waxman was seeking, he could only speculate. "You can say that the contract was awarded on favorable terms. You could not have dreamed up a better contract. Whether somebody in the administration interfered in the process . . ." Yeager paused, caught himself, and rephrased, "Unless someone has the evidence, no one should say that. But there is a history of political gaming."

• • •

In response to the attacks on his company, Halliburton CEO Dave Lesar mounted a spirited public relations campaign to control the damage. He wrote an op-ed piece in the *Wall Street Journal* in October 2003 that defended his company's actions under the guise of patriotism. Commenting on the RIO contract, he stated that "A lengthy bid process simply wasn't feasible," and directed some of his comments directly at the troops in Iraq—"you can count on us." For a time, there seemed to be some momentum behind defending Halliburton. The *National Review* said the claims against Halliburton were "All smoke, no fire." Steve Kelman, the head of the Office of Federal Procurement Policy under Clinton wrote an op-ed piece in the *Washington Post* in early November defending the work of the procurement officials involved and called the allegations against Halliburton "absurd." David Brooks, the conservative columnist for the *New York Times* titled his November 11, 2003 defense of Halliburton "Cynics Without a Cause," which relied heavily on Kelman's views published the week before. Indeed it seemed the political pendulum had swung the other way.

But when I asked Steve Kelman, who is now a professor of public management at Harvard, whether he thought there was anything wrong with the Iraq contracts awarded to Halliburton, he had a lot to say. "It's a fair criticism to say that the government needs to put more work into contract management," said Kelman, who said he worries "about very, very broad contracts that just say 'battlefield support.'" Kelman feels that a better way to dole out the LOGCAP contract would be to have two companies own the contract, and compete on individual task orders awarded under the one-umbrella contract. That would solve the problem of expediency and build in some limited competition to keep the overall costs of the contract down. He added, "The procurement policies of the Bush administration have not helped, we should focus more on managing the contract once it is awarded."

Meanwhile, Halliburton wasn't exactly backing up its public words with honorable actions. Over the summer, while the debate over Halliburton's involvement in Iraq was reaching a steady boil, the company revealed "improper payments of approximately $2.4 million" to a Nigerian tax authority in exchange for contracts to build a liquefied natural gas plant. The Nigerian president, Olusegun Obasanjo immediately ordered an investigation into bribery charges, saying that "the administration will not tolerate anything that undermines the integrity of the government." By December, the French magistrate, Reynaud van Ruymbeke was looking into the possibility of bringing charges against Dick Cheney for complicity in the bribery case and allegations that $243 million in secret commissions were paid from the late 1990s to 2002—a French company was involved in Halliburton's Nigerian business. Since then, the United States Justice Department and the SEC are looking into accusations that Halliburton made $180 million in illegal payments to win other contracts in Nigeria.

In addition, Waxman's constant prodding had finally hit its mark. For months during the fall of 2003, Waxman had been doing the math in Iraq, and feared that Halliburton was grossly overcharging the army for bringing much-needed gasoline into Iraq. In December, the Pentagon agreed. A Department of Defense audit showed that Halliburton was charging $2.27 a gallon for more than 56 million gallons brought into Iraq, from Kuwait, since the war began. That figure was $1.09 higher per gallon than the government was paying for the gas itself from another contractor. The result was a difference of $61 million. The company was losing friends fast. Even President Bush couldn't protect them now. "If there is an overcharge, like we think there is, we expect that money to be paid back," he told reporters.

The company claimed that due to the constraints placed on it by the U.S. Army, it was forced to use a Kuwaiti distributor that charged higher rates. "KBR should be commended, not chastised," said Randy Harl, KBR's chief executive, in a conference call with financial analysts on December 17. By February 2004, Halliburton was under investigation by no fewer than four government agencies, including the Department of Defense, the SEC, the Department of Justice, and the General Accounting Office. The investigations span four different countries (Afghanistan, Bosnia, Iraq, and Nigeria). And Halliburton had already admitted that two employees took kickbacks of $6.3 million; they were also accused of overcharging for everything in Iraq from gas to food. Yet despite all of this, the Army Corps of Engineers could not find a better option than KBR when it awarded the re-competed $1.2 billion contract for rebuilding the oil infrastructure in southern Iraq.

Lost in all the political maneuvering surrounding Halliburton's Iraq work is the fact that the military outsourcing business of KBR is not terribly profitable for the company. Halliburton is lucky if it makes pennies on the dollar from LOGCAP, a fact that has led many in the Wall Street community to openly call for KBR to be spun off, or somehow separated from the books of its far more profitable parent company. It is, in many ways, a business that no one else wants, and no one else can do. But the structure of KBR's contract in Iraq is, like it was in Vietnam, a cost-plus award contract. This means that the more money the company bills the American taxpayer, the more money it makes. When the figures start to climb into the $2 billion range, even if the margin is only 2 or 3 percent, the company is looking at a profit of between $40 million to $60 million, which is not bad for less than a year's work.

In an election year, Halliburton is understandably a political lightning rod. Its current situation is unique in American history. With its former CEO now the sitting vice president, the company is in a position to profit from the decisions Dick Cheney makes, or influences, while in office, even if he had no direct involvement in the awarding of contracts. Many political experts believe that Cheney led the case for war within the White House, a fact that further inflames the ire of those concerned with the proliferation of the so-called Iron Triangle, the confluence of politics, business, and the military.

Though some may be tempted to disregard the Halliburton hot button because of its obvious political overtones, we should all be reminded of whose money it is that is being spent. It's not just small business owners, like Bob Grace, that lose out when contracts are awarded without competition, or when management of those contracts is crippled by a dangerous and growing dependency on a single contractor. Taxpayers cringe at the thought of opening up their wallets every April 15, but rarely think hard about how that money is being spent and whether the ultimate destination of their taxes is directly improving their lives. Taxpayers deserve to feel good about the money they give to their government, and in the case of the $2 billion plus currently feeding into Halliburton's coffers, the government has sullied that right. Even if Halliburton is the best company for the job in Iraq, the appearance of the no-bid contract, coupled with the company's history of over-charging at the taxpayer's expense, should have raised a red flag in the administration that maybe giving Dick Cheney's old firm, which was in dire need of a cash infusion because of decisions made while Cheney was CEO, was not such a good idea.

In a December 2003 *New York Times* story, an anonymous member of the secret task force that awarded the RIO contract to Halliburton was quoted as saying that as far back as September 2002 "I immediately understood there would be an issue raised about the vice president's former relationship with KBR," the official said, "so we took it up to the highest levels of the administration, and the answer we got was, 'Do what was best for the mission and we'll worry about the political' fallout." Depending on which side of the political spectrum you reside, a comment like that could be seen as courageous and patriotic. But it can also be seen as a brazen act that blatantly disregarded public opinion and gave one of the most lucrative contracts in the history of war time to the vice president's former company. The no bid selection of Halliburton to perform the billions of dollars of reconstruction work in Iraq to the exclusion of all others including "coalition" members has marred the image of American democracy throughout the world, and has proven to be a serious misstep in foreign policy on the part of Bush and Cheney. Halliburton continues to be a hot issue throughout the 2004 presidential campaign, and will no doubt influence Bush's reelection. As public servants Bush and Cheney have demonstrated little regard for public opinion. How long can Halliburton and companies like it hide behind the cloak of patriotism, spending American tax dollars with abandon at our country's most vulnerable moment while our economy is enduring one of its most weakened states of the past decade? And what of the politicians who support its behavior? In the coming months, Bush and Cheney will have to answer for their actions and the ultimate judgment on those actions will lie in the hands of the voters.

NOTES

The most significant source for this book is the one that never commented. The Halliburton public relations staff declined to comment on this project or participate in any way. The company gave no explanation as to why they chose not to comment. In fact, they chose not to respond to phone calls and e-mails requesting comment. Fortunately, there were many other qualified sources who were willing to add their insights.

For the historical research, there were several crucial texts used, but some were more heavily relied on than others. The most important was *Builders: Herman and George R. Brown* by Joseph Pratt and Christopher Castaneda. *The Legend of Halliburton* by Jeffrey Rodengen was also critical for piecing together Halliburton's early history. And Robert Caro's trilogy of Lyndon Johnson biographies was indispensable in documenting Johnson's relationship with Brown & Root.

Following are the notes organized by chapter.

Prologue

Page ix   " 'I can tell you, . . .' " Jonathan Alter, "Al Gore and the Fib Factor," *Newsweek* (October, 16, 2000), p. 43.

Page ix   " 'But no matter . . .' " Jeffrey Rodengen, Foreword, *The Legend of Halliburton* (Fort Lauderdale, FL: Write Stuff Syndicate, 1996).

Page x   "In the five years . . ." Dan Baum, "Nation Builders for Hire," *New York Times Magazine* (June 22, 2003), p. 32.

Page x   "Halliburton went from seventy-third . . ." Chalmers Johnson, "The War Business," *Harper's,* (November 2003), p. 57.

Page xi   "It was also investigated . . ." Jeff Gerth and Don Van Natta, "In Tough Times, Company Finds Profits in Terror War," *New York Times* (July 13, 2002), p. 1A.

Page xi   "The company was also . . ." "Financial Post" and "FP Investing," *National Post* (May 10, 2003).

Page xiv   "KBR designed the contract . . ." Johnson, "The War Business"; Baum, "Nation Builders for Hire"; "Business on the Battlefield: The Role of Private Military Companies," Corporate Research E-Letter No. 30 (December 2002); and Peter Singer, *Corporate Warriors: The Rise of the Privatized Military Industry* (Ithica, NY: Cornell University Press, 2003), p. 142.

Page xiv   " 'Once a company gets . . .' " Interview with Peter Singer (2003).

Page xv   " 'Now that I'm chairman . . .' " "Weathervane," *Dallas Morning News* (November 30, 1997).

Chapter 1   Erle P. Halliburton and the Million-Dollar Boast

Page 3   "But Erle Halliburton . . ." J. Evetts Haley, *Erle P. Halliburton: Genius with Cement* (Halliburton Company Research Library, 1959).

Page 4   "He was an excellent student, . . ." Jeffrey Rodengen, *The Legend of Halliburton* (Fort Lauderdale, FL: Write Stuff Syndicate, 1996), p. 14.

Page 4   "But he brimmed with confidence, . . ." See previous note.

Page 4   ". . . 'fired by the stern . . .' " Haley, *Erle P. Halliburton: Genius with Cement*, p. 5.

Page 5   "It was a far cry . . ." Rodengen, *The Legend of Halliburton*, p. 14.

Page 6   "At first, the noisy, . . ." Daniel Yergin, *The Prize: The Epic Quest for Oil, Money, Power* (New York: Free Press, 1991), p. 80.

Page 6   "Automobile registrations in the . . ." See previous note.

Page 8   "It was a time . . ." Ron Baker, *A Primer of Oil Well Drilling,* 6th ed. (Austin: University of Texas, 2001).

Page 8   "It also served . . ." See previous note, p. 140.

Page 8   " 'The two best things . . .' " Haley, *Erle P. Halliburton: Genius with Cement,* p. 11.

Page 9   "The Halliburtons sccmcd . . ." Rodengen, *The Legend of Halliburton,* p. 16.

Page 10   " 'At any other time . . .' " Haley, *Erle P. Halliburton: Genius with Cement,* p. 15.

Page 10   ". . . 'drilled, drained, and . . .' " See previous note.

Page 10   ". . . 'low, seriously low. . . . The . . .' " Rodengen, *The Legend of Halliburton,* p. 18.

Page 10   "But still, the family . . ." See previous note, p. 19.

Page 10   "The company had a balance . . ." Haley, *Erle P. Halliburton: Genius with Cement,* p. 32.

Page 12   "He did business over . . ." See previous note, p. 35.

Page 12   "What seems like . . ." Rodengen, *The Legend of Halliburton,* p. 20.

Page 12   "The dispute was settled . . ." See previous note.

Page 13   "Erle himself was earning . . ." Haley, *Erle P. Halliburton: Genius with Cement,* p. 35.

Page 13   "In 1924, Halliburton . . ." Rodengen, *The Legend of Halliburton,* p. 21.

Page 13   "The Halliburton family owned . . ." See previous note.

Page 14   "They even began to win . . ." See previous note, p. 29.

Page 15   ". . . 'those people in . . .' " See previous note, p. 31.

Page 16   "Halliburton was undaunted by . . ." See previous note, p. 33.

Page 17   " 'If the courts will . . .' " See previous note, p. 34–37.

Chapter 2   The Road to Riches

Page 20   "This was about . . ." John D. Huddleston, *Good Roads for Texas: A History of the Texas Highway Department* (College Station: Texas A&M University Press, 1981).

Page 20   ". . . 'endless and everlasting . . .' " General Vicente Filisola, leader of the Mexicans at the Alamo, as quoted by Huddleston in *Good Roads for Texas: A History of the Texas Highway Department.*

Page 21   "Due to the poor roads, . . ." John Spratt, *The Road to Spindletop* (Dallas: University of Texas Press, 1955).

Page 21   "General Roy Stone, . . ." John D. Huddleston, *Good Roads for Texas: A History of the Texas Highway Department* (Austin: University of Texas Press, 1981).

Page 22   " 'More deceitful people . . .' " Riney L. Brown, "Riney Brown's Diary," in Joseph A. Pratt and Christopher J. Castaneda, *Builders: Herman and George R. Brown* (College Station: Texas A&M University Press, 1999), p. 8.

Page 22   "This was the Belton of Herman . . ." Jeffrey Rodengen, *The Legend of Halliburton* (Fort Lauderdale, FL: Write Stuff Syndicate, 1996), p. 69.

Page 22   ". . . 'they were just . . .' " Pratt and Castaneda, *Builders: Herman and George R. Brown,* p. 11–12.

Page 22   "He went on to the . . ." See previous note, p. 13.

Page 22   "Pulling down $2 a day . . ." Everett Collier, "Brother Team's Success Story: Mules to Millions," *Houston Chronicle* (December 18, 1950).

Page 23   "In fact, he rarely . . ." Transcript of George R. Brown interview with Paul Bolton (April 6, 1968), from LBJ Library in Austin, TX.

Page 23   " 'I had not been paid . . .' " Raymond Klempin, *Houston Business Journal* (August 30, 1982), p. 16, from Pratt and Castaneda, *Builders: Herman and George R. Brown.*

Page 23   "He sold rabbits . . ." Transcript of Mrs. Lyndon B. Johnson interview with Christopher Castaneda (November 15, 1990), from Oral History of George and Herman Brown, Rice University, Woodson Research Center (box 33, folder 14).

Page 24   "Having grown up in . . ." Kemplin, *Houston Business Journal,* p. 18.

Page 24   ". . . 'gains his power . . .' " Rodengen, *The Legend of Halliburton,* p. 72.

Page 24   "One night, while . . ." Transcript of George R. Brown interview with David G. McComb (August 6, 1969), from LBJ Library in Austin, TX.

Page 24   " 'I pressed the vein . . .' " Robert A. Caro, *The Years of Lyndon Johnson: The Path to Power* (New York: Alfred A. Knopf, 1982), p. 371.

Page 24   "That was enough . . ." Pratt and Castaneda, *Builders: Herman and George R. Brown,* p. 28.

Page 25   "The growing demand . . ." Rodengen, *The Legend of Halliburton,* p. 72.

Page 26   "He died in 1929 . . ." Linda Gillan, "Brown & Root: From Moving Texas Dirt to Spanning the World" (March 2, 1980), p. 18.

Page 26   "One night, he was . . ." Pratt and Castaneda, *Builders: Herman and George R. Brown,* p. 24.

Page 26   " 'I grew up in . . .' " See previous note.

Page 27   "The company was eventually . . ." Huddleston, *Good Roads for Texas: A History of the Texas Highway Department,* p. 69.

Page 29   "Not exactly a standard . . ." George and Herman Brown of Texas' Brown & Root: In Front as Builders, Backstage as Politicians, *BusinessWeek* (May 25, 1957), p. 93.

Page 29   " 'They had to become . . .' " Pratt and Castaneda, *Builders: Herman and George R. Brown,* p. 36.

Page 30   " 'It was real simple . . .' " Author interview with Bill Trott (2003).

Page 30   "The notes were secured . . ." Transcript of George R. Brown interview with David G. McComb.

Page 30   " 'You're broke and . . .' " Pratt and Castaneda, *Builders: Herman and George R. Brown,* p. 39.

Page 33   " 'The way things were . . .' " See previous note, p. 44.

Page 33   "They also had a brief . . ." See previous note.

Chapter 3   The Man Behind the Dam That Built Brown & Root

Page 38   " 'He was very deliberate . . .' " Transcript of George R. Brown interview with Paul Bolton (April 6, 1968), from LBJ Library in Austin, TX.

Page 38 "Acquaintances referred to him . . ." Letter, Lyndon B. Johnson to George R. Brown (October 10, 1942), from LBJ Library, "Brown, George," LBJA Selected Names (box 12).

Page 38 ". . . 'mind as quick . . .' " Robert A. Caro, *The Years of Lyndon Johnson: The Path to Power* (New York: Alfred A. Knopf, 1982), p. 373.

Page 39 " 'A. J. Wirtz, I believe, . . .' " Transcript of George R. Brown interview with Paul Bolton.

Page 40 "It created a number . . ." Bechtel web site, www.bechtel .com.

Page 42 "Wirtz was appointed chief counsel . . ." Statement of A. J. Wirtz (May 3, 1937), from LBJ Library, "Wirtz, A.J.," LBJA Selected Names (box 36).

Page 43 " 'Well then, I . . .' " Caro, *The Years of Lyndon Johnson: The Path to Power,* p. 378.

Page 44 " 'When we'd take on . . .' " "Roadbuilders," *BusinessWeek* (May 25, 1957), p. 105.

Page 44 " 'We originally were . . .' " Joseph A. Pratt and Christopher J. Castaneda, *Builders: Herman and George R. Brown* (College Station: Texas A&M University Press, 1999), p. 48.

Page 46 " 'And they were illegal. . . .' " Caro, *The Years of Lyndon Johnson: The Path to Power,* p. 380.

Page 48 " 'Under federal law, . . .' " See previous note, p. 383.

Page 48 " 'We had put . . .' " See previous note, p. 384.

Page 49 "He was a tender 28 years . . ." Pratt and Castaneda, *Builders: Herman and George R. Brown,* p. 51.

Page 50 " 'To Lyndon Johnson, . . .' " Caro, *The Years of Lyndon Johnson: The Path to Power,* p. 393.

Page 50 "Wirtz immediately made . . ." See previous note, p. 396.

Page 51 " 'He enters his . . .' " See previous note, p. 400.

Page 51 "To win the seat, . . ." See previous note, p. 409.

Page 51 "Though he contributed a token . . ." Transcript of George R. Brown interview with Paul Bolton.

Page 52 "In the meantime, . . ." Transcript of Mrs. Lyndon B. Johnson interview with Christopher Castaneda (November 15, 1990), from Oral History of George and Herman

Brown, Rice University, Woodson Research Center (box 33, folder 14).

Page 53   " 'The project known . . .' " Caro, *The Years of Lyndon Johnson: The Path to Power,* p. 459.

Page 54   " 'Give the kid . . .' " See previous note, p. 460.

Page 54   " 'We are doing this . . .' " Letter, Lyndon B. Johnson to James Roosevelt (August 9, 1937), from LBJ Library, Johnson House Papers (box 167).

Page 55   "Brown & Root stood . . ." Letter, George R. Brown to Lyndon B. Johnson (May 27, 1939), from LBJ Library, "Brown, George," LBJA Selected Names (box 12).

Page 56   "He called the New Deal . . ." Caro, *The Years of Lyndon Johnson: The Path to Power,* p. 469.

Page 57   "The new issue begged . . ." "Marshall Ford Dam, Texas" author unknown, Memorandum from LCRA, from LBJ Library, report in House Papers of Lyndon Johnson (Box 167).

Page 59   " 'The fellow [Johnson] relied . . .' " Transcript of George R. Brown interview with Michael L. Gillette (July 11, 1977), from LBJ Library in Austin, TX.

Page 60   " 'The gentleman is . . .' " Caro, *The Years of Lyndon Johnson: The Path to Power,* p. 467.

Page 60   "The House voted . . ." "Marshall Ford Dam, Texas," author unknown, Memorandum from LCRA, from LBJ Library, report in House Papers of Lyndon Johnson (box 167).

Page 61   ". . . 'a joint venture . . .' " Transcript of George R. Brown interview with Michael L. Gillette (July 11, 1977), from LBJ Library in Austin, TX.

Page 61   " 'It is needless for me . . .' " Letter, Lyndon B. Johnson to Herman Brown (April 18, 1939), from LBJ Library, "Brown, Herman," LBJA Selected Names (box 13).

Page 61   " 'Why do you send . . .' " Telegram from Lyndon B. Johnson to George Brown (November 23, 1940), from LBJ Library, "Brown, George," LBJA Selected Names (box 12).

Page 62   " 'Lyndon Johnson's whole world . . .' " Caro, *The Years of Lyndon Johnson: The Path to Power,* p. 468.

Page 62   " 'Lyndon and Herman would . . .' " Transcript of Mrs. Lyndon B. Johnson interview with Christopher Castaneda.

Page 63   " 'Listen, you get . . .' " Caro, *The Years of Lyndon Johnson: The Path to Power,* p. 475.

Page 63   " 'Dear Lyndon, In the . . .' " Letter, George R. Brown to Lyndon B. Johnson (October 27, 1939), from LBJ Library, "Brown, George," LBJA Selected Names (box 12).

Chapter 4   Guns and Butter

Page 67   "The company made several . . ." Letter, George R. Brown to Lyndon B. Johnson (May 27, 1939), from LBJ Library, "Brown, George," LBJA Selected Names (box 12).

Page 68   "Business was booming, . . ." Jeffrey Rodengen, *The Legend of Halliburton* (Fort Lauderdale, FL: Write Stuff Syndicate, 1996) p. 44.

Page 69   " 'It is not my . . .' " See previous note, p. 45.

Page 70   " 'As the politicians have . . .' " See previous note, p. 50.

Page 72   " 'New Dealer or no, . . .' " Ronnie Dugger, *The Politician: The Life and Times of Lyndon Johnson* (New York: W.W. Norton & Company, 1982), p. 274.

Page 74   " 'I hope you know, . . .' " Letter, George R. Brown to Lyndon B. Johnson (May 2, 1939), from LBJ Library, "Brown, George," LBJA Selected Names (box 12).

Page 74   " 'I wish I could dictate . . .' " Letter, Lyndon B. Johnson to George R. Brown (February 27, 1940), from LBJ Library, "Brown, George," LBJA Selected Names (box 12).

Page 74   "Over the course of . . ." Dugger, *The Politician: The Life and Times of Lyndon Johnson,* p. 279.

Page 75   " 'I'll do all I can . . .' " See previous note, p. 277.

Page 75   "After the contract was . . ." Letter, Lyndon B. Johnson to George R. Brown (November 5, 1941), from LBJ Library, "Brown, George," LBJA Selected Names (box 12).

Page 75   "He was humbled by . . ." Robert A. Caro, *The Years of Lyndon Johnson: The Path to Power* (New York: Alfred A. Knopf, 1982) p. 583.

Page 77   ". . . 'every member of the . . .' " See previous note.

Page 77   " 'I have been sitting . . .' " Letter, George R. Brown to Lyndon B. Johnson (October 27, 1939), from LBJ Library, "Brown, George," LBJA Selected Names (box 12).

Page 78	"One commander even . . ." "Army Should Do More to Control Contract Costs in the Balkans," GAO Report (September 2000).
Page 78	"Thomas had a reputation . . ." Caro, *The Years of Lyndon Johnson: The Path to Power,* p. 583.
Page 79	"In addition to this . . ." See previous note. p. 584.
Page 80	"Other contractors never . . ." See previous note, p. 585.
Page 81	"He set up a company . . ." See previous note.
Page 81	" 'We needed someone . . .' " See previous note.
Page 81	"The Browns were known . . ." Letter, Lyndon B. Johnson to George R. Brown (October 8, 1942), from LBJ Library "Brown, George," LBJA Selected Names (box 12).
Page 82	". . . 'twisted a hell of . . .' " Caro, *The Years of Lyndon Johnson: The Path to Power,* p. 586.
Page 82	"By the time the project . . ." Joseph A. Pratt and Christopher J. Castaneda, *Builders: Herman and George R. Brown* (College Station: Texas A&M University Press, 1999), p. 71.
Page 82	"He admitted that Johnson . . ." Transcript of George R. Brown interview with David G. McComb (August 6, 1969), from LBJ Library in Austin, TX.
Page 82	". . . 'getting the Corpus Christi . . .' " Pratt and Castaneda, *Builders: Herman and George R. Brown,* p. 71.
Page 82	" 'I never recommended . . .' " Dugger, *The Politician: The Life and Times of Lyndon Johnson,* p. 274.
Page 82	". . . 'this was a most . . .' " See previous note.
Page 83	". . . 'those plants and organizations . . .' " Pratt and Castaneda, *Builders: Herman and George R. Brown,* p. 73.
Page 85	" 'We didn't know . . .' " Caro, *The Years of Lyndon Johnson: The Path to Power,* p. 664.
Page 85	" 'We are hopeful . . .' " Pratt and Castaneda, *Builders: Herman and George R. Brown,* p. 77.
Page 86	"Brown Shipbuilding was fast . . ." Transcript of George R. Brown interview with David G. McComb (August 6, 1969), from LBJ Library in Austin, TX.
Page 86	" 'Destroyer Escorts were . . .' " *Time,* (January 11, 1943).
Page 87	" 'An unnecessarily severe . . .' " Pratt and Castaneda, *Builders: Herman and George R. Brown,* p. 84.
Page 88	" 'Slacker is a rough word . . .' " See previous note.

Page 88   "But many workers . . ." See previous note, pp. 84–87.

Page 89   ". . . 'the draft board . . .'" Dugger, *The Politician: The Life and Times of Lyndon Johnson,* p. 288.

Page 89   "'I say it's unfair . . .'" See previous note, p. 292.

Page 90   "'I don't know . . .'" Author interview with Bill Trott, 2003.

Chapter 5   Collateral Damage: The Leland Olds Story

Page 94   ". . . 'have some effect . . .'" Robert A. Caro, *The Years of Lyndon Johnson: Master of the Senate* (New York: Alfred A. Knopf, 2002), p. 232.

Page 95   "Either by owning . . ." See previous note, p. 234.

Page 95   ". . . 'evil of poverty.' . . ." See previous note, p. 241.

Page 98   "The construction, done on . . ." Christopher J. Castaneda and Joseph A. Pratt, *From Texas to the East: A Strategic History of Texas Eastern Corporation* (College Station: Texas A&M University Press, 1993), pp. 4–32.

Page 99   ". . . 'political entrepreneurship,' . . ." See previous note, p. 5.

Page 101   ". . . 'immediately commence an . . .'" See previous note, p. 45.

Page 102   "After he deposited . . ." See previous note, p. 53.

Page 105   " . . . 'even the most brazen criminals . . .'" Letter, Charles Francis to Lyndon B. Johnson (April 13, 1949), from LBJ Library, "Brown, George," LBJA Selected Names (box 12).

Page 107   "'He [Johnson] would call . . .'" Caro, *The Years of Lyndon Johnson: The Path to Power* (New York: Alfred A. Knopf, 1982), p. 250.

Page 108   "'I am here to . . .'" See previous note, p. 256.

Page 109   ". . . 'traitor to our country, . . .'" See previous note, p. 276.

Page 110   "'Even after everything . . .'" See previous note, p. 299.

Page 110   ". . . 'quite possibly the least . . .'" See previous note, p. 303.

Page 112   "'Both the Federal Power Commission . . .'" Castaneda and Pratt, *From Texas to the East: A Strategic History of Texas Eastern Corporation,* p. 104.

Chapter 6 Our Man in Office

Page 115 " 'I have some money . . .' " Robert A. Caro, *The Years of Lyndon Johnson: Master of the Senate* (New York: Alfred A. Knopf, 2002), p. 407.

Page 115 " 'They would contribute substantially . . .' " Transcript of Edward A. Clark interview with Christopher Castaneda (August 15, 1990), from Oral History of George and Herman Brown, Rice University, Woodson Research Center (box 32, folder 2).

Page 117 "Lyndon Johnson had as much . . ." Robert A. Caro, *The Years of Lyndon Johnson: The Path to Power* (New York: Alfred A. Knopf, 1982), p. 599.

Page 118 "Each contribution included . . ." Letter, Lyndon B. Johnson to George R. Brown (October 21, 1940), from LBJ Library, "Brown, George," LBJA Selected Names (box 12).

Page 118 "Letters poured in . . ." Letters, A. F. Maciejewski, Andrew May, Rudolph Tenerowicz, and Garrett Heyns, to Lyndon B. Johnson (October 26–28, 1940), from LBJ Library, Johnson House Papers (box 6).

Page 118 "Herman Brown knew that the . . ." Caro, *The Years of Lyndon Johnson: The Path to Power,* p. 628.

Page 118 "Dozens of congressmen . . ." See Letters from dozens of congressmen to Lyndon Johnson following the November 1940 elections, LBJ Library, Johnson House Papers (box 6).

Page 118 " '[Johnson's] power base . . .' " Caro, *The Years of Lyndon Johnson: The Path to Power,* p. 659.

Page 119 " 'I have thought . . .' " See previous note, p. 577.

Page 120 "And the orders they were . . ." See previous note, p. 685.

Page 120 " 'I did everything . . .' " Transcript of George R. Brown interview with David G. McComb (August 6, 1969), from LBJ Library in Austin, TX.

Page 120 "The Browns began systematically . . ." Caro, *The Years of Lyndon Johnson: The Path to Power,* p. 685.

Page 120 "Bags of cash, . . ." Robert A. Caro, *The Years of Lyndon Johnson: Means of Ascent* (New York: Alfred A. Knopf, 1990), p. 272.

Page 121   "Radio ads, transportation costs, . . ." Drew Pearson, "The Washington Merry-Go-Round," *Washington Post* (March 26, 27, and 28, 1956).

Page 121   " 'Now listen, we've made . . .' " Caro, *The Years of Lyndon Johnson: The Path to Power,* p. 717.

Page 121   "Votes were openly purchased . . ." Caro, *The Years of Lyndon Johnson: Means of Ascent,* p. 191.

Page 122   "Though it will never be . . ." See previous note, p. 717.

Page 122   "Some people believe that . . ." See previous note, p. 718.

Page 123   "The investigation had . . ." See previous note, p. 743.

Page 124   "Johnson alerted the president . . ." See previous note.

Page 124   "It was the kind . . ." Pearson, "The Washington Merry-Go-Round."

Page 124   "Helvering told Johnson . . ." See previous note.

Page 125   "Bonuses were found worth . . ." Caro, *The Years of Lyndon Johnson: Means of Ascent,* p. 746.

Page 125   "Brown & Root subsidiaries, . . ." Pearson, "The Washington Merry-Go-Round."

Page 125   "A typical scam was . . ." Caro, *The Years of Lyndon Johnson: Means of Ascent,* p. 746.

Page 125   " 'We have certainly . . .' " See previous note, p. 749.

Page 125   "Herman Brown, as straightforward . . ." See previous note.

Page 126   "Meanwhile, Wirtz and Johnson . . ." Letter, George R. Brown to Lyndon B. Johnson (October 5, 1942), from LBJ Library, "Brown, George," LBJA Selected Names.

Page 126   "Though Woods originally gave . . ." Caro, *The Years of Lyndon Johnson: Means of Ascent,* p. 750.

Page 126   "The report gave clear . . ." Pearson, "The Washington Merry-Go-Round."

Page 127   "The original team of agents, . . ." See previous note.

Page 127   "After all was said . . ." Caro, *The Years of Lyndon Johnson: Means of Ascent,* p. 753.

Page 128   " 'If the United States . . .' " See previous note, p. 136.

Page 129   " 'They [Brown & Root] were . . .' " See previous note, p. 274.

Page 130   "One thing that the Browns . . ." See previous note, p. 274.

Page 130   " 'They were spending . . .' " See previous note, p. 286.

Page 130   "Historical documents have shown . . ." See previous note, p. 304.

Page 131   " 'It was necessary . . .' " See previous note, p. 339.

Page 131   " 'In a material way . . .' " Transcript of George R. Brown interview with Paul Bolton (April 6, 1968), from LBJ Library in Austin, TX.

Page 133   ". . . 'healthy business climate, . . .' " Joseph A. Pratt and Christopher J. Castaneda, *Builders: Herman and George R. Brown* (College Station: Texas A&M University Press, 1999), p. 159.

Page 134   ". . . 'to relax—drink . . .' " Fran Dressman, *Gus Wortham: Portrait of a Leader* (College Station: Texas A&M University Press, 1994), p. 103.

Page 134   "In 1953, riding . . ." Joe R. Feagin, *Free Enterprise City: Houston in Political and Economic Perspective* (New Brunswick, NJ: Rutgers University Press, 1988), p. 154.

Page 135   ". . . 'and all you have . . .' " Pratt and Castaneda, *Builders: Herman and George R. Brown,* p. 167.

Page 136   "George Brown, who had been . . ." See previous note, p. 163.

Page 137   " 'They're looking for . . .' " See previous note, p. 169.

Page 138   "The airport purchase . . ." See previous note, p. 170.

Page 138   " 'If it wasn't . . .' " See previous note, p. 172.

Page 139   " 'I want to go . . .' " See previous note, p. 173.

Page 139   " 'It's very easy . . .' " See previous note, p. 166.

Chapter 7   Vietnam and Project Rathole

Page 147   "The post-war boom . . ." Jeffrey Rodengen, *The Legend of Halliburton* (Fort Lauderdale, FL: Write Stuff Snydicate, 1996), p. 60.

Page 147   "Erle Halliburton's health was . . ." See previous note, p. 61.

Page 148   "All of the faith that . . ." Joseph A. Pratt and Christopher J. Castaneda, *Builders: Herman and George R. Brown* (College Station: Texas A&M University Press, 1999), p. 131.

Page 149   ". . . 'the biggest mistake . . .' " Rodengen, *The Legend of Halliburton,* p. 184.

Page 149 "Brown feared that . . ." See previous note.

Page 150 "'I just thought it . . .'" Transcript of George R. Brown interview with David G. McComb (August 6, 1969), from LBJ Library in Austin, TX.

Page 150 "'Herman Brown, who . . .'" Pratt and Castaneda, *Builders: Herman and George R. Brown,* p. 185.

Page 150 "'George Brown was deeply . . .'" Interview with Joseph Pratt (2003).

Page 151 ". . . 'a builder of his . . .'" Pratt and Castaneda, *Builders: Herman and George R. Brown,* p. 222.

Page 152 "As part of the negotiation, . . ." "Price is $36,750,000 in Halliburton Purchase of Brown Properties," *Wall Street Journal* (December 24, 1962), p. 18.

Page 155 ". . . 'in a class . . .'" Herbert Solow, "How NSF Got Lost in Mohole," *Fortune* (May 1963), p. 198.

Page 156 ". . . 'a work of art.' . . ." See previous note, p. 204.

Page 156 "'Perhaps we were wrong, . . .'" See previous note.

Page 158 "After Thomas' death . . ." Arlen J. Large, "Mohole Melee," *Wall Street Journal* (January 19, 1967).

Page 158 "'Perhaps this is all . . .'" "Mohole Contractor Is Linked to Gifts to Democrats," *New York Times* (August 19, 1966).

Page 159 ". . . 'do not influence . . .'" "Johnson Denies Any Favoritism in the Award of Contracts," *New York Times* (August 24, 1966).

Page 160 "'Now, Lyndon, I . . .'" William Lambert and Keith Wheeler, "The Man Who Is President," *Life* (August, 1964).

Page 161 "'Albert and Lyndon worked . . .'" Transcript of George R. Brown interview with David G. McComb (August 6, 1969), from LBJ Library in Austin, TX.

Page 162 "Brown & Root picked up . . ." Pratt and Castaneda, *Builders: Herman and George R. Brown,* pp. 208–211.

Page 163 "'. . . we had been . . .'" Scowcroft Bush, *A World Transformed,* p. 489.

Page 164 "As part of the single most . . ." See previous note, p. 239.

Page 165 "The remaining 3 percent . . ." Hanson Baldwin, "U.S. Is Changing Face of Vietnam: Vast Construction Program Combats War Bottlenecks," *New York Times* (November 28, 1965).

Page 165 "Twenty-three employees died . . ." Hanson Baldwin, "Vast U.S. Construction Program Is Changing the Face of South Vietnam," *New York Times* (December 10, 1967).

Page 165 "Even as early as 1966, . . ." "Corruption Is Taking Up to 40 percent of U.S. Assistance in Vietnam," *New York Times* (November 13, 1966), p. 1.

Page 165 "Dozens of employees were sent home . . ." See previous note.

Page 166 "He ordered an immediate . . ." "Ribicoff Says Millions Are Squandered in Vietnam," *New York Times* (May 12, 1968).

Page 166 "It said that 'normal . . ." Pratt and Castaneda, *Builders: Herman and George R. Brown,* p. 240.

Page 167 "During the ceremony, . . ." See previous note.

Page 168 " 'Brown & Root . . . had gotten . . .' " See previous note, p. 241.

Page 168 "Bechtel pulled out of the running . . ." Neela Banerjee, "Bechtel Ends Move for Work in Iraq, Seeing Done Deal," *New York Times* (August, 8, 2003), p. C1.

Chapter 8   Empty Pockets

Page 171 "It seemed for a time . . ." "Biography of John Connally," Texas Politics, University of Texas at Austin, http:// texaspolitics.lamc.utexas.edu.

Page 171 "In 1972, Connally even . . ." "200 Texans Hear Nixon Reaffirm Vietnam Pledge," *New York Times* (May 1, 1972), p. 1.

Page 173 " 'We're still doing . . .' " Rodengen, *The Legend of Halliburton* (Fort Lauderdale, FL: Write Stuff Snydicate, 1996), p. 143.

Page 173 "Two Brown & Root executives . . ." See previous note, p. 141.

Page 174 "That would support . . ." Robert Lindsey, "Puzzle of Executive's Death Stuns Texas," *New York Times* (February 7, 1977), p. 48.

Page 176 "In 1985, Brown & Root . . ." Rodengen, *The Legend of Halliburton,* p. 155.

Page 177 "Like its fiercely independent . . ." See previous note, p. 173.

Page 177   "Hussein released the prisoners . . ." See previous note, p. 180.

Page 178   "Seven million barrels . . ." Robert D. Grace, *Blowout and Well Control Handbook* (Boston, MA: Gulf Professional Publishing, 2003).

Page 179   "Meanwhile, Brown & Root won . . ." Rodengen, *The Legend of Halliburton,* p. 183.

Chapter 9   The Big Score

Page 181   "That resulted in the massive . . ." Peter Singer, *Corporate Warriors: The Rise of the Privatized Military Industry* (Ithica, NY: Cornell University Press, 2003), p. 54.

Page 183   " 'In fact, providing for . . .' " See previous note, p. 7.

Page 184   "Sensing the need to bolster . . ." Chalmers Johnson, "The War Business," *Harper's* (November 2003), p. 57; Dan Baum, "Nation Builders for Hire," *New York Times Magazine* (June 22, 2003), p. 32; "Business on the Battlefield: The Role of Private Military Companies," Corporate Research E-Letter No. 30 (December 2002); and Singer, *Corporate Warriors: The Rise of the Privatized Military Industry* (Ithica, NY: Cornell University Press, 2003), p. 142.

Page 184   "It was a massive contingency . . ." Singer, *Corporate Warriors: The Rise of the Privatized Military Industry,* p. 142.

Page 184   "The company was paid . . ." "Business on the Battlefield: The Role of Private Military Companies"; Singer, *Corporate Warriors: The Rise of the Privatized Military Industry,* p. 142.

Page 185   ". . . 'mother of all . . .' " Anthony Bianco and Stephanie Anderson-Forest, "Outsourcing War" *BusinessWeek* (September 15, 2003), p. 68.

Page 186   "And in October of 1994, . . ." Interview with Joan Kibler, Public Affairs Officers, USACE, Transatlantic Programs Center (December 1, 2003).

Page 186   "They attended the staff meetings . . ." "Contingency Operations: Opportunities to Improve the Logistics Civil Augmentation Program," GAO Report (February 1997).

Page 187 "'I had an unlimited budget . . .'" Interview with Bob Borroughs (2003).

Page 189 "'Company A receives . . .'" Code of Federal Regulations, http://www.access.gpo.gov/nara/cfr/waisidx_02/48cfr9_02 .html.

Page 189 "As they had done . . ." Barry Yeoman, "Full Metal Racket: How Private Contractors are taking on the role of the U.S. Military," *Mother Jones* (June 2003), p. 41.

Chapter 10 Backseat Cheney

Page 192 "Casper was a typical . . ." Jeffrey Rodengen, Foreword, *The Legend of Halliburton* (Fort Lauderdale, FL: Write Stuff Syndicate, 1996), p. vi.

Page 193 ". . . 'she wasn't interested . . .'" Nicholas Lemann, "The Quiet Man; Dick Cheney's Discreet Rise to Unprecedented Power," *New Yorker* (May 7, 2001), p. 56.

Page 193 "In 1968, Cheney took . . ." See previous note.

Page 193 "Cheney himself avoided . . ." See previous note.

Page 195 "In fact, since the Cold War . . ." "Business on the Battlefield: The Role of Private Military Companies," Corporate Research E-Letter No. 30 (December 2002).

Page 196 "The world had become . . ." Richard Cheney biography, defenselink. http://www.defenselink.mil.

Page 196 "At the time, concerned . . ." See previous note.

Page 197 "Without Cheney there . . ." Lemann, "The Quiet Man: Dick Cheney's Discreet Rise to Unprecedented Power."

Page 198 "After a loss of $91 million . . ." SEC Filings.

Page 199 "In short, Brown & Root . . ." "Army Should Do More to Control Contract Costs in the Balkans," GAO Report (September 2000).

Page 199 "The initial feasibility project . . ." Chalmers Johnson, "The War Business," *Harper's* (November 2003), p. 57.

Page 200 "Brown & Root's cash flow . . ." "Contingency Operations: Opportunities to Improve the Logistics Civil Augmentation Program," GAO Report (February 1997).

Page 201 ". . . 'intended to be . . .'" See previous report.

Page 202 ". . . 'is the Army's customer . . .'" "Army Should Do More to Control Contract Costs in the Balkans."

Page 202 ". . . 'half of the crews . . .'" See previous report.

Page 203 "'The next day, . . .'" Interview with Bob Borroughs, 2003.

Page 203 "'We did have real . . .'" Interview with Dan Schilling (2003).

Page 204 ". . . 'sometimes you have to . . .'" Interview with Bob Borroughs.

Page 204 "'Was there waste . . .'" Interview with General Nash (2003).

Page 204 "'[Iraq] is different. . . .'" See previous note.

Page 205 "'It is a false dichotomy . . .'" Barbara Slavin, "Sanctions May Be Losing Favor as Top Policy Weapon," *USA Today* (June 25, 1998), p. 10A.

Page 205 "'Our government has become . . .'" Jim Landers, "Halliburton Chief Calls U.S. 'Sanctions Happy,'" *Dallas Morning News* (June 24, 1998), p. 3D.

Page 206 "He favored carving out . . ." Christopher Marquis, "Over the Years, Cheney Opposed U.S. Sanctions," *New York Times* (July 27, 2000), p. 21.

Page 207 "When stricter sanctions . . ." Raymond Bonner, "Libya's Vast Desert Pipeline Could Be Conduit for Troops," *New York Times* (December 2, 1997), p. A1.

Page 207 "The tunnels are slated . . ." Raymond Bonner, "Mysterious Libyan Pipeline Could Have Military Purpose," *New York Times News Service* (December 5, 1997).

Page 208 "The report that came . . ." Wendy Blake, "Thompson Blasts Halliburton's Iran Biz" *Crain's New York Business* (December 13, 2003).

Page 209 "Worse, the United States . . ." "Sources of Revenue for Saddam and Sons: A Primer on the Financial Underpinnings of the Regime in Baghdad," Coalition for International Justice (September 2002).

Page 209 "The Oil for Food program . . ." Edward Simpkins, "Where Are Iraq's Missing Oil Billions?" *Sunday Telegraph* (London, May 18, 2003), p. 8.

Page 209 "That comes to about $170 . . ." Joy Gordon, "Cool War: Economic Sanctions as a Weapon of Mass Destruction," *Harper's* (November 2002).

Page 210   "The two subsidiaries, . . ." Colum Lynch, "Firm's Iraq Deals Greater than Cheney Has Said," *Washington Post* (June 23, 2001).

Page 210   "Executives at both subsidiaries . . ." See previous note.

Page 210   "James Perrella, the former chairman . . ." See previous note.

Page 211   "In 1995, just before Cheney . . ." Marego Athans, "Cheney Profited Richly from His Time in Office," *Baltimore Sun* (August 16, 2000).

Page 211   "Halliburton soared from seventy-third . . ." Johnson, "The War Business."

Page 212   "During the five years . . ." Dan Baum, "Nation Builders for Hire," *New York Times Magazine* (June 22, 2003), p. 32.

Page 212   " 'I can tell you, . . .' " Jonathan Alter, "Al Gore and the Fib Factor," *Newsweek* (October, 16, 2000), p. 43.

Page 212   " 'I made a long-term commitment . . .' " "Cheney Says He Would Not Join Bush Administration," *Associated Press* (May 18, 2000).

Page 213   "When Cheney did leave, . . ." Maura Reynolds and Esther Schrader, "Bush Tries to Quell Halliburton Uproar," *Los Angeles Times* (December 13, 2003), p. 17.

Page 213   "The company settled . . ." Dana Calvo, "Halliburton Going Strong Amid the Clamor," *Los Angeles Times* (June 1, 2003).

Page 213   "The company maintains that . . ." Charlene Oldham, "SEC Investigating Halliburton Books," *Dallas Morning News* (May 29, 2002).

Page 213   "In May of 2002, . . ." Alex Berenson, "Halliburton and SEC Inquiry," *New York Times* (May 30, 2002).

Page 214   " 'When I was Secretary . . .' " Eli Pariser, "Who Is Dick Cheney?" MoveOn.org (July 11, 2002).

Chapter 11   Fall from Grace

Page 219   " 'We never had . . .' " Interview with Bob Grace (2003).

Page 220   ". . . 'in the event that . . .' " Letter from Mac Thornberry to Bob Grace (October 10, 2002).

Page 220   ". . . '[t]he Department is aware . . .' " Letter from Alan F. Estevez to Louisiana Senator John Breaux, on behalf of anonymous contractor (December 30, 2002).

Page 221 "The work assigned to KBR . . ." United States Army Corps of Engineers Web Site, http://www.hq.usace.army.mil/CEPA /Iraq/TaskOrders.htm.

Page 221 " 'When [KBR] finished with . . .' " Interview with Bob Faletti, Public Affairs Officer, U.S. Army Corps of Engineers (2003).

Page 222 " 'When you compete . . .' " See previous note.

Page 223 " 'You often hear . . .' " Interview with Peter Singer (2003).

Page 225 "In fact, Halliburton officials . . ." Jeff Gerth, "Cheney's Role in Acquisition Under Scrutiny," *New York Times* (July 31, 2002), p. A1.

Page 225 "In presenting the risks . . ." See previous note.

Page 225 "It wasn't until March 1999 . . ." See previous note.

Page 226 "Halliburton's stock began . . ." See previous note.

Page 226 "By December 2003, . . ." Transcript of Halliburton Company conference call to discuss the Chapter 11 proceedings, Fair Disclosure Wire (December 17, 2003).

Page 226 " 'I think either he . . .' " Interview with anonymous financial analyst currently covering Halliburton (2003).

Page 227 "That's one way . . ." Michael Scherer, "The World According to Halliburton," *Mother Jones* (July/August 2003), p. 24.

Page 229 "The language in the report . . ." Congressional Research Service, American Law Division. Memorandum to Senator Frank Lautenberg of New Jersey (September 22, 2003).

Page 229 ". . . '[a]s vice president, . . .' " Transcript from *Meet the Press* with Tim Russert (September 14, 2003).

Page 230 " 'Cheney is very loved . . .' " Interview with anonymous financial analyst currently covering Halliburton (2003).

Page 231 " 'We hope to understand . . .' " Interview with Mike Yeager (September 2003).

Page 233 " 'A lengthy bid process . . .' " Dave Lesar, "Halliburton's Mission," *Wall Street Journal* (October 17, 2003).

Page 233 " 'All smoke, . . .' " Byron York, "All Smoke, No Fire: The Administration's Critics Are Wrong about Halliburton and Iraq," *National Review* (July 14, 2003).

Page 233 "David Brooks, the conservative . . ." David Brooks, "Cynics Without a Cause," *New York Times* (November 11, 2003).

Page 234 "'the administration will not . . .'" "Nigerian President Orders Bribery Probe," *Associated Press* (June 18, 2003).

Page 234 "By December, the French . . ." "Bribery Probe Checks Cheney," *Herald Sun* (Melbourne, Australia; December 22, 2003).

Page 234 "Since then, the United States . . ." "Legal Troubles," *Dallas Morning News* (February 6, 2004).

Page 234 "'If there is an overcharge, . . .'" Richard W. Stevenson, "Bush Sees Need for Repayment if Fee Was High," *New York Times* (December 13, 2003).

Page 235 "'KBR should be . . .'" Halliburton Company conference call to discuss the chapter 11 proceedings (December 17, 2003).

BIBLIOGRAPHY

Abdi, Ali Musa. "Osman Atto Grabs for Power." *Agence France Presse,* May 8, 1995.

Abdi, Ali Musa. "UN Troop Pull-Out Sparks Fear of Upsurge in Fighting." *Agence France Presse,* November 5, 1994.

Abdi Hosh Askir v. Brown & Root Services Corp. U.S. District Court for the Southern District of New York. 1997 U.S. Dist. Lexis 14494.

"A Brief History of Money in Politics: Campaign Finance—and Campaign Finance Reform—in the United States."

"A Deal Maker Turns to Getty." *New York Times,* January 2, 1984.

"Aerospace Corp. Gets $5,924,752 Air Force Engineering Contract." *Wall Street Journal,* September 18, 1964.

Annan, Kofi. Letter dated April 15, 1998, from the Secretary-General Addressed to the Security Council. United Nations, April 15, 1998.

Annan, Kofi. Letter dated July 2, 1999, from the Secretary-General Addressed to the President of the Security Council. United Nations, July 2, 1999.

"Anti-U.S. Somali Chief Is Ousted by His Faction." *New York Times,* June 13, 1995.

Applebomes, Peter. "Houston Loses Piece of Heritage with Sale of *The Chronicle.*" *New York Times,* March 14, 1987.

Apple, R. W., Jr. "Vietnam Building Curtained by U.S.: Pentagon Decides to Review Program of Consortium." *New York Times,* August 29, 1966.

"Armed Somalis Attack Private Convoy under U.S. Protection." *Agence France Presse,* November 15, 1993.

"Army Should Do More to Control Contract Cost in the Balkans." GAO Report to the Chairman, Subcommittee on Readiness and Management Support, Committee on Armed Services, U.S. Senate, September 2000.

Athans, Marego, and Ann LoLordo. "Cheney Profited Richly from His Time in Office: His D.C. Connections Served Business Well." *Baltimore Sun*, August 16, 2000.

Autopsy of a Disaster: The U.S. Sanctions Policy on Iraq. Institute for Public Accuracy.

Axebank, Albert. "Bush Vows to Ease Trade with Soviets." *Journal of Commerce*, October 19, 1989.

Babcock, Charles R. "Big Donations Again a Campaign Staple; Not Since 1972 Have Presidential Races Seen Such Money." *Washington Post*, November 17, 1988.

Bagdikian, Ben H. "The 'Inner Inner Circle' Around Johnson." *New York Times*, February 28, 1965.

Baker, David R. "Oil Firm's Work for Terrorist Sponsors Challenged; Giving Contracts to Halliburton Questioned." *San Francisco Chronicle*, May 1, 2003.

Baldwin, Hanson W. "Bigger Blows in Pacific." *New York Times*, April 26, 1944.

Baldwin, Hanson W. "13,600 Prisoners Still on Islands." *New York Times*, August 12, 1946.

Baldwin, Hanson W. "U.S. Is Changing the Face of Vietnam." *New York Times*, November 28, 1965.

Baldwin, Hanson W. "Vast U.S. Construction Program Changing the Face of South Vietnam." *New York Times*, December 10, 1967.

Ballard, Tanya N. "GAO Drops Cheney Lawsuit." *Government Executive*, February 7, 2003.

Bamberger, Werner. "Rigs That Drillers Swear By." *New York Times*, March 31, 1974.

Barry, John, and Evan Thomas. "The Unbuilding of Iraq." *Newsweek*, October 6, 2003.

Basham, Patrick. "It's the Spending, Stupid! Understanding Campaign Finance in the Big-Government Era." The CATO Institute, July 18, 2001.

Baum, Dan. "Nation Builders for Hire." *New York Times*, June 22, 2003.

Beamish, Rita. "Political News." *Associated Press*, October 9, 1988.

Benedict, Roger W. "Russia Negotiating to Sell Siberian Gas to Tenneco, Texas Eastern, Halliburton." *Wall Street Journal*, June 15, 1972.

Bernstein, Peter W. "Reagan's Economic Redeal." *Fortune*, January 21, 1984.

Bianco, Anthony, and Stephanie Anderson Forest. "Outsourcing War." *BusinessWeek*, September 15, 2003.

Bigart, Homer. "Far-Right Groups Flourish in Texas, but Birch Society Declines." *New York Times*, October 10, 1962.

"Big U.S. Contractor in Vietnam Ends Operations After 10 Years." *New York Times*, July 4, 1972.

"Biography of George Herbert Walker Bush." George Bush Presidential Library and Museum.

Birnbaum, Jeffrey H. "Mr. CEO Goes to Washington." *Fortune*, March 19, 2001.

Biswas, Soma. "Honeywell Points to Asbestos Accords." *Daily Deal*, January 22, 2003.

Blair, William M. "First Lady Takes 'Flight to Moon.'" *New York Times*, November 24, 1968.

Boland, Vincent. "Freddie Mac Crisis 'Will Blow Political Cover.'" *Financial Times*, June 18, 2003.

Bonner, Raymond. "Libya's Vast Desert Pipeline Could Be Conduit for Troops." *New York Times*, December 2, 1997.

"Bosnia: Costs Are Exceeding DOD's Estimates." GAO Briefing Report to Congressional Requestors, July 1996.

"Bosnia: Costs Are Uncertain But Seem Likely to Exceed DoD Estimates." GAO Report to Congressional Requestors, March 1996.

Braestrup, Peter. "Bases in Vietnam Hurt by Strikes: Enemy Drive Against New Building Projects Feared." *New York Times*, May 26, 1966.

Braestrup, Peter. "President Spurs Negro Job Rights." *New York Times*, June 23, 1962.

Braestrup, Peter. "U.S. Acts to Ease Saigon Crowding." *New York Times*, October 7, 1966.

"Break-In to Pardon: A Chronology." *Associated Press*, June 7, 1997.

Bresnahan, John. "Cheney Has His Own Inner Circle of Lobbyists." *Roll Call*, September 11, 2000.

"Bricker Flays New Deal Record on Employment." *Los Angeles Times,* October 12, 1944.

"Brown & Root-Northrop, NASA to Negotiate a $10 Million Contract." *Wall Street Journal,* July 13, 1967.

"Brown & Root Worker, 6 Other Americans Wounded in Somalia." *Houston Chronicle,* August 5, 1993.

Bryce, Robert. "The Candidate from Brown and Root," sidebar: "Cheney Makes a Bundle off War." *Texas Observer,* October 6, 2000.

Bryce, Robert. "Cheney's Multi-Million Dollar Revolving Door." MoJo Wire, August 2, 2000.

Brzezinski, Zbigniew. *The Grand Chessboard: American Primacy and Its Geostrategic Imperatives.* New York: Basic Books, 1997.

Bumiller, Elisabeth, and Eric Schmitt. "Cheney, Little Seen by Public, Plays a Visible Role for Bush." *New York Times,* January 31, 2003.

Burnett, Victoria, Thomas Catan, Joshua Chaffin, Stephen Fidler, and Andy Webb-Vidal. "From Building Camps to Gathering Intelligence, Dozens of Tasks Once in the Hands of Soldiers Are Now Carried Out by Contractors." *Financial Times,* August 11, 2003.

Burnham, David. "The Abuse of Power." *New York Times,* September 3, 1989.

Bush, Janet. "Dresser to Pay Dollars 100 M for Henley Group Unit." *Financial Times,* November 30, 1987.

"Business Groups Move to Offset Labor's Campaign Power." *Bulletin's Frontrunner,* January 24, 2001.

Cahlink, George. "Army of Contractors." *Government Executive,* February 1, 2002.

"Californian David Gribbin Named Executive Director of 1996 Republican Platform Committee." *U.S. Newswire,* June 4, 1996.

"California Faces Power Cut Threat." BBC News, August 2, 2000.

"California Orders Statewide Blackouts." BBC News, March 20, 2001.

Calvo, Dana. "Halliburton Going Strong Amid Clamor." *Los Angeles Times,* June 1, 2003.

"Camp Bondsteel." GlobalSecurity.org.

Carney, James. "7 Clues to Understanding Dick Cheney." *Time,* December 30, 2002/January 6, 2003.

Caro, Robert A. *The Years of Lyndon Johnson: Master of the Senate.* New York: Alfred A. Knopf, 2002.

Caro, Robert A. *The Years of Lyndon Johnson: Means of Ascent.* New York: Alfred A. Knopf, 1990.

Caro, Robert A. *The Years of Lyndon Johnson: The Path to Power.* New York: Alfred A. Knopf, 1982.

Chatterjee, Pratap. "Soldiers of Fortune." *San Francisco Bay Guardian,* May 1, 2002.

"Cheney's Quiet Loyalty Earns Thanks." Foxnews.com, February 3, 2003.

Clark, Evert. "Mohole Planners Hold Wake Today." *New York Times,* August 29, 1966.

Cohn, Marjorie. "Balkans Pacification and Protecting an Oil Pipeline." *San Diego Union-Tribune,* August 16, 2001.

Commercial Activities Panel, Public Hearing, June 11, 2001, Speaker's Summary Statement, Submitted by Dennis Wright, Director of Marketing, Brown & Root Services.

"Construction Combine Plans to Leave Vietnam in 1971." *New York Times,* June 4, 1969.

"Contingency Operations: Defense Cost and Funding Issues." GAO Briefing Report to Congressional Requestors, March 1996.

"Contingency Operations: Opportunities to Improve the Logistics Civil Augmentation Program." GAO Report to Congressional Requesters, February 1997.

"Contract for Mohole." *New York Times,* March 18, 1962.

"Corruption Is Taking up to 40 Percent of U.S. Assistance in Vietnam." *New York Times,* November 13, 1966.

"Court Extends Government Contractor Defense to Service Contracts with United Nations." Government Contract Alert.

Dao, James. "Rumsfeld Pays Visit to Troops in Balkans." *New York Times,* June 6, 2001.

"Dave Gribbin, Longtime Friend of Vice Pres. Cheney, Joins Lobbying Firm Clark & Weinstock." *Wall Street Journal,* June 22, 2001.

"Dave Gribbin Named Vice President for Government Relations." *PR Newswire,* August 20, 1996.

"Defense Awards Rose by 35 Percent to $33.5 Billion in Fiscal '66 From '65." *Wall Street Journal,* November 29, 1966.

Deliso, Christopher. "South Balkan Oil Transit-I." *United Press International,* December 30, 2002.

de Onis, Juan. "Arabs Are Buying American." *New York Times,* October 7, 1973.

de Onis, Juan. "Iraq Seeks Rise in Oil Production." *New York Times,* December 23, 1974.

"Deputy Secretary Wolfowitz Media Availability at Camp Bondsteel, Kosovo." U.S. Department of Defense, News Transcript, May 17, 2003.

Despeignes, Peronet. "Mortgage Giants Fannie and Freddie Look Likely to Escape Deepest of Reforms." *Financial Times*, July 1, 2003.

Diamond, John. "Company Headed by Former Defense Secretary Gains Millions in Bosnia." *Associated Press*, March 22, 1996.

Dobbs, Michael. "Halliburton's Deals Greater than Thought." *Washington Post*, August 28, 2003.

DoD Mission for Repair and Continuity of Operations of the Iraqi Oil Infrastructure. ww.hq.usace.army.mil/cepa/iraq/factsheet.html.

"Dresser Founder Dies." *Associated Press*, March 2, 1983.

Dresser Rand official web site.

Dressman, Fran. *Gus Wortham: Portrait of a Leader*. College Station: Texas A&M University Press, 1994.

Dugger, Ronnie. *The Politician: The Life and Times of Lyndon Johnson*. New York: W.W. Norton & Company, 1982.

Dunnigan, James. "Prisoners of Fear." StragtegyPage.com.

Durkin, Tish. "The U.N.'s Oil-for-Food Program Is a Windfall for Saddam." *National Journal*, September 21, 2002.

Economides, Michael, and Ronald Oligney. *The Color of Oil: The History, the Money and the Politics of the World's Biggest Business*, Katy, TX: Round Oak Publishing Company, 2000.

Elliott, Michael, and James Carney. "First Stop, Iraq." *Time*, March 31, 2003.

"Emergency Employment of Army and Other Resources: USACE Support in the Theater of Operations." Department of the Army, U.S. Army Corps of Engineers, October 30, 1995.

"Enron 'Manipulated Energy Crisis.'" BBC News.com, May 7, 2002.

Erlanger, Steven. "The Ugliest American." *New York Times*, April 2, 2000.

"Ex-Im Bank's Way of Extending Loans to Russia Doesn't Obey Law, GAO Says." *Wall Street Journal*, March 11, 1974.

Feagin, Joe R. *Free Enterprise City: Houston in Political and Economic Perspective*. New Brunswick, NJ: Rutgers University Press, 1988.

Fineman, Howard, and Michael Isikoff. "Big Energy at the Table." *Newsweek*, May 14, 2001.

Fineman, Mark. "U.N. Funds Yield Little in Somalia." *Los Angeles Times,* November 28, 1993.

Fineman, Mark. "U.N.'s Water Funds Go Down Drain in Somalia." *Los Angeles Times,* September 27, 1993.

Finney, John W. "Moon Race Spurs Boom in Houston." *New York Times,* October 7, 1963.

"First U.S. National Commercial Exhibition in Moscow." *PR Newswire* October 4, 1989.

Flanigan, James. "U.S. Shows Two Faces on Oil Issue." *Journal of Commerce,* July 21, 1989.

Flanigan, James. "Why Oil Prices Don't Behave the Way They Used To." *Los Angeles Times,* March 1, 1998.

Fleishman, Jeffrey. "Kosovo Could Be Place Where Bush Decides Future of Missions." *Philadelphia Inquirer,* February 1, 2001.

Fleming, Stewart. "The U.S. Elections; Will the Real George Bush Please Stand Up Now?" *Financial Times,* November 10, 1988.

Franklin, Ben A. "20 Johnson Aides Form Cadre for an Enlarged Personal Staff." *New York Times,* November 24, 1963.

"Further Improvements Needed in Navy's Oversight and Management of Contracting for Facilities Construction on Diego Garcia." GAO Report to the Secretary of Defense, May 23, 1984.

Gall, Carlotta. "Albanians in Kosovo Grateful U.S. Army Is There." *New York Times,* November 24, 1999.

Gall, Carlotta. "Details Emerge in Kosovo Girl's Slaying." *New York Times,* February 19, 2000.

"GAO Sues Cheney over Energy Task Force Records." *Congress Daily,* February 22, 2002.

Gerstenzang, James. "Cheney Is Named in Suit Alleging Corporate Fraud." *Los Angeles Times,* July 11, 2002.

Gibbs, David N. "*Realpolitik* and Humanitarian Intervention: The Case of Somalia." *International Politics,* March 2000.

Gordon, Gregory. "Pentagon Pays Travel Tab for Congress' Watchdogs." *United Press International,* February 12, 1984.

Gordon, Joy. "Cool War." *Harper's,* November 2002.

Gordon, Michael R. "U.S. Force Ready to Take Last Aides from Somalia." *New York Times,* June 29, 1994.

Grace, Robert D. *Blowout and Well Control Handbook.* Boston: Gulf Professional Publishing, 2003.

Graham, Victoria. "Prospects Uncertain as UN Scrambles to Replace American Soldiers." *Associated Press,* December 17, 1993.

Green, Mark. *Selling Out: How Big Corporate Money Buys Elections, Rams through Legislation, and Betrays Our Democracy.* New York: Harper-Collins, 2002.

Grimaldi, James. "SEC Continues Halliburton Investigation." *Washington Post,* November 13, 2002.

Gruening, Ernest. "Our Era of 'Imperialism' Nears Its End." *New York Times,* June 10, 1934.

Gullo, Karen. "Criticized by Bush, Missions Aided Cheney; One-time Halliburton Boss Oversaw $2 Billion in Federal Contracts, Including Ones GOP Presidential Hopeful Campaigns Against." *Contra Costa Times,* August 29, 2000.

Gullo, Karen. "Reagan, Bush Officials Help Cheney." *Associated Press Online,* October 26, 2000.

Gwynne, S. C. "Did Dick Cheney Sink Halliburton (And Will It Sink Him?)." *Texas Monthly,* October 2002.

Hackworth King, David H. "Balkans Good for Texas-Based Business." *Sun-Sentinel* (Fort Lauderdale, FL), August 16, 2001.

"Halliburton and Trusts Agree to Buy All Stock of an Insurance Company." *Wall Street Journal,* February 27, 1964.

"Halliburton Co. Says 1969 Net Climbed 19 Percent." *Wall Street Journal,* February 9, 1970.

"Halliburton Co. Unit Gets $120 Million Order for Persian Gulf Work." *Wall Street Journal,* September 25, 1973.

"Halliburton Co. Unit Says It Has Received Big Contract." *Wall Street Journal,* December 12, 1969.

"Halliburton Estimates 9-Month Net Led '65 by 7 Percent." *Wall Street Journal,* October 27, 1966.

"Halliburton Is Said to Discuss Merger with Brown & Root." *Wall Street Journal,* December 11, 1962.

"Halliburton Names Connally." *New York Times,* February 15, 1969.

Halliburton official web site, SEC documents.

"Halliburton to Buy Brown & Root from Foundation." *Wall Street Journal,* December 13, 1962.

"Halliburton Updates Progress on Proposed $4 Billion Asbestos Settlement." *Associated Press,* June 6, 2003.

Harrington, Walt. "Born to Run: On the Privilege of Being George Bush." *Washington Post,* September 28, 1986.

"Harry W. Morrison Dies at 86; Headed Construction Concern." *New York Times,* July 20, 1971.

Henderson, David R. "The Real Campaign Finance Problem: Money Is Big in American Politics Because Government Is Big." *Red Herring,* June 1997.

Hennessey, Kathleen. "A Contract to Spend." *Mother Jones,* May 23, 2002.

"Herman Brown, Builder, 70, Dies." *New York Times,* November 16, 1962.

Holsendolph, Ernest. "Consumer Suits Seen Endangered." *New York Times,* May 3, 1973.

Hoover, Kent. "Pro-Business Election Efforts Coordinate under Project 2000." Bizjournals.com, January 31, 2000.

Horowitz, Rose A. "U.S., Soviet Officials to Discuss Trade Ties." *Journal of Commerce,* May 12, 1989.

Hoyos, Carola. "Block on Russian Contracts to Iraq Lifted." *Financial Times,* April 3, 2002.

Hoyos, Carola. "U.S. Oil Groups Find a Discreet Way of Doing Business with Iraq." *Financial Times,* November 3, 2000.

Huband, Mark. "U.N. Departs Failed Mission; Warlords Fight to Take Control." *Plain Dealer,* February 28, 1995.

"Hughes Shuns Plan for T.W.A. Board." *New York Times,* January 27, 1961.

Ifill, Gwen. "More Military Bases Weighed for Closing." *New York Times,* June 1, 1991.

Ignatieff, Michael. "The Reluctant Imperialist." *New York Times,* August 6, 2000.

"Inquiry Requested on Work in Vietnam." *New York Times,* May 18, 1968.

Interview with James A. Duff, J. Kenneth Fasick, and Charles D. Hylander. GAO International Activities 1956–1981, March 1991.

Ivins, Molly. "Cheney's Mess Worth a Close Look." *Baltimore Sun,* June 10, 2002.

Janssen, Richard F. "New Treasury Chief: Choice of Connally Is Seen Aimed at Congress Ties, '72 Texas Vote." *Wall Street Journal,* December 15, 1970.

Jolidon, Laurence. "Somalis Fear U.S. Departure." *USA Today,* January 4, 1993.

Jordan, Michael J. "Settling in for a Long Kosovo Run." *Christian Science Monitor,* November 22, 1999.

"Justice Agency Sues to Force Halliburton to Sell Ebasco, Which It Acquired Jan. 22." *Wall Street Journal,* April 25, 1973.

Kaplan, Jeffrey A. "Iraq's Reconstruction." *Boston Globe,* March 21, 2003.

Kaus, Mickey. "Somalia Syndrome." *New Republic,* October 17, 1994.

Keller, Amy. "For Reiser, Promotion to Chief of Staff Means Miller Time on the Hill." *Roll Call,* August 29, 1996.

Keller, Amy. "Shop Talk." *Roll Call,* February 1, 2001.

Keller, Amy. "Shop Talk." *Roll Call,* June 6, 1996.

Kiley, Sam. "Factions Head for New Somali War." *New York Times,* November 8, 1994.

Kleinfield. N. R. "The Whistle Blowers' Morning After." *New York Times,* November 9, 1986.

Komarow, Steven. "Army Base in Kosovo Will Try to Give Troops Taste of Home." *USA Today,* August 26, 1999.

"Labor Letter." *Wall Street Journal,* June 18, 1974.

Lake, Eli. "Analysis: Cheney and Sanctions Debate within GOP." *United Press International,* July 31, 2000.

Landler, Mark. "German City Tries to Persuade Pentagon to Keep Bases Open." *New York Times,* November 16, 2003.

Large, Arlen J. "Mohole Melee." *Wall Street Journal,* January 19, 1967.

Lemann, Nicholas. The Iraq Factor: Will the New Bush Team's Old Memories Shape Its Foreign Policy? *New Yorker,* January 22, 2001.

Lemann, Nicholas. "The Quiet Man: Dick Cheney's Discreet Rise to Unprecedented Power." *New Yorker,* May 7, 2001.

Leonard, Terry. "Dollars Are Leaving Somalia along with the Tanks and Guns." *Associated Press,* March 25, 1994.

LeSar, Dave. Memo to all Halliburton employees. October 17, 2003.

LeSar, Dave. "The Truth—From the Top—About Halliburton." *Houston Chronicle,* May 30, 2003.

Letters to the *Times,* Harold L. Ickes, C. L. Littel, Morris W. Herbst. *New York Times,* October 21, 1946.

Leviero, Anthony. "U.S. Reconverting Military Stations to Pacific Airways." *New York Times,* January 30, 1947.

Lindsey, Robert. "Puzzle of Executive's Death Stuns Texas." *New York Times,* February 7, 1977.

Locklin, Mike, Testimony. President, Local 2302 Fort Knox, KY, American Federation of Government Employees, AFL-CIO regarding contracting out before the General Accounting Office Commercial Activities Panel, August 8, 2001.

"Logistics Civil Augmentation Program (LOGCAP) Army Regulation 700-137." Headquarters Department of the Army, December 16, 1985.

"Logistics Civil Augmentation Program: A USACE Guide for Commanders." U.S. Army Corps of Engineers, December 5, 1994.

Logsdon, John M. "Space and Power Politics." *New York Times,* July 17, 1969.

Lorch, Donatella. "In Somalia, a Chameleon Thrives." *New York Times,* July 31, 1995.

Lydon, Christopher. "Connally, Hailed by Nixon, Reported to Look to 1976." *New York Times,* March 5, 1973.

Lynch, Colum. "Firm's Iraq Deals Greater than Cheney Has Said; Affiliates Had $73 Million in Contracts." *Washington Post,* June 23, 2001.

Lynch, Colum. "U.S. Firms Aiding Iraqi Oil Industry; Commerce with Baghdad Grows Quietly as Washington Urges Regime Change." *Washington Post,* February 20, 2000.

Lyons, Richard D. "25 on Boards of Oil Companies Scrutinized in Antitrust Inquiry." *New York Times,* March 12, 1974.

Manjoo, Farhad. "To the Cronies Go the Spoils." Salon.com, October 9, 2003.

Mann, James. "Young Rumsfeld." *Atlantic,* November 2003.

Maren, Michael. "Spoiled." *New Republic,* December 12, 1994.

Margasak, Larry. "Halliburton to Lose Iraq Oil Project." *Associates Press,* December 31, 2003.

Marshall, Joshua Micha. "Vice Grip: Dick Cheney Is a Man of Principles. Disastrous Principles." *Washington Monthly,* January/February 2003.

McElheny, Victor K. "Houston Space Center Is Rededicated to Johnson." *New York Times,* August 28, 1973.

Mendels, Pamela. "Inaugural Committee Lists $100,000 Lenders." *Newsday,* January 19, 1989.

Metz, Robert. "Market Place: S.E.C. Continues Talley Hearings." *New York Times,* June 10, 1969.

Milbank, Dana. "For Cheney, Tarnish from Halliburton; Firm's Fall Raises Questions about Vice President's Leadership There." *Washington Post*, July 16, 2002.

Miller, Ian. "Pro-Business Strategy Hopes to Gain Worker Votes." *The Hill*, September 20, 2000.

Mintz, John. "Transition Advisors Have Much to Gain." *Washington Post*, January 17, 2001.

"Mobil Discloses Libya Settlement on Dollar Shift." *Wall Street Journal*, May 5, 1972.

"Mohole Contractor Is Linked to Gifts Made to Democrats." *New York Times*, August 20, 1966.

"More Letters to the Editor." *The State* (Columbia, SC), December 9, 2003.

Morris, David. "Cheney's Former Firm Paid Fines on Prior Contracts." *Congress Daily*, April 16, 2003.

Morris, Ted. "Important Dates of the Provisional People's Republic of Diego Garcia." Personal web site, http://www.zianet.com/tedmorris /dg/realhistory.html.

Morrissey, Siobhan. States News Service. June 20, 1988.

MoveOn Bulletin, Thursday, July 11, 2002.

Mullins, Brody. "Business Changes Course; Turnout Becomes Focus." *Roll Call*, July 9, 2003.

Naval Postgraduate School. Official biography of David Gribbin.

"News From Guam." *New York Times*, April 7, 1947.

"Nomination of David J. Gribbin III to Be an Assistant Secretary of Defense." George Bush Presidential Library Papers, May 2, 1989.

Norman, James R., Terri Thompson, Cynthia Green, and Jo Ellen Davis. "The Scrappy Mr. Penzoil." *BusinessWeek*, January 27, 1986.

"Nostalgia for Sale at a Houston Hotel." *New York Times*, July 21, 1983.

"Now Hear This." *Fortune*, August 29, 1988.

Nyden, Paul J. "Asbestos Victims Threatened Orrin Hatch Bill Would Protect Industry." *Charleston Gazette*, July 6, 2003.

Oberdorfer, Don. "Equipment Is Shipped to Soviets; U.S. Promptly Sets Sanctions against Two Firms Involved." *Washington Post*, August 27, 1982.

Office of the Iraq Program Oil-for-Food, Chronology of Implementation August 2, 1990—June 26, 2003. U.N. web site.

Office of the Iraq Program Oil-for-Food, Summary of the Program. U.N. web site.

"Oil Well Servicing Cited in Trust Case." *New York Times,* July 28, 1961.

Oliphant, Thomas, and Diane Alters. "A Day of No Respect for Candidates Bush Heckled in Oregon, Dukakis Taunted in Illinois." *Boston Globe,* September 7, 1988.

"1962 Nixon Tactic Was Held Illegal." *New York Times,* October 28, 1972.

"On the Move: Halliburton Picks Politician." *Lloyd's List,* August 22, 1996.

"Option on Secrecy Given Contributors to Johnson Park." *New York Times,* January 9, 1967.

"Osman Atto Offers to Mediate between Aidid and His Rivals." *Agence France Presse,* October 2, 1997.

"Pan-American Road Link Drafted." *New York Times,* August 29, 1966.

Pasternak, Judy. "Bush's Energy Plan Bares Industry Clout." *Los Angeles Times,* August 26, 2001.

Paumgarten, Nick. "Where's the Veep?" *New Yorker,* November 19, 2001.

Payne, Darwin. "Dresser Industries." *The Handbook of Texas Online.* http://www.tsha.utexas.edu/handbook/online.

"Peace Operations: Withdrawal of U.S. Troops from Somalia." GAO Briefing Report to Congressional Requestors, June 1994.

Pfleger, Katherine. "U.S. Embassies Assisted Cheney Firm." *Washington Post,* October 26, 2000.

"Pilot's Release Lets Clinton Call Off Manhunt for Aideed." *Herald* (Glasgow), October 15, 1993.

Pincus, Walter, and Bob Woodward. "Bush Opened up to Secret Yale Society." *Washington Post,* August 7, 1988.

Pincus, Walter, and Bob Woodward. "Doing Well with Help from Family, Friends; They Pointed Bush to Jobs, Investments." *Washington Post,* August 11, 1988.

Potter, Beth. "Texans Busy with Kosovo Construction." *United Press International,* August 18, 1999.

Pratt, Joseph A., and Christopher J. Castaneda. *Builders: Herman and George R. Brown.* College Station: Texas A&M University Press, 1999.

Pratt, Joseph A., and Christopher J. Castaneda. *From Texas to the East.* College Station: Texas A&M University Press, 1993.

"President of Dresser Industries—Tass Interview." The Russian Information Agency ITAR-TASS, June 12, 1989.

"Price Is $36,745,000 in Halliburton Purchase of Brown Properties." *Wall Street Journal,* December 24, 1962.

"Privatizing Combat, the New World Order," International Consortium of Investigative Journalists, October 28, 2002.

"Profile: How to Turn a Warmonger into a Hero; General Aideed, Top Bad-Guy on America's Hit List." *Independent* (London), July 17, 1993.

Purvis, Andrew. "The Somalia Syndrome." *Time Europe,* May 22, 2000.

"Puts Guam Blame on Roosevelt." *New York Times,* October 12, 1944.

"Quality of Life for U.S. Soldiers Deployed in the Balkans." GAO Report, December 14, 2000.

Randal, Jonathan. "Enemy Sinks U.S. Dredge; Three Other Vessels Damaged." *New York Times,* January 10, 1967.

Report of the Group of United Nations Experts Established Pursuant to Paragraph 30 of the Security Council Resolution 1284 (2000). United Nations, March 2000.

"Report to the Chairman, Subcommittee on Readiness and Management Support, Committee on Armed Services, U.S. Senate." GAO, September 29, 2000.

"Ribicoff Says 'Millions Are Squandered' in Vietnam." *New York Times,* May 12, 1968.

Rodengen, Jeffrey L. *The Legend of Halliburton.* Ft. Lauderdale, FL: Write Stuff Syndicate Inc., 1996.

Roff, Peter. "Analysis: Why Not Ridge?" *United Press International,* December 21, 2000.

Rothenberg, Randall. "In Search of George Bush." *New York Times,* March 6, 1988.

Royce, Knut, and Nathaniel Heller. "Investigative Report: Cheney Led Halliburton to Feast at Federal Trough: State Department Questioned Deal with Firm Linked to Russian Mob." The Center for Public Integrity, August 2001.

Rubin, Alissa J. "Cheney Voted a Conservative Conscience." *Los Angeles Times,* July 29, 2000.

Rugaber, Walter. "Agencies Rebuked in Peru Project." *New York Times,* December 26, 1971.

Rugaber, Walter. "The Helpful Americans: In Peru 'No.'" *New York Times,* August 23, 1970.

S. 1125: To create a fair and efficient system to resolve claims of victims for bodily injury caused by asbestos exposure, and for other purposes. 108th Congress.

Salant, Jonathan D. "Business Organizing for Republicans." *Associated Press Online,* January 20, 2000.

Sammakia, Nejla. "Lull in Fighting Nurtures Banditry by Somalia's Young." *Associated Press,* January 2, 1994.

Sanger, David E. "Bush Makes Clear Troops Will Remain in Troubled Balkans; President Visits Largest U.S. Base in Kosovo on Last Day of Trip." *Milwaukee Journal Sentinel,* July 25, 2001.

Sarasohn, Judy. "Puerto Rico Shells Out for Big Guns." *Washington Post,* June 28, 2001.

Savage, David G. "Senate Panel Approves Asbestos Victims' Trust Bill." *Chattanooga Times Free Press,* July 20, 2003.

Savage, David G. "The Nation; Asbestos Bill Could Be Windfall for Business." *Los Angeles Times,* July 14, 2003.

Scheer, Robert. "Dick Cheney's Nightmare of Peace; War Could Be Just the Thing to Banish the Halliburton Specter." *Los Angeles Times,* September 3, 2002.

Schmitt, Eric, and James Dao. "A Nation Challenged: Military Planning; U.S. Is Building up Its Military Bases in Afghan Region." *New York Times,* January 9, 2002.

Schneider, Andrew, and Lise Olsen. "Cheney's Firm Backed Asbestos Legislation." *Seattle Post-Intelligencer,* August 4, 2000.

Schneider, Greg, and Tom Ricks. "Profits in 'Overused' Army; Cheney Slams Deployments That Benefit His Former Firm." *Washington Post.* September 9, 2000.

Scully, Megan. "Cheney's Vice Presidency to Boost Wyoming Pride." *Wyoming Tribune-Eagle,* December 24, 2000.

Semple, Robert B. "200 Texans Hear Nixon Reaffirm Vietnam Pledge." *New York Times,* May 1, 1972.

Shaw, Angus. "Americans Wounded in Blast, Gunmen Resume Attacks." *Associated Press,* August 4, 1993.

Simpkins, Edward. "Where Are Iraq's Missing Oil Billions?" *Sunday Telegraph* (London), May 18, 2003.

Singer, P. W. *Corporate Warriors: The Rise of the Privatized Military Industry.* Ithaca, NY: Cornell University Press, 2003.

"Six Killed in Clash between Two Somali Clans." *New York Times,* June 26, 1994.

Smith, Bradley A. "Campaign Finance Regulation: Faulty Assumptions and Undemocratic Consequences." Cato Policy Analysis No. 238, September 13, 1995.

"Somalia: Boutros-Ghali Deplores Killings, Backs Italians." *Inter Press Service,* September 7, 1993.

"Somali Financier Splits with Warlord Aideed." *Deutsche Presse-Agentur,* March 27, 1995.

"Somalia: U.N. Holds Three Somalis in Attack on Indians." *Inter Press Service,* August 23, 1994.

"Somalis Protest Dismissals by a U.S. Company." *New York Times,* November 6, 1994.

"Sources of Revenue for Saddam and Sons: A Primer on the Financial Underpinnings of the Regime in Baghdad." Coalition for International Justice, September 2002.

"South Vietnamese Strikers Due Back on Jobs Today." *New York Times,* June 29, 1966.

"Space Agency Speaker." *New York Times,* April 11, 1967.

Spiegel, Peter. "Cheney Staff Held Series of Meetings with Enron." *Financial Times,* January 9, 2002.

Spiegel, Peter. "Power Politics: The Furore over Enron Is Starting to Raise Some Uncomfortable Questions about the Bush Administration's Links with the Collapsed Energy Giant." *Financial Times,* January 11, 2002.

Spivak, Jonathan. "NASA's Jim Webb a Rare Bureaucrat." *Wall Street Journal,* October 11, 1968.

Stephen S. Stephens v. Halliburton Company, filed by Judicial Watch, July 11, 2002. http://www.judicialwatch.org/cases/92/complaint.htm.

Sterba, James P. "Refugees Say Hanoi Reacts to Pressure." *New York Times,* July 21, 1979.

Stuart, Paul. "Camp Bondsteel and America's Plans to Control Caspian Oil." World Socialist web site, April 29, 2002. http://www.wsws.org.

"Texas Rightists Assail Johnson." *New York Times,* August 2, 1964.

Thayer, George. *Who Shakes the Money Tree: American Campaign Financing Practices from 1789 to the Present.* New York: Simon & Shuster, 1973.

"Third Top Enron Executive Arrested." BBCNews.com, June 3, 2003.

"Threat by Vietcong Fails to Block Vote." *New York Times,* June 9, 1966.

"Tiger Cage Camp to Get New Cells." *New York Times,* February 21, 1971.

"Time line of Enron's Collapse." *Washington Post,* May 1, 2003.

Timmons, Bascom M. *Jesse H. Jones: The Man and the Statesman.* Westport, CT: Greenwood Press, 1956.

Toth, Robert C. "Mohole Advisors Are Discharged in Controversy with Contractors." *New York Times,* May 31, 1963.

Toth, Robert C. "Mohole Concern Backed by Panel." *New York Times,* August 7, 1963.

Toth, Robert C. "Mohole Project Runs into Snags." *New York Times,* September 14, 1962.

Toth, Robert C. "Mohole's Planning under Investigation." *New York Times,* April 14, 1963.

Transcript of Halliburton conference call for financial analysts, *CCBN Street Events,* December 17, 2003.

"Triumph in Pacific Followed Steady Course after Early Days of Japanese Advances." *New York Times,* October 10, 1945.

Trumbull, Robert. "Guam to Be Base for War on Japan." *New York Times,* December 11, 1944.

"2 to 3 Months; Cheney Says U.S. Role in Somalia Won't Drag On." *The Record,* December 7, 1992.

U.N. Resolution 687. April 3, 1991.

U.N. Resolution 986. April 14, 1995.

"Unit of Halliburton Co. Revamps Its Management." *Wall Street Journal,* June 25, 1974.

"U.S. Army Corps of Engineers Modifies Contract Synopsis for Possible Future Work on Iraqi Oil Infrastructure." USACE news release, June 27, 2003.

U.S. Army. "U.S. Army in Somalia: Chronology of Key Events."

"U.S. Building Group Raises Vietnamese Worker Wages." *New York Times,* July 4, 1966.

"U.S. Commandos Grab Aideed Aide." *Courier-Mail,* September 23, 1993.

"U.S. Company Is Granted $117-Million Iraq Contract." *New York Times,* September 24, 1973.

U.S. Department of Defense. Official biography of Richard B. Cheney.

"U.S. Errs on Costs of War Contracts: Vietnam Projects Estimate Is $200-Million Too Low." *New York Times,* September 11, 1966.

"U.S. to Spur Work on Mohole Project; Contract to Be Let." *New York Times,* February 28, 1962.

"U.S. Wants No 'Second Vietnam' on Balkan, Free Democrats Conclude." *MTI Econews,* December 8, 1992.

"Very Real Effect on Some Building Costs Is Seen from Davis-Bacon Act Suspension." *Wall Street Journal,* February 26, 1971.

Vidal, Gore. *Dreaming War: Blood for Oil and the Cheney-Bush Junta.* New York: Nation Books, 2002.

Vieth, Warren. "CEO Assets Now a Debit for Cheney; Inquiry: His Tenure Atop Halliburton Has Become a Liability for the White House as Corporate Scandals Unfold." *Los Angeles Times,* July 29, 2002.

"Vietnam Workers for U.S. Get Raises." *New York Times,* July 2, 1966.

"Vietnamese Strike Halts Work at Port." *New York Times,* June 25, 1966.

Waldron, Martin. "Foundation Paid Connally $225,000 While Governor." *New York Times,* February 1, 1971.

Walz, Jay. "U.S. Pacific Base Plan Has Wide Implications." *New York Times,* November 10, 1946.

"War and Piecework." *Economist,* July 10, 1999.

"Washington News." *United Press International,* August 27, 1982.

"Waste Charged in Vietnam Buildup." *New York Times,* May 19, 1967.

"Watergate." BBC.com, December 8, 2003.

Wayne, Leslie, Richard A. Oppel Jr., and James Risen. "Gulf War Led Cheney to the Oil Boardroom." *New York Times,* July 27, 2000.

Weintraub, Richard M. "Reagan and the Trade Agreement; Link with Sanctions' End Said to Surprise the French." *Washington Post,* November 15, 1982.

Whitefield, Debra. "Pennzoil's Liedke Still in a Hurry; Winning Battle with Texaco Would Make Firm a Major Player." *Los Angeles Times,* December 16, 1985.

Whitney, Craig R. "Children Sing Requiem in Land of Unrest." *New York Times,* April 11, 1971.

Wicker, Tom. "Lyndon Johnson Is 10 Feet Tall." *New York Times,* May 23, 1965.

Wicker, Tom. "The Other Prisoners." *New York Times,* September 28, 1971.

Wilford, John Noble. "$24-Billion for Big Push to the Moon." *New York Times,* July 17, 1969.

Woodruff, Judy. "Does Everybody Do It? Big Money, Politics Go Way Back in U.S. History." CNN.com, October 7, 1997.

Yergin, Daniel. *The Prize: The Epic Quest for Oil, Money & Power.* New York: Free Press, 1991.

Zieman, Mark. "NASA Agrees with Small Start-Up Firm to Launch Industry's First Shop in Space." *Wall Street Journal,* August 21, 1985.

INDEX